In our complex fast moving world u *the good, the worth-while, the inspiring. Angel of the Garbage Dump is a well-written story that can guide any person with lofty dreams of making a difference. This book is not a book just for the non-profit geek or the inspiring story lover, it is packed full of practical examples of how to create something remarkable, be it a school built on a dump or a successful commercial business. Hanley Denning would be happy with Jacob's portrayal of her life. (Not so much the angel bit) He allows us to see that what is remarkable about Hanley was simply that she made choices that inspired people to get along, to work together, to co-oper-ate and to love. Today the world needs more Hanley's. If you're 17 or 70, Angel of the Garbage Dump will inspire you to action, and nothing would make Hanley more excited than for you to read this book and say, "I can do that!"*

PAUL SUTHERLAND, Chairman, Utopia Foundation

There are few endeavors more daunting, and yet more rewarding, than that of creating a true account of another human being's dreams, life and impact. Painstakingly researched and crafted through the accom-plished eye of one with intimate experience working alongside Hanley Denning, Jacob Wheeler has achieved a work of immense beauty and power. He has not only paid homage to Hanley and her legacy, but also to the organization and community to which she gave so much.

TRAE HOLLAND, Safe Passage executive director

Angel of the Garbage Dump *is a literary and spiritual triumph — one that I simply could not put down. Like Hanley Denning herself, biogra-pher Jacob Wheeler dives into the horror and darkness, emerging with a book full of love's elusive light. His achievement is all the more notewor-thy for finding success in a way that honors the work — and the ethics — of its protagonist.* Angel of the Garbage Dump *is not just a compen-dium of praise for the hero at the story's center. Rather, as Hanley herself would have demanded, it is a sensitive and thoughtful investigation of the world inhabited by* los gaujeros, *the human beings who suffer and struggle to create passionate lives inside the Guatemala City garbage dump, where Ms. Denning committed her life's work. As Hanley did in her all-too-brief time on this planet, Wheeler treats those men, women, and children with dignity, respect, and empathy — not the paternalistic pity so common in the Global North.*

Now, it's worth noting that were she still with us, Hanley might well suggest putting down any book written about her and focusing our energies instead on our brothers and sisters who could use a helping hand. But I trust that you, like me, will find that very, very hard to do. Wheeler's storytelling is far too compelling — and his prose is far too eloquent — to set this book aside. Angel of the Garbage Dump *reads like a balance between an adventure story and a love poem. Whether you knew Hanley personally or are meeting her for the first time inside Wheeler's words, you will close the back cover of* Angel *with a deeper appreciation for daring compassion and human love.*

So, perhaps we can find a compromise: Read Wheeler's book at night before you sleep, at the end of your own hard day. Learn from the story he tells of this singular, incredible woman and her improbable, beautiful life just before you dream. Let the narrative work through you. Let the art of the language Wheeler employs work through you. Let those entwined graces lead you toward your natural, empathic core. Then, in the morning, rise with the intention to change this world in some meaningful way. Of that, both author and subject would approve.

Hanley, thank you for your life.

Jacob, thank you for writing it all down.

MICHAEL TALLON, author of the soon-to-be-published *Incompatible With Life: A Memoir of Grave Illness and Great Love*

Marathoning is a metaphor ... you never know what is going to meet you around the next bend in the road. Hanley didn't know what was going to meet her in the Guatemala City dump, but the skills and resiliency she learned as a runner helped her to meet the challenge head on and with an even stride — never wavering and never wanting to give up on setting a course to improve and inspire the lives of so many children.

JOAN BENOIT SAMUELSON, Olympic marathon gold medalist

Angel of the Garbage Dump

Published by Mission Point Press
2554 Chandler Rd.
Traverse City, MI 49696
(231) 421-9513
MissionPointPress.com

ISBN: 978-1-958363-16-4
Library of Congress Control Number: 2022911934

Printed in the United States of America

ANGEL
of the Garbage Dump

How Hanley Denning
Changed the World,
One Child at a Time

JACOB WHEELER

MISSION POINT PRESS

For my children, Nina and Leo.
Because of you, I understand.

Children often ate whatever the garbage trucks left in the dump—
from tortillas, to a leftover sandwich, to scraps from a restaurant.
(JOHN SANTERRE)

Contents

Hanley smiled a lot and seemed ebullient whenever she was around the children, remembered Danish volunteer Joan Andersen.

Prologue

THIS IS A STORY ABOUT HOPE AND OPTIMISM, bravery and idealism, and finding light in the darkest of places. It's about seeing and empathizing, and overcoming the convenient urge to look away from suffering and forget it exists. It's about one woman who refuses to avert her gaze and refuses to believe that the poor are disposable. This is a story about the lives she changes, and the people she inspires to walk alongside her and carry on her mission, even after she's gone. It's about a privileged American who leaves her wealth behind and chooses a life of service. The legend of Hanley Denning, the "angel of the garbage dump" in Guatemala City, depicts her as a saint—and yet she was also human. Like each one of us, she was complex. She could be stubborn, and manic in devotion to her cause. She was difficult to emulate. She inspired thousands.

Many of us idealistic citizens from the global north travel to places like Guatemala to seek adventure, learn the local language, and try out humanitarian work. Most of us eventually return home to our comfortable lives. But Hanley, who hailed from a prominent family in Maine, saw the garbage dump as she was preparing to leave Guatemala. She saw people competing with vultures for food. She saw children playing amidst the rot and despair. The experience changed her. It prompted her to, as Mother Teresa said, "find her own Calcutta." Hanley chose not to come home. She stayed and launched Safe Passage, or *Camino Seguro* in Spanish—a nonprofit that for more than two decades has worked to break the cycle of poverty through education, healthcare, nutrition and social services for the families of the garbage dump. Long after her death, the stone she cast continues to ripple.

What was it about Hanley that prompted her to forsake the comfort of home and light a torch of hope in one of the darkest, most dangerous urban environments in the western hemisphere? How did the characters Hanley met along the way influence her and spur her to action? What was the unfulfilled need that she carried, and did she satisfy it in the end? What can we learn from such a selfless individual—albeit one as human and flawed as each of us—as the global pandemic loosens its grip, and we feel the call to action once again from the forgotten corners of the world? Those questions inspired me to research and write this book about Hanley Denning.

Readers should note a few things: I chose the book's title *Angel of the Garbage Dump* because that's what the people of the Guatemala City garbage dump called Hanley, particularly following her tragic death. To them she was *el angel del basurero*. Though the words suggest a hint of white saviorism, I chose this title because it accurately reflects the emotions and words of the "guajeros"—the garbage pickers, themselves. Readers should also note that I use the names "Safe Passage" and "*Camino Seguro*" interchangeably. Hanley's project touched thousands of people, both Guatemalans and expats alike. As such, I didn't attempt to include every character in this book.

As you take this journey with me, I hope you'll come away inspired by her life, and moved to action when you see injustice and inequality. Daily headlines warn us that we live in an age of painful polarization, but even as we shout about our differences, let's not ignore the common call to service and working to build a better world. As Hanley's friend and confidant, Paul Sutherland, said, "Anyone in this room could be Gandhi, or Mandela, or Hanley Denning. We all have those attributes."

List of Characters

The Denning family from Yarmouth, Maine

Hanley Denning — *founder, Safe Passage*

Marina Denning — *Hanley's mother*

Michael Denning — *Hanley's father*

Jordan Denning — *Hanley's brother*

Seth Denning — *Hanley's adopted brother*

Lucas Denning — *Hanley's adopted brother*

Volunteers, staff & board members in Guatemala

Sister Regina Palacios (U.S.) — *Texan nun who shows Hanley the garbage dump*

Padre Luís Gonzalo Pérez Bámaca (GUATEMALA) — *priest who lends Hanley the church*

Joan "Juanita" Anderson (DENMARK) — *Hanley's first volunteer*

Maribel Cholotio (GUATEMALA) — *Safe Passage's first employee*

Claudio Ramos (GUATEMALA) — *Safe Passage's first social worker*

Fredy Maldonado (GUATEMALA) — *colleague of Hanley's at God's Child Project, Antigua*

Billy Burns (U.S.) — *owner, Monoloco*

Petra Gress (GERMANY) — *volunteer*

Rachel Meyn (U.S.) — *volunteer, Hanley's friend, later ran U.S. office*

Ed Mahoney (U.S.) — *accountant*

Lety Mendez (GUATEMALA) — *Hanley's assistant*

Camino Seguro student Sucely Cifuentes Pérez stands in her barrio near the garbage dump. (JOHN SANTERRE)

Guajeros wait for a city garbage truck to dump its payload. (UNKNOWN)

Mary Jo Amani (U.S.) — *volunteer who launched library, literacy program*

Marc Wuthrich (SWITZERLAND) — *accountant under Ed Mahoney*

Vilma Garcia (GUATEMALA) — *worked in Casa Hogar*

Juan Mini (GUATEMALA) — *land owner, board member*

Sandra González (GUATEMALA) — *volunteer, later board member*

Carlos & Lorena Quisquina (GUATEMALA) — *Safe Passage employees*

Beth Kloser (U.S.) — *long-term volunteer from Indiana*

Bayron Aroldo Chiquito de Leon (GUATEMALA) — *Hanley's driver*

Rob Tinsley (U.K.) — *volunteer*

Shannon Moyle (CANADA) — *long-term volunteer*

Amilcar de Leon (GUATEMALA) — *Ed Mahoney's assistant*

Barbara Nijuis (NETHERLANDS) — *Safe Passage director from 2007–2010*

Richard Schmaltz (CANADA) — *Safe Passage director from 2011–2014*

Todd Amani (U.S.) — *Safe Passage director from 2014–2018*

Trae Holland (U.S.) — *Safe Passage director, 2018–present*

Donica Wingett (U.S.) — *volunteer coordinator from Washington, D.C., post-Hanley*

Guajeros & students
Mamá Roque, son Ángel
Mamá Forunda, daughter Gloria
Mamá Vasquez

Mirnia Lazario Días

Irina Rodríguez Cotto

Nancy Gudiel

Iris Ramírez

Daniél Osorio

Gustavo Lías

Marco Tulio

Ingrid Mollinero

Christián Chiche

U.S. supporters & board members

Danny Paul — *Hanley's high school running coach, Maine*

Doug Pride — *supporter, 5K race organizer, Maine*

Cathy Mick — *supporter, Oregon*

Arthur Berg — *key financial supporter, Oregon*

Jane Gallagher — *supporter and organizer,
  Hanley confidant, Maine*

Jim Highland — *provided office space, board member, Maine*

Charlie Gendron — *key financial supporter, Maine*

Joan Benoit Samuelson — *Olympic runner, Maine*

Dean DeBoer — *supporter, North Carolina*

Leah Katz — *volunteer, North Carolina*

Arnie Katz — *supporter, board member, North Carolina*

Marilyn Alexander — *supporter, North Carolina*

Chip Griffin — *supporter, Maine*

Christine Slader, and son Wilson — *supporters, Maine*

Phil Kirchner — *supporter, Maine*

Joe Delconzo — *photographer, New Jersey*

Susan Attermeier — *literacy program, supporter, North Carolina*

Susanna Place — *supporter, Hanley confidant, board member, Boston*

Marty & Frank Helman — *key financial supporters, Maine*

Marilyn Fitzgerald — *supporter, Michigan*

Paul Sutherland — *first board chair, Michigan*

Sharon & Wayne Workman — *board chairs, Michigan*

Barbara Davis — *Safe Passage employee, Maine*

Drew Casertano — *supporter, board member, New York*

John McCarthy — *supporter, Michigan*

Deb Walters — *supporter, board member, Maine*

"Safe Passage" and *"Camino Seguro"* are used interchangeably throughout the book.

Hundreds of children helped their parents in the garbage dump, which deprived them from going to school. Hanley's program sought to break that cycle of poverty. (JOHN SANTERRE)

PART I

Entire guajero families often lived in tiny shacks they built out of recycled metal or wood on the edge of the dump. (JOHN SANTERRE)

Staring into the Abyss

BLACK VULTURES SOAR IN THE SKY above the garbage dump. They glide in meandering circles, carried by the updrafts of the wind as it whispers over the hills and volcanoes of this beautiful, rugged, haunting land. The buzzards wait, watching, smelling for opportunity below them. Something fresh, or something rotting. They follow a pecking order that determines which vultures will eat first. A meat carcass. A bag of rotting fruit. A stack of moldy tortillas. These scavengers are not picky. Far below, a truck arrives, dumping more trash into the teeming filth, its contents spilling into the ravine below. Creatures that look like ants scurry around the vehicle, carrying away their own treasures.

Suddenly the vultures sense opportunity. They turn and dive down, down—passing over the city cemetery and its tapestry of crosses and ornately decorated mausoleums. Like the trucks, this cemetery also feeds the garbage dump. The deceased whose families don't pay "rent" for their vaults here sometimes get evicted, their corpses tossed over the cliff and into the landfill that seems to suck everything into its grotesque, hungry maw. Only the vultures glide effortlessly between the filth and the volcanic views above.

As the birds sweep down to eat, those ants swarming the yellow garbage truck evolve, suddenly becoming people. A second truck leaves the city streets and enters the *basurero*, the

1

garbage dump, to drop its payload, and four men jump onto its back fender and hold on. Others jockey for position, placing their palms on the sides of the truck as it moves toward the ravine, then when it stops they box out their fellow scavengers like bouncers blocking the entrance to a nightclub. The truck's hopper opens, and they climb up onto the trash as it tumbles down. One man grips the rope attached to the hopper, swings back and forth while peering inside to see what treasure the garbage yields today.

Each dump truck bears three digits written on its side, which broadcasts the zone of the city from which this garbage comes. Could it be whole, uneaten pizzas and discarded electronics from Zone 1, where the wealthy live? Or chicken scraps and plastic bags? Rotting fruits and vegetables? Even plastic bags and sheet metal command value in these parts of the city. They could be used for shelter, or sold on the underground market.

The industrious scavengers at work here are the *guajeros*, the waste pickers of Guatemala City. The forgotten, the damned, the abused, the recycling class of society who make their living on the scraps and refuse of others. They live off the *basura*, the garbage. They are destitute vagabonds; some are drug addicts. They are survivors of broken families, of forced migration, of a civil war. The *guajeros* have worked here for decades. Their community grows whenever the rural coffee crop in the western highlands fails, or the price of corn and beans—Guatemala's staple foods—rises, or in the 1980s when the army marched into villages and left massacres in its wake, forcing rural Mayan Indians to migrate to the anonymity of the capital city. Nothing is easy in the desperate and violent city, but a strange opportunity always awaits here in the abyss of the garbage dump—even for unskilled migrants.

They don baseball caps, hoods, and rags to shield themselves from the heat, the smells, the dust, the noxious methane gases that bubble below the surface, even from pecking vultures. The women wear their babies in slings on their backs. Or they place the infants carefully in a cardboard box, enclosed to keep out the sun and the greedy birds. As soon as they are old enough to walk, the children are put to work, too. Their skinny arms reach into the piles of garbage. The boys use broomsticks to stir the trash, always in search of treasures.

Here now, a skinny boy in a soiled orange soccer jersey runs among the vultures, shooing them away with his stick, and throwing an elbow to keep other kids away from *his* pile of trash. The rumble of the yellow truck grows distant, replaced by the sound of children playing. Three boys wrestle in the dirt, as mangy puppies nip at their ankles. The *varónes* look no older than four, but the malnutrition that has long plagued the Guatemalan poor mean they could be eight. Raised in the dump, they learn a toughness that makes them act like teenagers.

There, a young girl with tiny dark olive eyes and wearing a flowery white dress coated in mud sits on a tire, holding a baby in her lap. She rocks and coos her sibling while the mother works nearby with the other *guajeros* picking through a mound of plastic in search of discarded tennis shoes.

"Espera, espera un rato," the mother tells her daughter. *Just wait a moment.*

The boy in the orange soccer jersey returns bearing gifts. He hands the girl an open yogurt container that has hardly been touched. He pulls a spoon from his pocket. And behold this: a chicken drumstick, still warm! The girl takes the chicken and uses her thin fingers to tear off strips of meat, which she slips into a clear plastic bag that she places in her pocket. A meal for later. She tosses the drumstick bone onto the ground, where it is immediately claimed by a vulture, who spreads its wings and hops 10 yards away before it discards the now worthless bone once again. It comes to rest in the dirt next to a cardboard box.

There, what is that sticking out of the box? A child's elongated arm, the hand hanging limp at the wrist. There is no movement.

The vulture hops closer for a look, but then stops, realized someone new is on the scene, someone far bigger than the bird, watching it. The scavenger spreads its wings and flees to a different corner of the garbage dump.

Half a football field away, inside the *basurero* garbage dump property but still removed from the hulking piles of trash, stand two white women: there is a nun dressed in a skirt and blouse and wearing a cross around her neck, and a younger, fair-skinned woman wearing a short-sleeved pink polo shirt, faded blue jeans and white tennis shoes, her blonde hair tied in a ponytail. She slings a dark backpack around her right shoulder. These are not *guajeros*. What are they doing here?

The two women freeze and stare at the arm protruding from the cardboard box.

"¿Está muerto?" they ask themselves silently. *Is the child dead?*

The blonde-haired woman in the polo shirt shifts the weight of her backpack and moves her right tennis shoe forward six inches in the dirt, a natural move she has made a thousand times before as she waits for the starting gun and prepares to run laps around the track. The nun notes that a look of silent determination has come across her friend's face.

Sister Regina Palacios feels tears welling in her own eyes. She feels a creeping in the pit of her stomach as she absorbs the scene around her: the smell of the trash, the vultures, the *guajeros* covered in dust, the tarps on the hillside held up by wooden stilts where people sleep at night, the shanty towns of corrugated tin roofs surrounding the dump where most in this community live, where these children grow up, the cemetery above the ravine from which bodies are thrown into the *basurero*.

The nun has not seen the Guatemala City garbage dump before. A native of Corpus Christi, Texas, she has been in the country for about 12 months, learning Spanish in the nearby colonial tourist town of Antigua. At 50 years old, she has seen poverty, but not like this. Nothing like this. Her role will be matchmaker. Sister Regina's job will be to broker a meeting between the fair-skinned *gringa* with the backpack and the priest of the local parish, where her friend hopes to borrow space to open a drop-in center for the children of the *guajeros*. She will give the children books and paper and crayons, rice and beans and bread, songs and hope and love—anything to keep them out of the garbage dump—among the most wretched and dangerous parts of the capital. But to do this she needs a space from the priest, and she needs to earn the trust of the *guajero* mothers.

Hanley Denning, this tall, slender, eloquent 29-year-old New England native, this compassionate social worker who studied psychology at Bowdoin College in Maine and early childhood education at Wheelock College in Boston, this competitive runner, this striving activist, studies the dump before her. She studies the arm protruding from the cardboard box (it is moving now—the little girl was just asleep), she studies the vultures, the boys wrestling, the girl eating the chicken drumstick, the *guajeros* hopping onto another dump truck as it arrives in the *basurero*. She studies all this. And she knows that she won't return to Yarmouth, Maine, the following week, or following month. She won't take her father's advice and get a well-paying job back in the States, perhaps meet a nice boy and settle down in New England. No, she will stay here in Guatemala. She has seen the garbage dump, and it has changed her life forever.

The Guatemala City garbage dump is the largest landfill in Central America. It has existed since the 1940s and grew through the second half of the twentieth century. The dump attracted refugees after the 1976 earthquake who never left as their homes were long gone.

It has continued to expand during this new millennium, as urbanization took hold, as plastics littered the Americas, as the country's 36-year Civil War from 1960–1996 displaced indigenous communities, and as the rural poor came here seeking opportunity. Each economic recession, each agricultural crisis has sent people to the capital in droves. Today, nearly a sixth of Guatemalans (about three million) live in greater Guatemala City. Those without marketable skills, without roots, without family have found their way to the underbelly of society. The *relleno,* or landfill. The *basurero.*

Waste pickers are not unique to Guatemala. Millions in cities around the world make their living by collecting, sorting, recycling, and selling what others have thrown away. In some countries, waste pickers provide the only form of solid waste collection, which offers a tangible public benefit. A network called Women in Informal Employment: Globalizing and Organizing (WIEGO) is dedicated to improving the working conditions of the working poor, women in particular, in the informal economy. Though they contribute to local economies and to environmental sustainability, waste pickers often face low social status, deplorable living and working conditions, and get little support from local governments. Some waste pickers even face competition for lucrative waste from powerful corporate entities.

The garbage dump in Zone 3, a long sliver of land in western Guatemala City, is the size of 12 football fields and consists of more than one-third of the country's total trash. Thousands live next to, and work inside, the dump. This is their only livelihood. Many follow in their parents' and grandparents' footsteps as *guajeros* because this is all they know. They and their families consume what they pull from the dump, they construct homes with it, and they sell it. There's money to be made here. Metal, plastic, paper refuse all command a price. Some *guajeros* can make 100 quetzales, or $14 if they work from 5 a.m. until 6 p.m., selling their wares in the scavenger economy. (Newcomers to the dump make far less.) That's close to the average daily wage for agricultural workers in Guatemala, and significant compared to the extreme poverty and meager wages of the rural highlands.

But the dangers are everywhere. Garbage trucks running over children or accidentally burying them in the trash heap. Cuts from hidden sharp objects. Lung disease and cancer from the air pollution and chemicals. Toxic methane gas bubbling underneath the trash that erupts in fires. Landslides during the rainy season. Desperation, violence, gang warfare. Children abandoned by their parents, sniffing glue to hallucinate and forget their hunger. Above all, an endless cycle of poverty.

By December 1999, when Hanley Denning first saw the Guatemala City garbage dump, there were hundreds of young children working and playing here. The Civil War had ended three years before, and Guatemala was nominally at peace. But the poverty and the root causes of the *guajero* economy still existed. In this squalid environment, she found her calling.

"What struck me was the enormity of it, and the over-whelming stench," she told a film crew years later. "I had never smelled anything like it. When I went down into the dump I saw the mounds of garbage, and so many children, spending their days in dangerous conditions scavenging in filthy garbage, looking for something to sell."

As to those who see the dump and turn away, she added, "I find a sense of pity for people who are working in the garbage dump, a sense of horror and disbelief that kids are working in the garbage dump. But there's this onlooker effect of people looking at it, and commenting on it, but reluctant to get directly involved."

Hanley refused to be a passive bystander.

DAYS LATER, THE TAXI RIDE from the Sisters of Notre Dame house in wealthy Zone 1 to the garbage dump felt more danger-ous than normal, as the driver used any space he could find to pass buses and semitrucks. He nearly hit a group of schoolchil-dren waiting by the roadside and treated telephone poles like they were flags on a ski course. Hanley normally projected calm level-headedness and focus in situations that stressed others—such as when she worked with the migrant children in North Carolina, an important track meet at Bowdoin College or Greely High School before that, or in the garbage dump that afternoon, where she showed Sister Regina her cool and deter-mined side. But in this cab as it hurtled through Guatemala City, she felt vulnerable and scared.

"*Por favor*, drive more cautiously," she pleaded with the driver, who nonchalantly pointed to his "*Dios es mi copiloto*" sticker on the dashboard. (God is my co-pilot.)

She and Sister Regina had an appointment to visit the priest who ran the Capilla Santa Maria church across Calle 30—dubbed the *Calle Sucia,* or "dirty street"—from the garbage dump. The nun had used her connections with the Sisters of Notre Dame to broker the meeting. But neither of them knew a thing about the priest and whether he would help. Hanley hoped that Padre Luís Gonzalo Pérez Bámaca would let her use the space as a drop-in center on non-mass days where *guajeros*—particularly the single mothers—could leave their children, before they went to work each day in the garbage dump. She hoped to give those children safety and food, crayons and books, music and lessons, and a passage out of misery. She hadn't yet thought of where the supplies or staff would come from. She'd improvise that later.

Padre Pérez could open his doors to Hanley, or he could slam them shut. He could ask her, "Why should these hardened people, perhaps already numbed to urban poverty, trust her—an optimistic but naive *gringa* from wealthy New England? What did she know about the Guatemala City grind? After all, this was the natural pecking order where the scavengers consumed what the capital's land-owning aristocracy threw out. They were lucky to subsist on the garbage." He *could* say that.

Some *guajeros* would say they are far more fortunate than their rural forefathers who toiled and starved in the provinces. Off in San Marcos province to the west, or Zacapa to the east, you lived off the beans and tortillas and sugarcane that you harvested yourself. If the crops didn't grow, because of a drought or a rainstorm or a mudslide, or if the military came and seized your land or massacred your farmers, you and your malnourished children starved to death. During the civil war that brutalized the rural Mayan Indian population, in particular, tens of thousands of Guatemalans left the land and moved to the capital.

Hanley couldn't expect that Padre Pérez would help her. As she and Sister Regina left the reckless taxi and walked toward the little church, she braced herself both for the encounter to come and for the acrid air on the edge of the garbage dump where they now stood. It was the dry season in Guatemala, and a mid-morning smog had settled over the city.

It took Hanley and Sister Regina some time to locate the rectory because the little church was like a fortress, barred and locked up. Zone 3 was a dangerous neighborhood, after all—considered the *zona roja* in Guatemala City. The chapel itself was homely and rustic. Its external white walls, the paint fading from neglect, were dwarfed in size by telephone poles whose power lines hung just over the roof of the church. The only thing that marked the structure as a place of worship was the simple metal cross mounted next to the electrical lines. To Hanley, who wasn't religious but understood the importance of Catholicism in Guatemala and the power of faith to organize people for good, the naked cross may have looked more utilitarian than holy. A black metal door was the entrance, and the small windows on either side were barred. If you looked closely, a yellowing poster of *la Virgen María* was taped to the wall outside the entrance. The women found the right door and a secretary led them to a sparsely furnished office where they sat in plastic chairs. The Padre soon entered, Regina introduced herself as a Sister of Notre Dame, then turned the conversation to Hanley, who spoke better Spanish than the nun. Hanley had spent more than two years already in Guatemala, working for a nonprofit called God's Child Project in nearby Antigua.

The conversation began as she feared. "Why do you want to help these children, *señorita*?" the priest asked. "They're already working as *guajeros*. Some are already 10 or 11 years old. For them, isn't it already too late? And you say you'll offer the mothers food in return for them dropping off their children. Won't they just come to expect your handouts?"

The priest's questions were logical, and Hanley expected him to ask them. She listened and waited, like the empathetic, trained social worker she was. When he finished, she answered in slow, articulate, albeit heavily-accented Spanish. Any Guatemalan could tell from her dialect that she was a *norteamericana*. Hanley also spoke her native English in a meticulous and deliberate fashion, giving each word, each image, more gravitas and relevance.

She described the dump, the desperation, the danger, the tragedy that children must follow their parents into the *basurero* and sacrifice themselves to the cycle of poverty. She spoke of the calling she felt to stay and help, even though she wasn't from Guatemala and would be perceived as foreign by the *guajeros*. She told the priest what she thought the children and their families needed. Food, yes, but also love and attention, books, art and music.

"Deberían poder soñar de su futuro," she said, pronouncing each word as though it carried the weight of the entire sentence. *They should be able to dream about their future.* "No es demasiado tarde para los niños." *It's not too late for the children.*

Hanley explained that the families who brought their children to her would be given bags of food once a week, but only if they showed up each day. She would incentivize their participation in her program.

Padre Pérez was formal, even stiff, Sister Regina remembers. But he listened to Hanley. He didn't project warmth, but he nodded his head, and after a 45-minute meeting, he offered her the church to store food and supplies and to hold a drop-in center on weekdays. But she couldn't count on him for financial help. The space would need a thorough cleaning, the priest told them. It was full of rats, and cockroaches, and who knows what else.

As they left the rectory, Hanley showed relief and exuberance. She told Sister Regina she had felt like a nervous wreck when they approached the priest.

Before they left Zone 3 of the capital, Padre Pérez toured the garbage dump with Hanley. The priest told them he had to overcome his own fears because he had once been surrounded by gang members there carrying knives. The experience traumatized him and he struggled to continue working in the area. He shared his concerns with her about safety—concerns voiced by other Guatemalans she knew.

"What, you're going to Zone 3, to the *basurero*? That's full of *maras*, gangs!" people told her over and over again.

But Hanley knew that she had to establish a friendship and sense of trust with the *guajeros* working in the dump if she were to be safe. To her, the relationship would be reciprocal. She would care for their children, and they would shield her from threats and violence.

On the hour-long public bus ride back to Antigua, the nun felt amazed by her friend Hanley. Minutes earlier she had stood outside the church on the edge of the garbage dump with nothing but a big dream, and now she had one small space where she could begin to grow that dream.

"She just had this tremendous faith that she could start with nothing and her project would grow," Sister Regina Palacios reflected years later.

BACK IN THE SAFETY, TRANQUILITY, and beauty of Antigua, the UNESCO World Heritage town adored for its cobblestone streets and ornate cathedrals and ruins, and nestled between *Volcán de Agua* to the south and the *Cerro de la Cruz* (hill of the cross) to the north, Hanley and Sister Regina met for lunch at their favorite restaurant, Doña Luisa Xicotencatl, an elegant two-story establishment a block and a half east of the Parque Central. Though the nun would soon move to San Marcos province in far western Guatemala, they would meet there whenever she was in town.

Hanley loved hamburgers, and Sister Regina watched her gobble up more than one would imagine her slender frame could handle. In particular, Doña Luisa's served a "California hamburger" with avocado and sprouts on the patty. Hanley packed it with lettuce, tomatoes and all the fixings, and French Fries, too. Here they were, two women from the United States, each in search of their calling, eating hamburgers and fries in Guatemala.

Perhaps Hanley preferred the burger because it reminded her of home. But she may also have been ravenously hungry. Sister Regina remembered that Hanley would go hours, even days it seemed, without eating. Hanley didn't sleep more than a few hours each night, those around her attested. And she didn't own more than a couple simple outfits of clothing. Faded blue jeans, a pink blouse, tennis shoes, the backpack—that was her uniform that she wore when traveling from Antigua to the dump in Guatemala City.

She was so busy, so inspired, planning her next moves to help the children of the garbage dump, that when she went out to eat, she ate heartily. "If you went out with her, she'd really eat," Sister Regina remembered.

They talked about how to help the poor in Guatemala,

about how to gain trust in the communities, and about the beauty they saw in the people. Hanley talked about how she would raise money for her project, and the limits she would place on how the money was used. She said she wouldn't spend money on lavish homes and décor like other, less frugal local nonprofits had done.

After pausing to listen to street musicians playing the marimba and local kids hawking textiles and jewelry affixed with jade stones, Hanley confided in Sister Regina about her family back home in Maine and about a tense dynamic there, and how she would tell them she wasn't coming home—not to pursue another degree nor a stable, traditional job. She had found her mission here in Guatemala. She also joked that, while she'd like to find a partner, she probably could never marry a macho Guatemalan man because of the cultural differences. Sister Regina found that humorous, but also recognized that observation may have been part of Hanley's internal debate about whether or not to return to the United States.

During one burger meal at Doña Luisa Xicotencatl, Hanley quizzed Sister Regina about the name she ought to give her project in the garbage dump. They quibbled over the name for a bit, hemming and hawing over a few options. Suddenly Hanley offered the name "Safe Passage" (or *Camino Seguro* in Spanish). The nun didn't care for it, she said, but once the words had left Hanley's mouth, they may as well have been etched in stone. "When she made up her mind about something, there was no changing her," said Sister Regina.

"I'm Not Coming Home"

IT WAS MID-MORNING WHEN THE PHONE RANG, Marina Denning remembered. It was December 1999, just weeks before the Christmas holidays. Hanley's mother was in the kitchen enjoying the radiating heat from the wood-burning stove— one of two which the family had acquired from the Portland Stove Foundry for their spacious, Colonial-style home. Hanging above the hearth were a collection of large antique decorative fireplace forks, which the Dennings had brought back from their time in London, where Hanley's father Michael had worked as an international banker when the kids were young. Whenever she was home, Hanley loved to sit in front of that wood-burning stove.

This was Yarmouth, Maine, a town of just over 8,000 residents, 12 miles north of Portland, the state's largest city. The Denning home in Broad Cove Woods sat just a stone's throw from the water of Broad Cove, and beyond that Cousins Island, beyond that rugged, finger-like rock islands that dot the Maine coastline, and beyond that Casco Bay and the North Atlantic Ocean. Out there in the blue, lobster boats cruised around the rocky shoals, hoping for a last catch as New England's fishing season wound down for the year.

Marina picked up the corded phone from its hook on the wall. She sat down at a little antique wooden desk with a calendar on it. On the other end of the line was Hanley, calling from Guatemala. A cacophony of noises accompanied her daughter's voice, as Antigua's noisy three-wheeled Tuc-Tuc taxis careened along the cobblestone streets, and as newspaper vendors, shoeshine boys, and Mayan women making fresh *licuado* smoothies hawked their wares in the nearby Parque Central.

"Mom, I'm not coming home," Hanley said in her clear and deliberate voice. Her tone was warm, but firm. "There's something I need to do here. I have found a project to help people in desperate need of hope."

The phone call was short. Hanley had paid for only a few minutes to chat. Those were the days before most ex-pats in Guatemala carried cell phones. She was calling from one of Antigua's call center internet cafés that double as travel agencies where tourists book trips to Lake Atitlán and other destinations.

Marina listened and nodded to herself. Perhaps she smiled in affirmation. She took the message in stride. She knew that Hanley was searching for a mission, a reason to stay in Guatemala. This was bona fide Hanley—ambitious, passionate, some might say spontaneous or impulsive, a tad stubborn—but her mother saw this trait, above all, as "committed."

This was the same Hanley who, at age 17, wouldn't allow herself to be "injured" and ran the state championship race for Greely High School with her foot in a cast. The same Hanley who, as a freshman at Bowdoin, spontaneously organized the baby shower for Lucas when the Dennings adopted him and brought him home. The same Hanley who, after she finished undergrad at Bowdoin, surprised her family when she decided to spend a year in Italy exploring her maternal roots. She spoke no Italian, and had no plan, but just went there. Marina had delivered Hanley to John F. Kennedy airport in New York City in the middle of the night for the flight across the Atlantic, not sure whether to feel excited or scared for her daughter.

"OK, Han. OK, Han," Marina nodded her head.

Marina thought of her father, Luigi Antonio Russo, who had encouraged Hanley to travel to Italy. Luigi's parents had immigrated to New York City from Castellammare di Stabia in Italy. The Russos lived comfortably in a huge apartment on Manhattan's Upper East Side. Luigi's father owned a grocery store and acquired apartment buildings in Greenwich Village. Nevertheless, Luigi's mother, Rosa Russo, who Marina remembered as being smart, stubborn and feisty, encouraged her son to be daring. She told him to climb onto the outside of the trolley and ride it to the end of the line on Madison Avenue and back without paying and without being seen. Quite the challenge and workout.

"If you make it back without getting caught, I'll fix you a bowl of spaghetti," Rosa told him. Marina's father Luigi worked hard, took advantage of his smarts, and ended up going to New York University followed by Harvard, after which he worked as general counsel for Chase Manhattan Bank and had a summer house in East Hampton on Long Island. Did Marina's oldest child get some of her ambition and audacity from her *nonno*, her Italian immigrant grandfather, she wondered?

Hanley had first traveled to Guatemala in 1997 to take Spanish language classes and work with families-in-need at the Guatemalan nonprofit called the God's Child Project, or *Nuestros Ahijados* in Spanish. She had received a master's degree in early childhood education from Wheelock College after her undergrad at Bowdoin, and then taught at the pre-kindergarten level for a Head Start program in North Carolina, but expressed frustration that she couldn't communicate with her

Spanish-language students and Hispanic, migrant worker communities in the United States. She had already lived in North Carolina and established residency in order to continue her studies in psychology and social work. But one year working for God's Child Project turned into two years. Then Hanley announced she would return to Guatemala and stay another few months, just to figure out what to do next. Nevertheless, by Christmas, by the millennial New Year, one could have surmised that she would be back in the United States to pursue the next chapter of her life.

It came as little surprise to Marina that her daughter was shifting gears yet again and planned to stay longer in Guatemala. But they both knew that the reaction from Hanley's father Michael would be a different story altogether. He loved Hanley, but he had a short fuse and didn't see the purpose of living in an impoverished country. Michael, who had worked in international banking in Maine, Texas, London, and the Middle East, saw professional success in a different light. A place like the garbage dump in Guatemala wouldn't have appealed to him. Marina figured he would react incredulously to the news that his daughter wasn't coming home. It would pose one more hurdle for his family. Hanley's decision to stay in Guatemala came on the heels of Marina and Michael finalizing their divorce just two months earlier, in October. Relationships within the family were shaky.

"Don't tell Dad yet," Hanley asked of Marina before ending the call. "I'll call again very soon and tell you more."

THE FOLLOWING MORNING Marina was sitting by the stove in the kitchen when the phone rang again. This time Hanley described to her what she had seen in the garbage dump with Sister Regina.

"Oh Mom, there were acres and acres of garbage before us. Some people pitch tents and live in it. Others live in shanty towns around the garbage dump. Their houses are made from reclaimed sheet metal, bricks, and anything the people of the dump can get their hands on. Piles of trash are everywhere. But what's really strange, Mom, is you can't tell where their neighborhood ends and the dump begins. It's all mixed together.

"Mom, my friend Regina and I saw a little hand sticking out of a cardboard box the other day. We hoped it was just a doll. But we were afraid there was a dead little girl in the box, and that the vultures would try to eat her. Mom, people bring their children, even their babies, into the dump with them to work."

"Han, was the girl dead? The girl in the cardboard box?" Marina asked.

"No. She was only sleeping."

"Han, I can tell you were moved by this experience. What do you want us to do?"

"Please don't tell Dad yet about this. I'm worried that he'll be upset with me. I know he wants me to come home and resume my studies and get a job."

"Your Dad is proud of you, Han, you know that, right? He's so proud of your academic accomplishments."

"I know. I just can't turn my back on this suffering I saw. These children living and working in the dump. I need to stay here and help them. I need to get them in school. Some of the things I learned at God's Child Project I can use here in the garbage dump. I want to show these kids hope."

"Han, how can we support you?"

"The priest leant me his church next to the dump so I can use it as a place where the moms can drop off their kids. But I'll need to raise money to buy school supplies, and food for the families. I need to convince them to leave their kids with me when they go work in the dump.

"Mom, can we can sell some of my things back in Yarmouth? Like my computer, my car. I won't need them anymore. Can you sell them for me?"

WHEN SHE PLACED THE PHONE back on the wall, Marina sat by the fireplace in the kitchen and again thought about Hanley, her daughter's determination, and her ability to see opportunity even in the toughest of situations.

Perhaps Han had a bit of her mother in her. Marina, too, had faced adversity and made her share of difficult choices. She thought of their time in London during the 1970s, where Michael worked as an international banker. They were wealthy, they took lavish vacations, they drove a Rolls-Royce, they attended social gatherings almost every evening. But their family didn't have continuity or happiness. Once they came home from a night on the town and Hanley's 18-month-old younger brother Jordan, whom they had left at home with a nanny, turned his head and wouldn't even look at Marina. He showed her he was unhappy. When Michael was given an opportunity to work in Beirut, Marina told him she had no desire to continue living what to her felt like a "fake life." She told her husband, "I've got to get out of here. This is not making my children happy." People told Marina she was nuts for leaving this lifestyle behind, but she knew it wasn't what she wanted.

When Michael left for Beirut, she took Hanley and Jordan back to the United States. His stint in Lebanon didn't last long—a civil war was brewing there, and bullets were once fired at Michael's taxi cab—so he took a different banking opportunity in Cairo. Marina didn't want to go there either. "Unfortunately for him, I was too independent," she recalled. Instead she contacted Bob Avaunt, Michael's childhood friend, and Hanley's godparent. He encouraged her to settle back in Maine where, he said, she could move into a great house on the water. Michael eventually quit international banking and moved to Yarmouth, too. They would raise their children at home in the United States, but their marriage wouldn't last.

All that day, as a chilly wind swirled off Broad Cove, Marina thought about the girl's hand sticking out of the cardboard box, with the vulture hopping nearby. She thought of Hanley's love for children and how important a role her daughter had played when they adopted Seth, and later Lucas.

The impetus to add to their family had come from Marina. Hanley was eight, and Jordan was six at the time, and they had a comfortable home with the means to feed more mouths. Marina contacted the Maine Department of Human Services to facilitate an international adoption. Michael followed along. But she faced several hurdles. The neighbors expressed opposition to the Dennings bringing home a dark-skinned child. Marina lied to the caseworker and said that the neighbors approved of the idea. Marina also had to show the agency that Han and Jordan had been baptized. At the time, adoption in the United States was usually facilitated by a religious organization, and the Dennings didn't belong to a community of faith. So, Marina told the kids to cross the street to the nearby Catholic church, so they could learn about the obligatory catechism and become baptized.

"I could have cared less, but Han was very into it," remembered Marina. "Why do you like this?" she asked her daughter. "Mom, I love it because they're teaching us about God, and that

God is love." Marina never forgot what Hanley said next. "God is everywhere, so that means love is everywhere," said the astute girl.

The Dennings were matched with a boy who had been abandoned on a street in Busan, Korea, at age three, and had spent a year living in an orphanage for mentally disabled children. A year later Seth arrived at JFK Airport in New York, and the family drove down to get him. Marina remembered that a little lady who spoke little English handed Seth to her and said "sick, very sick." On the return trip to Maine, they paused for a picnic, where they drank orange juice and ate sandwiches on rye bread with seeds. But Seth picked out every seed and dropped them on the ground, acting as though they were bugs. Marina learned later that the orphanage where he had lived in Korea had a slug infestation in the food. When they got home to Yarmouth, Marina and Michael saw that Seth's body was covered in scabs. And he couldn't tolerate their pet dogs, which were promptly moved outside. Seth was not mentally disabled, however. It seemed he had been misplaced in the Korea orphanage.

Marina remembered that 8-year-old Hanley showed a patience and tolerance unusual for her age. She had far more emotional stamina to help Seth than anyone else in the family did. "It was like she was older than her age. She handled the transition with such maturity," the mother thought. Hanley would spend hours pushing Seth on the big rope swing in the yard. He didn't yet understand English, but Marina would walk onto the back porch every so often to hear what she was saying to him.

"Your life is going to be wonderful," Hanley said as she played with her little brother. "Everything is going to be fine. You're going to be very happy."

Seth struggled with anger in those early weeks in his new home. He threw temper tantrums and kicked the kitchen cabinets for a solid year. But Hanley was always there for him, Marina remembered. She understood him.

Much later, when 19-year-old Hanley was in her freshman year at Bowdoin College up the road in Brunswick, Maine, the Dennings adopted another boy. This time it was Lucas, an African-American boy originally from Atlanta. Marina figured that most teenage children would think she was nuts for adding to the family, but Hanley organized a huge baby shower for Marina and invited all her friends. Hanley loved to hold her little brother. Marina and Jordan both remembered that Han was particularly fond of babies.

"HAN'S NOT COMING BACK? What do you mean Han's not coming back?" Michael's voice sounded flabbergasted, incredulous when Marina told him the news.

"She's going to stay *in Guatemala*? But what about her work in North Carolina? What about her career? She has a degree from Bowdoin College! She's wasting her education!"

Jordan, too, remembers that Michael "flipped out a little bit" and disapproved of Hanley's decision when he first learned of it. Jordan also learned the news via telephone. He had moved to Charleston, South Carolina, to work for a law firm there. "Mother was on board and kind of understood," Hanley's brother reflected later. "My father was much more pragmatic— at the time anyway. He wanted her to come back here, to get a job, and build on the career she had started."

And who could fault Michael Denning for wishing his

only daughter would return home? Home to a familiar, comfortable, and safe setting. Home to apply her compassionate social worker skills in a community here in the United States that needed them. Home to be closer to family, to enjoy meals together, to run together or shoot hoops together with him. Christmas was nearly upon them, after all. Who could fault a father for that wish?

Michael's fears that Hanley was putting herself in danger launching a project in the Guatemala City garbage dump in Zone 3, a violent, gang-infested and polluted hellhole—a place whose fortunes almost no one of wealth had cared about, until now—those fears were legitimate. There were a hundred scenarios in which the ambitious, naive *gringa's* adventure in the *basurero* could end badly. And yet, the white-collar banker, the pedigree of standout athletes, would have to accept the choice his 29-year-old, strong-willed, independent daughter was making.

If Hanley's audacity and spontaneity came partly from her *nonno* Luigi hopping trolleys in Manhattan, her grit almost certainly came from her paternal side, too. Michael's father, Francis "Rock" Denning, was a legendary high school football coach and boxer in steel country Bradford, Pennsylvania, in the 1950s. Michael followed his dad to the line of scrimmage, playing both football and basketball at Hobart College with his buddy Bob Avaunt—Hanley's Godparent. Then Michael took to running in the '70s and '80s, to be kinder on his body after his collegiate sports career ended. Jordan remembered that their father fanatically trained and obsessed with running and finishing marathons. Jordan and Lucas would become standout basketball players in their own right. Seth's athleticism led him to join the U.S. Coast Guard.

The running bug was what bit Hanley. She dabbled in basketball, but hoops—or perhaps team sports in general—weren't really her thing. "She used that long-distance running time to think, and plan stuff, and map out her individual challenges," Jordan said. "I think she enjoyed running so much because it gave her time to organize her thoughts without having 100 different voices coming at her, or people asking her things, or for her to delegate things. It was her time to lay out in her mind what she had to do that day."

Athletics were always part of the Denning family's daily ritual. In the mornings, at 5:30 or 6 a.m., Michael would send the kids out the door to run up and down the hill where they lived, five times, just to get their blood flowing. The kids would do it in rain, sleet, or snow. It didn't matter. "He instilled that in all of us," reflected Jordan.

Hanley developed a rock-like determination and will of steel, both while wearing her running shoes and when she had her nose buried in books. For her freshman year of high school, Marina sent her to Hebron Academy, a college prep boarding school an hour from Yarmouth, but the school had no running coach. She called Marina and said, half seriously, "I guess I'll have to start my own running program here." Instead, she transferred to Greely High School in the town of Cumberland in order to train with Maine Hall of Fame coach Danny Paul. "She had a stubborn force," said Marina. "Her motto was 'when the going gets tough, the tough get going.'"

Coach Danny Paul's cross-country runners at Greely were a dynasty in the 1980s. They won the Maine state championship each year that Hanley was in high school, and she was the team's top runner both her junior and senior years. The cross-country course was five kilometers, or 3.1 miles: Hanley also ran the 2-mile distance on the track team. "She didn't have explosive speed or kick," recalled Danny, "but she just set a pace."

One story from Hanley's high school running career

exemplified her drive and determination. She suffered a stress fracture prior to the 1987 state championship meet, which was held up the road at Bowdoin College during the spring of her junior year. Despite the painful injury, Hanley told Danny after seeing the doctor that she could still run on it. But the coach was cautious. He asked her to get a note from the doctor and have the physician call him. What followed wasn't an argument. Danny remembered Hanley as being among the nicest and most gracious people he had ever met. "But she was almost in tears when I said that 'I don't think you should run (on the injury). I don't want you to do real damage.' She was devastated." By the time Danny returned home for dinner, Michael was calling him, asking the coach to let her run the state championship. "I said I need something official from the doctor.... I got it by the next day."

The doctor, Dr. John Godsoe, an orthopedic specialist in nearby Cumberland, put Hanley's foot in an air cast, which allowed her to wear her running shoes, but with a brace above the ankle that would stop her from experiencing any further pain or doing any further harm. The doctor sent the coach a letter, the coach gave permission, and she won the state championship meet while wearing it. Danny remembers that everyone stared in wonder at her leg during the race. Everyone except Michael, who Danny remembered "was upset with me for being overly cautious." Later, Danny said that "Hanley probably apologized to me 10 times for the miscommunication."

"My nickname for her—between me, her, and her parents—was 'Zeal.' She gave everything she had in whatever she was doing."

Hanley also excelled in the classroom, getting all A's. But when the time came for her to apply for colleges the following year, her guidance counselor at Greely tried to dissuade Hanley from attending Bowdoin. He thought that if she worked this hard in high school, academics would be difficult for her once she got to college—and an elite school at that. But Hanley worked hard to get A's, no matter what effort it took. Hers was a self-imposed discipline.

"If she says, 'I'm doing this', then there's no stopping her," reflected Jordan. "There's no changing her mind. It's going to happen. Period."

HANLEY ASKED MARINA to sell her computer and car to generate seed money to launch her project in the Guatemala City garbage dump, and the devoted mother did so. She advertised both items in the classified section of the local Yarmouth shopping notice, and within a day a girl came to look at the computer, which Marina had placed on the dining room table. "Does it work?" the girl asked. Marina didn't know. But she bought it anyway and took the computer away. The car, an old Nissan station wagon which Marina remembers never ran properly, didn't sell quite as quickly. A few weeks may have passed: the car might not have sold until Christmas. She estimated that she may have gotten $500 for the car and $450 for the computer. The amount that Hanley used to launch Safe Passage has since been inflated in lore around the story. Marina thinks it was no more than $1,000.

The Denning family Christmas typically featured tree decorating on Christmas Eve with Hanley putting an angel made of an old toilet paper roll on top of the tree. The family would string outdoor lights around the house, then wrap any last-minute gifts. For dinner they would eat an oyster stew. When the kids were little, the family would hang high-quality wool

Christmas stockings before falling asleep. Christmas morning featured a huge breakfast of cinnamon rolls, sausage and bacon, toast, and eggs, followed by opening presents in the living room. Marina's parents would arrive on Christmas Day, and her father Luigi generously poured a whole bottle of vodka into the Christmas pudding, which may have been one reason why Hanley abstained, for the most part, from drinking alcohol. The Christmas Day meal was traditional Italian fare, with a cocktail hour, an antipasto, and dinner around two o'clock. Marina usually made a pie, and everyone else had an assigned duty for dinner. But Hanley's absence in December 1999 marked a void.

Sometime during the holiday season—perhaps only a few weeks after Michael's initial reaction to the news that Hanley wasn't returning from Guatemala—he ran into his buddy Doug Pride in the YMCA locker room, just off Route 1 between Yarmouth and Freeport. Michael beamed as he told Doug, "Hanley is starting this new program in Guatemala. My daughter is doing this!"

Doug, who at the time knew nothing about Guatemala other than where to find it on a map, noted an unmistakable sense of pride in Michael's voice. The father was clearly in awe that his daughter could go to a foreign country and start a program from scratch to help children in need. Doug would get updates from Michael from time to time in the YMCA locker room about Hanley. Michael had come around fast.

Opening the Church Doors

Inside La Iglesia, the little church across the street from the garbage dump entrance that the priest had leant to Hanley, a thick coat of dust covered the floors, shelves, and window sills. The building had three rooms. In the chapel, a grimy cheerless image of Jesus hung on the wall and looked down on a row of heavy wooden benches. A couple plastic flowers were set up on the wooden altar chair. The floor was made of concrete tiles and the roof was tin and plastic. So, when the sun rose in the morning, it baked everything and everyone inside La Iglesia.

Cockroaches were often seen scurrying across the floor and flies swarmed the air. Aside from the three rooms, the church had a dark, foul toilet. The irrigation didn't work well, and stagnant water lingered in the pipes. It was through the bathroom that rats entered the church. Like in a horror movie.

That's how Hanley's first volunteer, Joan "Juanita" Andersen from Denmark, remembered the filthy locale where the project started. The Dane wrote about her experience working with Hanley, and helping her launch Safe Passage, which they called by its Spanish name *Camino Seguro*, in a 2016 Danish-language memoir called "Drømmenes Losseplads: Blandt engle og skraldebørn I Guatemala Citys slum" *(The Garbage Dump of Dreams: Among angels and garbage children in Guatemala City's slum)*.

Joan Andersen had met Hanley in 1999 while living in Antigua and volunteering at God's Child Project, a nonprofit that works with orphaned and abandoned children. Hanley was finishing a two-year stint there as a teacher and social worker with first-grade students. Hanley smiled a lot and seemed ebullient whenever she was around the children, remembered the Danish woman, who as a volunteer wasn't allowed to accompany her friend on visits to the nearby shanty towns, where Hanley encountered families suffering from violence and alcoholism. What a contrast between that world and the casual nightlife, salsa dancing and party scene that Antigua offered the ex-pat community and wealthy *Guatemaltecos*.

Dubbed "Juanita" by her Spanish teacher—a name that stuck, even back in Denmark—the 19-year-old, free spirited and idealistic Dane fell in love with Guatemala, its rugged volcanoes, friendly people, and fascinating and complex modern history. She was smitten, like so many others before her. Juanita returned to Copenhagen that summer to begin her university studies, but she couldn't shake the impact her Latin American experience had on her. She wrote an essay about her "vacation" for a Denmark-wide competition, and in particular about befriending a 4-year-old at God's Child Project named Kevin, who would warm up to no one else but her. Juanita won the competition and used the earnings to buy a plane ticket back to Guatemala in January 2000. She would only stay for six weeks, she told her parents.

Within days of landing in Antigua a second time, she ran into Hanley on the street. Perhaps it was at the popular fresh-squeezed orange juice stand near the city's attractive Parque Central. The 29-year-old American woman was eager to bring the younger Dane up to speed on what she had witnessed at the Guatemala City garbage dump since they had last seen each other six months before. Hanley's time with God's Child Project was up, but instead of fulfilling her plan and returning to the United States, she had found a desperate, forgotten community with children who no one wanted to help, who no one cared about. This is where she would make her impact.

"Juanita, you should have seen the place!" said Hanley. "You think you've seen poor people. But this place, Oh my God! I went to talk with the kids sitting around in the streets. Many of their fathers were lying there drunk—their mothers out there somewhere looking for garbage. And these kids, Juanita, they have never gone to school!" Hanley sighed. "I thought, 'I must do something ... I have to do something.'"

Hanley told Juanita how she had called her parents in Maine and asked them to sell her belongings and how she would use the money to start a new project that would offer educational reinforcement to the children of the dump three afternoons a week—as long as they attended half-day classes at a local public school. She wouldn't start a new school; Guatemala City already had enough of those. What the kids needed was support. With the money from selling her car and her laptop, and a donation from a group of nuns, Hanley planned to launch the project in the filthy church next to the dump, even though, as of yet, she knew very few of the *guajeros*, themselves.

"Come with me to the garbage dump, Juanita," Hanley encouraged.

The Danish woman got butterflies in her stomach again, like the first time she had landed in Antigua and beheld Volcán de Agua arching skyward south of town.

"Sure," Juanita replied. She figured she'd check out the dump, and once she got home to Copenhagen in a few weeks, she could help Hanley raise funds for the project.

"You need to see this place," insisted Hanley.

Two days later, the phone rang at 6:30 a.m. in Veróni-ca's boarding house in Antigua where Juanita rented a room.

"Wakey-wakey," said Hanley in the cheery tone of a morning person. She guessed, correctly, that the Danish girl had been out salsa dancing and drinking beer the night before. "Let's catch the bus into the capital."

What Juanita didn't know yet was that Hanley hadn't slept much either. She didn't sleep much in general. Half the night she would sit awake in bed, in her own rented room in Antigua, wondering if the *guajeros* would trust her and send their children to the drop-in center at the church. To pass the time she jotted notes about the project she was about to launch, about pedagogical and social work tools and methods she had learned at Wheelock and honed at God's Child Project that she could emulate here in the Guatemala City garbage dump. About people and organizations she could approach for donations back in Maine. About ex-pat travelers and students at Antigua's growing number of language schools that she could tap as volunteers. She figured she just had to show people the garbage dump, and they'd understand the gravity of the situation and the need for this project. They'd support her. They just had to see it with their own eyes.

An hour later the two young women hopped on a *camioneta* one of those old yellow American school buses that had retired to Guatemala and been converted into a public bus. One could still make out the letters that spelled out which American school district this bus had once served. Parts of the bus had been painted and adorned with religious messages ("Dios es mi piloto"—*God is my driver*). The foreign backpackers and tourists in Guatemala call these "chicken buses" because they are used to transport everyone and everything, including live poultry.

The bus jostled back and forth as it lumbered down Antigua's cobblestone streets and then onto a curvy, switchback highway in the hills between Antigua and Guatemala City. The constant jostling prevented them from falling back asleep.

"I already talked to a few families in the dump about signing up their children for the project," Hanley told Juanita. "The priest will let us use the church next to the dump for signing them up. He'll meet us there today. We'll sign up those families.... Don't worry, Juanita, it's only about 10 families."

It dawned on Juanita, still rubbing sleep from her eyes, that she wasn't emotionally prepared to see the garbage dump and this rough part of the capital. Just days before, she had been enjoying the Christmas holidays with family and friends in her home village near Copenhagen. Eating roasted duck, dancing around the Christmas tree, and singing Danish holiday carols. Here she was now, a world removed from that carefree life. During her previous time in Guatemala, she had heard a lot about the capital city and how most of it should be avoided.

"It's a very poor area," Hanley interrupted her daydream. "There are lots of gangs in the dump. But it's the daytime, so they are sleeping now."

When the bus reached the Trébol commercial district of downtown Guatemala City, Hanley motioned that it was time for them to hop off. They walked at a brisk pace north for 15 minutes, about one kilometer, toward Zone 3 and the garbage dump. "Come on, this way," Hanley led Juanita while speaking in high-pitched, excitable American English. Hanley's mood was quick but nonchalant, even as Juanita noticed the houses around them getting smaller and smaller, and the neighborhood more and more impoverished.

They reached the little white church across the street from the dump, and entered with the few supplies they had brought with them to sign up children interested in the project. Outside, Juanita could hear, and smell, the garbage trucks barreling by, on their way to drop their payloads into the waiting hands of the *guajeros* and vultures. She could also hear the shouts and banging of people outside who wanted to get into the church. But she wasn't prepared for what would happen when they opened the door.

THE OPENING CHAPTER of Juanita's book, *Garbage Dump of Dreams*, narrates the bizarre scene that followed.

Hanley clapped her hands together. Her tone was a little too cheerful and nonchalant for Juanita's taste. "Well, should we open up the doors?"

She unlocked the black metal doors, but when they looked outside both of their jaws dropped. It wasn't 10 families waiting for them outside the church, but Juanita estimated there must have been 100! Women were pushing and shoving and yelling at each other for the right to reach the doorway and enter the church first. It was total chaos. Clearly the word had spread throughout the *basurero* and surrounding community.

"Oh my God, I only told 10 families about this," Hanley promised Juanita and Padre Pérez, the priest who had agreed to join them on the first day of the project in the church he was lending them.

"¡Seño Hanley, Seño Hanley!" called out a portly woman as she shoved her way to the front of the mob. (Seño is the polite colloquial expression, short for "Señora" or "Señorita.")

"¡Cinco a la vez, Cinco a la vez!" Hanley's gentle voice tried to break through the yelling and cursing. *Five at a time.*

The shoving mother reached the doorway. She was dragging

a spindly woman behind her, as well as four children. Hanley, Juanita and the priest let them enter, then shut the door to control the crowd.

"I have four children I want to sign up," the stocky woman's voice boomed in Spanish. "Their names are Juan Luís, Angel David, Claudia, and Emily. They all want to join your project."

Juanita described Mamá Lety Roque as being large and terrifying. The *guajero* must have been in her late 20s, but looked 10 years older than she was. Her four children in front of her looked puzzled. The Danish woman noticed that only the oldest child was wearing shoes, and that each one had large wounds on their arms and legs. Their hair was greasy, and their skin was sunburned and dirty.

"When does it begin, and what will you give us?" Mamá Roque asked. "My children want to sign up. They all work with me down in *la oficina*. But I want them to go to school."

Her family would become one of the few, proud "first families" that would join Hanley's project. A distinction they would carry years into the future.

"*¿La oficina?*" asked Juanita.

"Yes, *la oficina*. The pit down there. The *basurero*," said Mamá Roque with a look that suggested the Danish woman was ignorant for not understanding.

"Well, are you going to sign up my kids or not?"

Juanita wrote in *Garbage Dump of Dreams* that Mamá Roque's blouse was dirty and full of holes, her hair was matted, and she wore a mis-colored cap with an imitation NIKE logo. Over her shoulder she carried an enormous garbage sack full of old plastic bags. Her commanding tone and in-your-face manner made it clear that no one messed with her. Hanley and Juanita wrote her children's names on the list.

Next in line was the more fragile-looking Mamá Forunda,

who Mamá Roque had been dragging behind her. Her children should also be on the list, came the order. Mamá Forunda was missing her front teeth, but she had tried to look presentable for the occasion by wearing red lipstick and a sparkling dress. Two little girls, named Gloria and Paola, held onto her hands. Juanita caught a little smile and wink from Gloria.

Suddenly Mamá Roque's authoritarian tone disappeared.

"Gracias, gracias, seño, for giving us this chance," she broke down and wept. "What would my poor children do without you? It's dangerous and disgusting in *la oficina*. And then you two angels showed up. May God bless you!"

Mamá Roque embraced Juanita with a hug that nearly knocked her over. Luckily, Hanley came to the rescue, a smile beaming across her face.

"We'll visit you in your home tomorrow," said Hanley.

The garbage dump worker's tears disappeared as quickly as they had arrived. "Good, seño, we'll see you tomorrow," she said in a stern tone.

THE NEXT FIVE MOTHERS and children entered the church. They were dirty and smelled of sweat and garbage, and bore deep furrows and sunspots on their faces, remembered Juanita. The children with bristled hair followed each movement in the room with big, curious eyes. Hanley warmly introduced herself and dutifully wrote down their names and, when possible, their ages, and promised a visit soon.

Five followed, then another five. It was almost midday by now, and the sun pouring in through the metal and plastic roof had turned La Iglesia into a sauna. Cockroaches tickled their toes, flies buzzed around their heads, and garbage trucks continued their racket outside on the street. The damp stench from the dump created dark snot in Juanita's nose. She used her nails to peal black, sticky tar-like residue off her arms.

"Seño, my children want to join, but do they need to be able to read and write?" asked Mamá Vásquez. She looked around tentatively, as if she were nervous about something. Juanita remembered her voice as confused and subdued, and she had to repeat her answers to the *guajero*.

Mamá Vásquez shoved her kids, Angelina Sofia and Luís Alfredo, forward and clapped each alongside the head. "Say hello to seño!" she ordered them. The mother raised a bamboo cane. "If they don't behave, just beat them," she told Juanita.

"No! There's no reason for that. We don't beat children here!" the Danish woman asserted.

The mother grinned, took Juanita's hands in hers and warmed up. "You're a good person," she said. "We just need food, and my children don't have any clothes or shoes. Please show us mercy."

"We'll come visit you next week," Juanita promised.

Hanley and Juanita worked their way through the crowd, signing up the names of children who were interested in the project. It was time for lunch. The priest left to pick up a pizza for the three of them, while Hanley showed the Danish girl around the filthy little church where they would launch the project. She explained to Juanita how she had seen the garbage dump with Sister Regina and felt compelled to act. They had toured the community around the garbage dump and met a few of the families.

"Most of the children have never been in school!" said Hanley, dismayed. "They scavenge in the dump to find things they can use or sell. Others work in the streets of Guatemala City, waiting at traffic lights to sell candy, pens, and chewing gum. Some kids as young as eight ride along and help on the garbage trucks."

Hanley explained that her idea was to start a project that would help and encourage kids to attend one of the local public schools and then visit the project in the church afterwards, three days a week, for help with their schoolwork and to get a meal. Hanley and Juanita talked about the schools they had seen while working for God's Child Project in Antigua. As many as 50–70 kids were often squeezed into a single classroom. Lessons were comprised of the teacher writing a line of letters, numbers, words or sentences on a chalkboard, and asking the students to copy the line over and over again in their notebooks. That's why many poor Guatemalan children never learn to read or write, and often end up on the street.

"I want to give them an alternative," said Hanley. "A place where they can come and be children. And where they get help with their schoolwork, a little care, and time to play. The more time they're off the street, the better."

Juanita wrote in *Garbage Dump of Dreams* that she was struck by Hanley's willpower almost as a physical presence between the two of them. Amid that presence, the older American woman seemed so nonchalant. She smiled, shrugged her shoulders and motioned with her hands as she described calling home to Maine and asking her parents to sell her belongings. It seemed so simple, the way Hanley told her story. She just approached the priest, borrowed his church, and launched her dream project. But did she realize that she would need help and support?

The banging on the metal door resumed, and the women could hear that some of the *guajeros* had run around back and climbed onto the church's flat, tin and plastic roof. "I hope the roof holds," said Hanley with a calmness in her voice that Juanita found ironic.

They moved to an adjacent room, which was a little cooler because its windows could be opened halfway. That's where they would store the school equipment, paper, plastic plates and cups. A few tables and plastic chairs were pushed up against the wall. That's when Juanita saw the black rodent crawling along the wall.

"A rat!" she yelled.

Hanley screamed and jumped into the air.

The priest, who had just walked in the door with pizza, laughed at them in a mocking tone.

"He doesn't think we'll last more than a day here," Hanley whispered. "But we'll show him!"

"WELCOME TO *LA OFICINA* or 'the vultures' shopping center,' another nickname the *guajeros* have for the garbage dump," said Hanley as she stretched out one arm to show Juanita a panoramic view of the dismal scene spread out before them. They were touring the dump after eating pizza in the church.

The Danish woman wrote in *Garbage Dump of Dreams* that a flock of little girls held their hands as they approached the *basurero* together with several toothless *guajeros* wearing tattered and dirty t-shirts and carrying plastic sacks over their shoulders.

"Seño, can I also learn to read?" one called out. "When does it begin?" yelled another. "Seño, can you lend me a few dollars," voiced a third.

"We'll meet with you soon enough and answer all your

questions," said Hanley as she gently pushed her way through the crowd. Juanita doubted whether anyone heard her words.

Suddenly she noticed a couple flimsy guys in dirty t-shirts and baggy jeans carrying yellow plastic bags filled with glue in their fists. They repeatedly lifted the bags to their noses to sniff them. Juanita shuttered with fear. She knew that street kids in Guatemala sniffed glue to get high and to dull their hunger. But Hanley continued walking, a calm and stoic look on her face. They ducked behind a dilapidated wall which formed a barrier between them and the glue sniffers. Juanita exhaled.

Her eyes burned from the fumes of the dump. Her skin felt like it was covered in grease. She gasped and turned away. The stench of the dump, of feces, smoke, rotten food waste, and death made her so nauseous that she plugged her nose. The air was full of dust, as smoke from countless small bonfires created a yellow smog that blanketed the dump. Enormous vultures flew silently and ominously in circles above the *basurero's* inferno of shame and hopelessness, she wrote in *Garbage Dump of Dreams*. Every once in a while, the scavengers dove down into the trash but were quickly chased away by *guajeros* and other vultures. It was a fight—all men, or vultures, for themselves.

Juanita looked down at her feet. She stood near the edge of a slope that dropped 100 yards. In the mounds of garbage down below, people slung large bags over their shoulders. Others carried babies in slings on their backs. Next to a mountain of plastic bags, bottles and cans, they bought lemonade and tortillas at a small makeshift stand made of sticks and plastic. Garbage trucks arrived every few minutes to dump a new load. Each time the rear door opened, *guajeros* pushed and shoved, jockeying for position.

"The biggest and strongest get first choice of the garbage," said Hanley as she followed Juanita's eyes. "The smaller and weaker ones have to wait for the leftovers...."

The Danish woman suddenly noticed in the distance a little girl in a frayed dress walking among the grownups, the vultures and scrawny street dogs. The girl's eyes focused intently on the mounds of garbage. Even though the girl was half a football field away, Juanita could tell that she was not wearing any shoes.

"Yep, it's kids like that who we need to get out of the dump and into school," said Hanley. "Before it's too late."

Their visit to the dump didn't last more than an hour, but Juanita never forgot the smells, the acrid air, and seeing that little girl.

"OH JUANITA, HOW WAS IT? What did you think?" asked Hanley as they boarded the bus at Trébol, bound for Antigua. Her huge backpack sat open on her lap as Hanley thumbed through manila envelopes with files she had created for each of the kids. This was her mobile office. "I could really use your help with this project."

Before she could answer, tears begin to run down the Danish woman's cheeks. The 19-year-old sobbed, completely overwhelmed by what she had just experienced, as the *camioneta* drove away from Guatemala City and up into the hills toward the tranquility of Antigua.

"I'm so sorry. I should have prepared you better," said Hanley as she touched the hand of her first volunteer. Juanita was grateful for Hanley's compassion and company. Nevertheless, she wept the entire hour-long ride home. Hanley said she would understand if the experience was too much, and she didn't want to return to the dump or to the church.

A day or two later Hanley called Verónica's house to check up on the Danish woman. Juanita came to the phone and told Hanley, without hesitation, that she *did* want to return to the project. Like Hanley, she couldn't ignore what she had seen.

On February 10, four days before Juanita was supposed to leave Guatemala and return to Denmark to study at the University of Copenhagen, she called her parents and asked if they could empty her apartment and sublet it to another student. She wasn't coming home. Juanita's father cried on the phone; her mother became angry. But the Danish woman felt compelled to stay in Guatemala for another four months and help Hanley launch this project in the garbage dump. Then in June, two days before Juanita was supposed to make her delayed return to Denmark, she broke her leg playing basketball and postponed her trip again. Guatemala had captured her heart. By then, Hanley had agreed to pay her and other long-term volunteers a stipend of $100 per month, an amount that would nearly cover her rent in Antigua.

Years later, Juanita could still hear Hanley articulating her motto, as if they were still standing next to each other that day, facing the garbage dump.

"If we can save just one child, we'll change the world—for that child."

Gaining Trust

AT FIRST, MANY OF THE *GUAJEROS* feared that Hanley had other intentions. Nasty rumors swirled around the dump, as they had around Guatemala for a decade or more, that *gringos* were coming to steal their children. To take them back to the United States and adopt them, perhaps even to harvest their bodily organs.

Who was this strange *gringa* who had appeared in the garbage dump, and why did she care so much about the *guajeros* bringing their children to her? She promised schooling for the *niños* and *niñas*, but what people really needed was comida. *Food.* Few of power and privilege had ever stood up for the people of the dump. The land they had claimed for their shanty villages, the shacks they had built with recycled metal and wood, the community they had created out of the garbage dump—they had done this with their own sweat, their own calloused hands. Why should they trust this tall, skinny blonde foreigner with the disarming smile and the lyrical laughter?

Mamá Roque had heard those rumors of babies being taken right out of the cardboard boxes in the dump, never to be seen or heard from again. Another mom, Rosalina, known as "La Chepa" had a husband who didn't trust Hanley. "She's gonna rob us," he insisted. Yet another mom, Mirna Lazario Días, remembered the story of foreign doctors arriving from the border, giving the *guajeros* medicine and bathing their children. When they left, it was said that a four-year-old girl from the dump disappeared with them and was never seen again. The mothers were convinced that the doctors had taken her. So when Hanley offered to bring Mirna's children to La Iglesia to shampoo their hair and feed them, Mirna at first said no. She didn't trust the *gringa*.

The fear of *robaniños* had a mysterious and dark history in Guatemala, particularly in the Mayan Indian highlands to the west, which was cut off from the outside world, and whose villages were victims of the worst of the atrocities committed during the country's brutal, 36-year civil war that lasted from 1960 until 1996.

Stories abounded of foreigners venturing into rural villages and staring too long at a child or saying the wrong thing in broken Spanish to a cautious highland mother. In one story, Mayan women wielding machetes attacked a foreigner during the waning days of the civil war for saying something like "Quiero tu niño" (which translates to "*I want your child*," whereas she probably meant to say "Quiero a tu niño" "*I love your child*"). The villagers may have heard the rumors that Guatemalan babies were being sold to foreigners to be chopped up for their organs.

The Guatemalan military may have intentionally spread those rumors in the highlands to scare the locals away from speaking with human rights observers and activists who were arriving in the 1980s to document the military massacres being committed against the Mayan Indians. The civil war claimed 200,000 lives, and a United Nations-backed truth commission report after the bloodshed ended found that 90 percent of the deaths, disappearances, and other human rights violations during the *conflicto armado* were committed by the military—which was trained, funded, and backed by the U.S. government, hellbent during the Cold War on destroying any movements in Latin America it perceived as leftist. The seeds for Guatemala's civil war had been planted in 1954 when the CIA used a covert operation backed by the Eisenhower admin- istration to overthrow the democratically-elected government of Jacobo Árbenz, a progressive president who pushed for agrar- ian reform and measures to tax multinational corporations such as the Boston-based United Fruit Company on all the land they owned in Guatemala, not just the land they used. Political pro- tests followed the coup d'etat, and the country descended into hell six years later—with blood on American hands.

The belief that children were sold or kidnapped for their organs, unfounded though it was, remained widespread among some Guatemalans years after the Peace Accords were signed in December 1996.

This was the traumatized and mistrustful environment that Hanley entered when she set foot in the garbage dump three years later. The *guajeros* didn't understand her and didn't trust her. Nevertheless, she offered something of value, so they cau- tiously played along.

"CAN WE JUST GET OUR BAG OF FOOD NOW?" a *guajero* mother demanded of Juanita, as she and other volunteers gath- ered with Hanley at La Iglesia to hand out the first rations of food to those families whose kids had attended school and taken part in Hanley's education reinforcement program in the church. Each bag contained staple foods and household items such as rice, beans, pasta, soap, laundry detergent, tomato sauce, soup bouillon, powdered milk, and cornmeal. The project was a month old. This was the first of what would become monthly, incentivized reward ceremonies for the families who complied with Hanley's wishes and sent their children to school. It was also the first harbinger that a power struggle existed between the *gringa* and the *guajeros*. Juanita described what happened next in *Garbage Dump of Dreams*:

The mothers shouted and clapped. As soon as the door to the church's exterior gate opened, they streamed in and nearly knocked over Hanley and the other volunteers.

"*Tranquilo, tranquilo, silencio,*" Hanley tried with her outstretched arms to dampen the noise. She waited until a calm fell over most of the crowd in the church. A small child cried in the back row. The garbage trucks outside rumbled down the street, sounded their horns and shook the church walls. People began to murmur and shout again. Hanley nevertheless decided to start her monologue.

"Thank you for coming today!" she shouted over the crowd. "As you know, the children have now been in school for one month. Or at least they should have been. Because we only have five food bags today. Only five of your children have actually been going to school."

Silence fell over the crowd. The mothers glanced nervously around the room.

"I hope that next month you'll try a little harder." Hanley took a few minutes to describe the project's vision and rules.

"And please say hello to our volunteers," her tone changed and lightened. The church filled with applause, cheers and whistling. "The kids can get their hair washed and trimmed by the volunteers, and they can draw and work on their homework while each of you wait to come talk with us. I'm asking for your patience and respect so the process moves quickly."

No sooner had Hanley finished did the mothers immediately

swarm the doorway to the adjacent room where the food bags were to be distributed. Chaos ensued. The mothers, and one *guajero* father, pushed and shoved to enter the room first.

"None of your children have been in school like we talked about, Doña Roque," said Hanley in a patient, but stern voice. "Unfortunately, there is no food bag for *Ústed*," she addressed Mamá Roque using formal language. But you'll have another chance next month. "Es muy importante que sus niños estudien." *It's very important that your children study.*

Mamá Roque leaned threateningly over the table where Hanley sat with her files. The *guajero* mother looked her directly in the eyes. Hanley fell silent.

"They're lying at the school! They're trying to keep us down, just because we're poor. I sent my kids to school every day. Clean and with their hair combed. They did all their homework. They sat in the dark and filled out their blackboards. And you have the nerve to tell me it's not true!"

"I have personally been in contact with your school almost every day," Hanley attempted to calm the situation.

"If you don't give us our bag of food, I'll call a few mean street kids that I know," said Mamá Roque. "Should I get them now? Is that what you want?"

"Yes, well we have no food bag for you," Hanley said calmly, her tone unwavering.

Suddenly Mamá Roque fell apart. Tears gushed out of her eyes and she pulled out a filthy scarf to blow her nose.

"But *seño*, haven't you seen how we live? I couldn't send my kids to school because then we would have died of hunger. And we also had to buy medicine. My mom is sick, and my kids are sick, too. And we were threatened by some gang members over by the school."

Everyone in the room waited for Hanley's reaction.

"Yes, we talked about this when I visited you in your home," she said calmly. "But you knew the rules. So there is no bag of food for you this month. But your children are diligent, and smart. So I'd like to give them a chance next month."

"Oh please, *seño* Hanley," Mamá Roque pulled back, as Hanley maintained her deep, calm gaze. Suddenly the *guajero* grew threatening again.

"You get one more chance, or I'll call the street boys!"

"Should I come visit you tomorrow, so we can talk more about this?" Hanley asked in a tone that disarmed the situation.

"Oh yes, *seño* Hanley, we'd be grateful for that. And if you happen to have an extra bag of food, you know where we live." Mamá Roque suddenly embraced Hanley. Then she slung her plastic sack over her shoulder, took her kids by their arms and left the church with a smile spread wide across her face.

The Danish woman was impressed by her friend's stamina and patience that knew no boundaries. She had watched Hanley launch this program in a state of chaos, with little in the way of structure or rules. But here, the *gringa* was improvising and developing a plan. As always, Hanley's unbridled optimism led the way. "Of course it's possible, Juanita," she said, time and time again. "Todo es posible." *Everything is possible.* The Danish woman saw in her both an angelic naivety, and also a battle-hardened strength.

Some *guajeros* thought they could manipulate Hanley. But with each child she befriended, each meal she served, each doctor's visit she paid for, they were growing more and more curious about her. She had something they wanted, so the people of the dump played along with Hanley's game. They sent their kids to school, and to La Iglesia in the afternoons for educational reinforcement. And the following month, Hanley and the volunteers passed out 30 food bags to the *guajero* families.

In the beginning, allies in Guatemala City were hard to find. Despite the loan of the building, the priest who leant Hanley La Iglesia didn't really understand or support the project. Juanita remembered that he got upset one time when the volunteers hung the letters of the alphabet on the interior walls. "This is a church, not a classroom," he scolded them. On another occasion, Padre Pérez drove Hanley and the Danish woman around the city in his air-conditioned car with tinted windows, introducing them to middle-class families who he claimed needed financial help. They all seemed to be related to the priest. When he dropped Hanley and Juanita off at the bus station, where they were to visit a family interested in the project, Padre Pérez warned them, "These people are criminals who want to take advantage of you. They won't amount to anything."

Convincing the principals of local schools to accept children from the garbage dump was another daunting battle. Juanita described their reaction when Hanley came calling.

"But they are so dirty," she quoted one of them in *Garbage Dump of Dreams*. "They have lice and fleas, and who knows what else? They stink, and their books are infested with cockroaches. Don't think for a second that we don't know their type. They've gone to school here before. They are uneducated, and even the smallest ones are criminals and drug addicts. Most are also involved in gangs. And their parents get drunk and create a scene at our meetings. It simply won't work."

The wall of prejudice was almost impenetrable. But despite their negative experiences with, and stereotypes about, the children from the dump, Hanley's gentle art of persuasion helped move the principals, one by one, to admit the children. The project would be responsible for the kids and make sure they behaved, did their homework, and showed up for school on time, she promised.

"Please remember that education is a human right," Hanley told the principal. Juanita admired that determination that always seemed hidden behind her angelic, innocent appearance.

"But we don't want their lice and fleas."

"We'll wash them," responded Hanley. "If you promise that our children can attend your school, we'll make sure that they show up to school clean. And we'll wash their uniforms, too.

"We'll pay the cost of enrollment, books, materials, calculators, uniforms, shoes, school bags and medicine," Hanley continued, as the principal moved her way through a long list of things that each child would need.

Eventually, the principal ran out of excuses and the 15 *guajero* children on their list were admitted into the school. So long as they were clean.

"Oh well, I guess we'll have to go out and buy a whole bunch of shampoo and combs," Hanley turned to Juanita with a tired expression on her face.

They converted one of the rooms in the church into a virtual hair salon. Hanley bought towels that quickly got so dirty and wet that they were permanently soiled. Each child sat in a tub filled with water. The Danish woman and other volunteers recruited from language schools in Antigua went to work with lice combs and scissors, removing huge colonies of them from the scalps of the children. Each child needed to be shampooed multiple times, depositing the army of lice into the tubs in front of them. Most of the girls had so much lice that large chunks of their hair had to be cut off.

The volunteers washed each child from head to toe, and they played gleefully in their layers of soap foam.

THE DEATH AND DESPAIR of the garbage dump could be overwhelming, wrote Juanita in *Garbage Dump of Dreams*.

One day a curly-haired girl named Marta told the Danish woman that a dead baby had been found in a cardboard box in the dump. "It's true, *seño*. It looked like a little doll," she said.

"Sometimes they also find dead grownups," a boy named Luís Antonio chimed in. "Once I saw a woman who had been raped and killed. She was almost completely naked and lay like this ..." he grimaced and bent his arms at an awkward angle.

"And sometimes they find men who have been shot in the head," yelled a boy named Daniél. "They smell really bad! And the vultures and dogs eat them."

Juanita shuddered at the scenes they had witnessed. They were not 10 years old.

She learned that many *guajero* children carried rocks in their pockets to throw at vultures or street dogs when they got too close.

BY THE LATE SPRING OF 2000, the rainy season had begun in Guatemala, pattering the city streets and sheet metal roofs with a torrential downpour for several hours each day, and bringing out the worst smells of the garbage dump. The rainy season was the most difficult time to work in the *basurero* because rivers flowed where there was once dry ground. In less than six months, Hanley's project had grown from 15 to 70 kids, Juanita estimated. The Danish woman had also helped recruit a flock of volunteers—many of them fellow Scandinavians. And Hanley's insomniac nights of work, her emails, phone calls, and correspondence with potential supporters back in Maine were paying off. She had raised enough money to begin hiring teachers and social workers for the project.

But even with money and volunteers, how would she gain the trust of *guajeros* who still kept their distance because she was a *gringa*? Juanita remembered that Hanley threw a pizza party for the volunteers in the room she was renting in Antigua, and that's where they met Maribel Cholotio Pérez, the project's first Guatemalan employee and first teacher. Hanley explained the importance of having someone the children could look up to and emulate—someone who wasn't a foreigner. "They think you all come from a Telenovela" television show, she told the European and American volunteers over pizza.

Maribel, 22 years old and a couple years removed from her university studies, was from San Juan La Laguna, an indigenous village on Lago de Atitlán, the strikingly beautiful volcanic lake in western Guatemala. Picturesque though it was, Maribel had found little in the way of teaching jobs in her home village, so she looked instead to the capital city for employment. A friend had told her to seek out the foreigner who had recently launched an educational program in the church near the garbage dump. "You can try this out for a little while and see if you like working with young kids," Hanley told her.

In the garbage dump, Maribel stood out in her traditional Mayan colorful embroidered *huipil* dress. The Danish woman's first impression was that the *indígena* came across as gentle and subdued. She later observed a proud strength that resonated with many families in the garbage dump. Maribel, who lived in a house two blocks from the *basurero*, conceded that she faced discrimination among some for being indigenous—racism was a chronic problem in Guatemala today—but that everyone around Hanley treated her well. "She was doing good things for my people, so I had to help her," Maribel reflected years later.

The presence of a proud, traditional Mayan woman alongside Hanley helped build trust in the *guajero* community that the *gringa* had no ulterior motives with their children. After all, in the western highlands it was the indigenous communities that were most protective of their children.

During the four years that Maribel worked with Hanley, the *indígena* would occasionally bring *guajero* children home to her apartment near the dump if their parents had disappeared or gone on a drunken bender, or if Maribel perceived that the children felt threatened at home. Being Guatemalan, it's possible that she could watch them for the night more easily and ethically than Hanley or the foreign volunteers could.

Once Hanley and Juanita took a child with them to Antigua for the night because they worried about her safety at home in the *colonia*. Karlita was 3 years old, and her mother was known to take drugs, hang out on the street, and beat her daughter. One afternoon the other children had gone home but Karlita remained alone at the church. No one came to pick her up. When nightfall neared, Hanley, Maribel and Juanita decided to bring the girl home. As they neared the shack where she lived near the garbage dump, Karlita grew tense and started to cry. "She was trying to get away from there," said Juanita who carried her. "She was afraid of going home."

Each time Hanley knocked on the door, Karlita hugged Juanita tighter. No one answered. A neighbor emerged from their house but refused to take the girl for the night, saying she worried the mother would react with anger. Though nervous about the situation—and afraid of reprisals if the *guajeros* perceived that the foreigners were taking their children away—Hanley suggested that Karlita come back to Antigua with them on the chicken bus. She left a note for the mother and told the neighbor that Karlita would return the following day.

"She fell asleep in Hanley's bed that night, looking like an angel," said Juanita. "I wondered if she had ever slept so well before." The experience convinced Hanley that she needed to open a dormitory away from the *colonia* for kids who were especially vulnerable to domestic abuse.

Maribel, the project's first paid employee, remembered Hanley more as a colleague than as a boss. The *gringa* had great faith in the young indigenous woman and trusted her, even though Maribel's roots seemed nearly as distant from the Guatemala City garbage dump as Hanley's community in Maine. The drug addicts in the dump, the kids high on glue, the gang members, they were as foreign and scary to Maribel as they were to Hanley. "Si, tú puedes, tú puedes." *You can do it*, the *gringa* told her, repeating a phrase of empowerment that would become ubiquitous with Hanley for so many employees of the project—both Guatemalan and international—in the years to come.

She sent Maribel to the market to buy food, refreshments, uniforms and school supplies for the kids. She sent her into the *colonias* around the dump on homes visits. Maribel also loved visiting the schools around the capital and providing educational reinforcement for the children inside La Iglesia. The two women shared a modesty in how they carried themselves when they were near the desperate and the poor. They never sported cameras or any valuables in the dump—not only for fear of getting robbed, but because they didn't want to flaunt their wealth.

In Hanley, Maribel also saw a pillar of strength—except for one day she'll never forget when the rain pounded on the roof so hard that it sent the rats, giant rats, running around the church. Both women jumped onto a table in La Iglesia, waiting for the rainstorm to stop, waiting for the rodents to disappear, waiting for someone, anyone, to help clear them out. But, of course, no one would come. "We had to take care of things ourselves," said Maribel. So it was no surprise that Hanley was already beginning to think about who they could talk to about expanding the project to a different building and getting out of that filthy church.

Some families in the dump still didn't trust Hanley. Their fears persisted that, if they gave her their children, she'd take them away, or sell them. Maribel tried to assuage those fears. "That's not the case," she told them. I'm a *Guatemalteca*, myself, and I'll be right there with her. Nothing will happen to your child. Don't be afraid." Poco a poco, *bit by bit*, their confidence in Hanley began to rise in part because they saw Maribel working with her.

BY THE END OF 2000 the project had grown to include more than 100 children, and Hanley knew she needed to hire more Guatemalans to help her—both teachers and social workers. But she didn't have enough money to pay for top-notch help in the capital, so she asked Maribel for help. She would have to hire young idealists in their 20s who would work for relatively low pay. The *indígena* made phone calls home to San Juan La Laguna, where she knew there were educated family members struggling to find work. Thus began the steady stream of employees arriving from Lake Atitlán. The first was Maribel's cousin Claudio Ramos, 21 years old, who would become Hanley's first social worker hire, and who would also become a constant presence by her side.

Claudio started in November 2000, and Hanley quickly learned to trust him. Juanita remembered that, once, Claudio was walking through the dump, across what was then a *fútbol* field to get home, when he was assaulted by armed thieves, who shook him down and left him in only his underwear. Yet he returned to work the following Monday. That's how committed he was to the project, to Hanley, and to the job opportunity he didn't have in his home village.

In return, Claudio remembered that Hanley put him and Maribel in charge of the project for a week or so when she needed to return to the United States to raise money. But Hanley was never far away. She called him each night from Maine to ask how the kids were doing, what had happened in the project that day, who ate, who was sick, and who was going to school. When Hanley was in Guatemala City, Claudio and Maribel worked together with her until 8 or 9 p.m. on many nights, paying home visits on families near the dump. As time went on, the *guajeros* built a protective forcefield around Hanley and her staff. The street kids knew her, the *maras*, or gangbangers, knew her, and few wanted to mess with her. They protected her as one of their own.

ONE STORY, ABOVE ALL, SHOWS how Hanley gained the trust of the last of the *guajero* holdouts who still worried that she would steal their children. That story would be passed down through the annals of *Camino Seguro* as a legend. But it was a true story, and Claudio had a front row seat.

One morning Hanley arrived at La Iglesia to find that some-one had stolen the *portón*, the metal gate. They had broken into the church and taken the plastic chairs, taken books and school supplies. She was aghast and overcome with anger. But Hanley was also determined. This wasn't right. She would find the thief and compel them to return what they had stolen. "Don't do it," said Claudio and Maribel. "These are dangerous gang members who could hurt you if you make them feel threatened.... It's not worth it." The metal gate, the other supplies could be replaced for a few hundred dollars. And by then, donations were rolling into the project. But to Hanley, that wasn't the point. Someone in Zone 3 couldn't just steal what was meant for the children— the community's own children. She needed to find the thief.

With Claudio by her side, Hanley asked the man who ran a small *tienda* store near the church if he'd seen anything suspicious. "I didn't see who did it, but I could imagine someone in the Colonia Landivar would know," he responded cryptically. Hanley walked straight through the colonia, down a dark street toward the house suggested by the store owner. Claudio followed close behind, wary of what his boss might encounter.

She banged on the door. A man's voice answered through a door grate. His face was cloaked in shadow, only his eyes were visible. His reaction was aggressive. "I don't know anything!" the man yelled. "It wasn't me! Go away because I'm in my house." Claudio guessed that he may have been on drugs.

"These things that were stolen are for the kids, not for me," Hanley said in a firm voice. "They are for *your* kids, the children of *this colonia.*"

By now a crowd had gathered. Noise and rumors of a fight traveled swiftly in the garbage dump community. What would the man inside the door do? What would Hanley do?

Contrary to some versions of this legend, the metal gate wasn't returned, neither were the plastic chairs or the school supplies. They had to be purchased again. But that didn't matter. Hanley's pursuit of the thief wasn't about the materials. Whether she intended it or not, she had passed an important test. Her show of force convinced the last of the holdouts that her commitment to the people of the garbage dump was genuine. She wasn't going to steal anyone's children. She was going to help them go to school and dream about a better future.

THE THEFT OF THE *PORTÓN* wasn't the only time that someone robbed the church. But the next time it happened, it was the *guajero* families, themselves, who took offense, as Hanley had done. Juanita narrated this scene in *Garbage Dump of Dreams*:

One morning they arrived at La Iglesia to find the roof panel torn off and tables and chairs strewn about inside. Someone had stolen the hot plate, which Hanley's volunteers used to warm up beans and rice for the children. The pencils, vitamin pills, and even the teddy bears were gone, too.

"Who the hell would steal teddy bears from children?" asked the Danish woman in disbelief.

Suddenly they heard Mamá Roque shouting angrily outside on the street. A flock of *guajero* mothers had gathered in front of the church with brooms and sticks. Some of their children gripped rocks in their hands. They were ready for battle.

Mamá Roque clenched the collar of a young man who was dressed in rags. He attempted to smile when he saw Hanley, but his eyes were filled with fear. A couple other mothers clutched another young man.

"We caught them! They stole from you—from *us*!" yelled Mamá Roque. "What should we do with them? Should we burn them or stone them to death? Or should we do both?"

The women began to wack the thieves with their brooms as the boys wept. It turned out that, high on drugs, they had broken into the church from above, and then fallen asleep on the hot metal roof. One boy still had the hot plate under his arm.

Hanley stepped forward and quickly calmed the situation.

"There's no reason to lynch anyone here," she said. "If they return what they stole, they can go free."

Mamá Roque released her grip on the boy in rags. A short time later the boy returned with a box of supplies he had stolen from the church. Juanita thought that Mamá Roque actually looked disappointed.

The teddy bears were never returned. But Hanley and the volunteers understood that the families of the garbage dump were starting to care about her project—*their* project. They were starting to care about their children's education.

It's possible that Irina Rodríguez Cotto had heard these dramatic stories through the gossip of the garbage dump when she decided to seek out the mysterious foreigner for help. For weeks she had asked people "Quién es la gringa?" *Who is this white woman?* But she was worried because she had also heard rumors of outsiders coming to the dump to steal their children. Still, Irina was willing to give this a try. She was desperate. The father of her four young kids had just left her. She had no work, and nowhere to go. She figured that her kids would have to drop out of school and work with her in the garbage dump. She needed help. But she had no idea how to find this foreigner.

Irina found herself outside La Iglesia, praying and sobbing. Looking for a sign. That's when she heard the sweet, but heavily accented voice: "¿Qué pasó? ¿Porqué estás llorando?" *What's wrong? Why are you crying?* She turned, and there was a tall, slender blonde woman wearing a pink blouse and blue jeans, with a compassionate face and a backpack slung over one shoulder. Irina figured the foreigner in front of her must work for the church. She wiped her tears and explained that she had heard rumors about a *gringa* who was paying for children of the garbage dump to go to school and helping them with their studies, and sending bags of food home for their families afterwards. But she didn't know if she could trust a stranger with her children.

"Do you have kids?" the woman asked Irina. Yes, four.

"Do you work in the garbage dump?" No, but the father of her children does. He left us.

"Why do you want to talk to this *gringa*?"

"Because I want my kids to continue studying in school," said Irina. "I don't want them to drop out."

"Would you come inside for a moment," asked the woman in the pink blouse. Once inside the church, Irina was offered bread. She looked around and saw children whose hair was being washed. Some of the children she recognized. They looked happy, and clean.

"Listen, *yo soy* Hanley. *Yo soy la gringa.* And I'm not stealing your children. I'm here because I want to help them."

Hanley is "loca"

HANLEY SLUNG TWO BACKPACKS, one over each shoulder, as she hurried—half walking, half jogging—by the Iglesia Santa Cruz on the outskirts of Antigua, where she would catch the bus for Guatemala City. Bread and tortillas filled one backpack, plastic bags of beans and cheese filled the other. Each felt as heavy as a watermelon, but Hanley adeptly balanced the weight as she strode forward along Antigua's cobblestone streets, her feet careful not to trip or roll an ankle.

An old green Toyota Hilux slowed and honked as it approached her and pulled over. The passenger side window rolled down, and the gringa heard a familiar, jovial voice call out, "Hanley, Hanley, Qué traes?" *What are you carrying?* Her former colleague Fredy Maldonado from God's Child Project hopped out of the pickup. He didn't yet know about her new project with the *guajeros* in the garbage dump, and he hadn't seen her in two months.

Fredy had worked with Hanley during her two years at the nonprofit that brought her to Guatemala for the first time in the Fall of 1997. Fredy was more or less the righthand man for that project's director, North Dakota native Patrick Atkinson. God's Child, known in Guatemala as *Nuestros Ahijados*, had launched in the early 1990s and had become one of the most visible and successful nonprofits in Antigua. It worked with

disadvantaged families, orphans and street children and com-
batted poverty through education. *Patricio*, as he was known
around Antigua, had hired Fredy after a mere 10-minute interview—presumably for his outgoing nature, his vast connections
around Antigua, and his English language skills and his famil-
iarity with Americans.

Once a soccer star for various professional club teams in
Guatemala, Fredy walked with the methodical, gingerly gate of
a *fútbolista* whose legs had suffered a few blows and was saving
them for the next important play at midfield. Fredy, 36 years
old, had also seen and experienced a lot growing up in Guatemala. Not much fazed him. The descendant of coffee-growing
campesino peasants from Mazatenango on Guatemala's Pacific
coast, and parents who had migrated to Antigua in the 1950s
to pursue better work opportunities, Fredy had studied teaching and social work at a university in Antigua because the town
was less affected by the civil war ravaging the countryside and
Guatemala City. He was one of the first in Antigua to initiate
programs to help street children, bringing them bread and juice.

Playing *fútbol* earned him an extra 300–500 quetzales per
month, which went a long way in Central America. Fredy traveled to Mexico, El Salvador, Costa Rica, and Cuba, which is
where his passion for social work blossomed. But being a social
worker in Guatemala at the time carried the burdensome impli-
cation of being a Communist, and in the 1980s that could get
you killed. Fredy had *compañeros* who talked too much or out-
wardly expressed their social causes who were disappeared, or
killed, or forced to leave the country. "We were careful what
words we used," he said. As such, Fredy also spent time in the
diaspora in Boston and California in the late '80s. But his
roots beckoned him home. Fredy returned to Antigua in 1990

and worked for a Franciscan hospital until 1994 when Patrick Atkinson came calling.

Post-civil war Antigua prospered as more and more Spanish language schools launched, local families opened their homes to foreign students, and the backpackers, adventure seekers, musicians, artists, retirees, and fine restaurants followed. One evening in September 1997—nine months after the Peace Accords had been signed—Patrick asked Fredy to drive his green Toyota Hilux to La Aurora airport in Guatemala City and pick up a new God's Child Project employee. It was a young woman from Maine who had committed to work for their project for two years, even though she spoke not a word of Spanish. Her name was Hanley Denning.

Years later, Fredy jokingly reminded Hanley that, when he picked her up at the airport that night, she didn't believe he worked for God's Child Project. She didn't believe that he and the old Toyota Hilux were supposed to be her ride to Antigua. She didn't trust him, at first.

Hanley spent her first few months in Guatemala taking language classes while Fredy oriented her and interpreted for her work at God's Child Project. She quickly adapted and became one of the most popular social workers among the families the project served. Fredy and Patrick soon figured out why. Hanley would observe what the families were missing in their homes—whether it was food, dishes, or silverware—and she would buy it for them.

"Her fame and reputation began to grow among the families," Fredy remembered. "And they took advantage of her." Hanley would bring peanut butter and jelly sandwiches for lunch and eat it together with the families, then give her food away. Needless to say, this caused problems for the other social workers at God's Child Project, and Fredy asked Hanley to stop giving things away.

Later, when she launched *Camino Seguro*, Hanley would tell her employees and long-term volunteers, "Working with poor people is a struggle between the 'cabeza' (*the head*) and the 'corazón' (*the heart*)." She had learned a lesson in those early months at God's Child Project. You can't give away things for free. You have to use some form of currency, as in food bags to offer an incentive to the families to send their kids to school.

"She changed somewhat, but not totally," reflected Fredy years later. She always remained generous with what she gave to the *guajero* families.

During her two years at God's Child Project working with street children, orphans, and poor, single-parent families on the outskirts of Antigua, Hanley learned about Guatemala's "educación básica," or *basic* compulsory education system (which encompasses ages 7–15), the large classroom sizes, the teachers who asked their students to copy letters and numbers over and over again, and how many children the system left behind. She learned about offering educational reinforcement through a nonprofit, and supporting existing schools rather than launching a new school. She learned about how to use both teachers and social workers, and long-term foreign volunteers who earned a stipend. All these lessons she would bring with her to this new project in the garbage dump.

"*Camino Seguro* wouldn't exist without the knowledge that Hanley gained at God's Child Project," Fredy concluded.

Hanley could have remained at God's Child Project beyond her two-year commitment. According to Fredy, Patrick offered to pay her a salary, rather than the initial meager stipend she earned. But Hanley had something else in mind. It's also possible that she was casting about, simply ready to branch off on her own, and search for where she could make the greatest impact.

In January 1999, a North Carolinian named Billy Burns, who had landed in Guatemala at about the same time as Hanley a year and half earlier, got hired to teach third and fourth grade at a school just outside of Antigua for upper-class and wealthy kids. Billy admitted that the job was "a way to kill some time and earn some beer money." Within a year he would open Monoloco, a popular magnet in the heart of Antigua for ex-pats to party and watch sports on television. Nachos, beer, raucous laughter, and Boston Red Sox pennant flags on the wall are all part of the Monoloco experience today.

On the first day of orientation at the school, Billy was excited to see a familiar face—Hanley, who had also taken a teaching job at the privileged school. At the end of the second day, just after the new hires had completed a training exercise, Hanley beckoned Billy over to her.

"Billy, I have a question for you," she said. "Do you think these children need us?"

He didn't understand what she meant.

"They need teachers," Hanley continued. "But somehow this doesn't feel right to me. I feel like there are so many other children in Guatemala that need us more than these kids do."

Hanley didn't show up the following day, or the day after that. She had decided not to serve the children of the Guatemalan upper class.

THE DAY THAT FREDY MALDONADO saw Hanley on the outskirts of Antigua waiting for the bus with her backpacks full of bread and beans, she told him about her new project in the garbage dump, about how desperate these children were for educational support, and about how she couldn't turn a blind eye to them. But she also told Fredy that the project had no money, and she feared it wouldn't last very long. She asked her friend for help, and though Fredy still worked for God's Child Project, he offered to assist her on a volunteer basis in his spare time. For nearly three years Fredy would deliver food, and run errands for Hanley—often at night, like a modern-day Robin Hood—before he officially joined *Camino Seguro* in 2003 as an employee.

During those years, Fredy was amazed by Hanley's work ethic, and how many hours in the day and night she toiled. His sister, who worked the early shift as a respiratory therapist at a local hospital, would drive by Hanley's room on her way to work at 5 a.m. and see Hanley's light on. Fredy sometimes delivered food at 10 p.m. and would see the *gringa* working away, trying to make her project succeed despite its meager funds.

Juanita wrote in *Garbage Dump of Dreams* that Hanley's quarters on the outskirts of Antigua consisted of only a bedroom, a toilet, an outdoor kitchen, and a small patio which she used for storage. The neighborhood was quaint, with flowers everywhere, and the neighbor's radio playing salsa music. This house where Hanley lived was the headquarters of her project. In her bedroom, Juanita saw large stacks of folders, papers, envelopes, photos of children from the dump, an old computer, pizza boxes, and piles of clothes and Hanley's hand-written notes. Needless to say, Hanley didn't cook or prepare meals at home. She ate as infrequently as possible, and usually it was something simple while on the go. Bread and cheese from the supermarket, fast food from McDonald's in the Trébol district of Guatemala City, where she would hop off the bus on the way to the garbage dump. A proper meal of California burgers at Doña Luisa's, where she went with Sister Regina, or the nachos at Monoloco were a rare luxury.

Hanley was so skinny that some of her clothes didn't fit her, including her brown jacket and skirt, which the Danish woman remembered as the only nice clothes that Hanley owned. "You could use some new clothes, or at least an ironing board," Juanita once joked with her.

"Oh, but I hate buying clothes," Hanley answered. "I'm losing weight because I forget to eat. There's just too much work to do."

Hanley never quit. The project had become her entire life. Late in the evening, when Antigua was dark and still, she continued to pursue possible donors, or write emails, or archive her files, or crunch numbers for the project's meager finances, or reach out to people who might sponsor one of these children. Her almost manic steadiness had already helped the project grow. But now Hanley would soon need more volunteers. She asked Juanita for help. "Would you be my volunteer coordinator? You're the one who has found all the volunteers we have now." The Danish woman accepted.

VOLUNTEERS CAME FROM EVERYWHERE. Language schools in Antigua, elsewhere in Guatemala, and from abroad. There were Danes, Swedes, Germans, and Dutch backpackers. There were French activists and American college students, people of faith, and self-professed world changers who ran into Hanley and were inspired by her story and her cause. In time, media attention, too, generated awareness and attracted people and money to Hanley's program.

There was Petra Gress, a German woman who traveled to Antigua to learn Spanish soon after she graduated from high school in June 2000. Her program "Experiment e.V." allowed her to visit several volunteer projects and pick one after she had spent several weeks in Guatemala. Petra saw an immediate need for help at *Camino Seguro* since Hanley didn't yet have money to hire many employees. Petra remembered arriving at the little church each morning and preparing snacks and filling buckets with water, since the water was often turned off later in the day. She also remembers organizing hundreds of packages of food and hygiene products and wrapping them in plastic bags, which the *guajero* mothers would come and carry away on their heads. Letters sometimes arrived from foreign donors who had agreed to sponsor a child. Petra and other volunteers would translate and read them aloud to the kids in Spanish, who would attempt to write "thank you" cards in return. Each Friday the volunteers would remove everything from the church so the priest could hold service on Sunday.

Many of the volunteers worked at *Camino Seguro* for only a few weeks or months. Nevertheless, in their first hours on the job, they saw the horrors of the garbage dump and came to understand the complex and painful existence that many *guajeros* led. Petra remembers that children who wore modern clothing would bully Mayan Indian kids who wore *trajes típicas* from the rural highlands. The bullying, and the racism behind it, bothered Hanley immensely. Petra overheard her consider requiring uniforms for the children in the program as a solution.

On another occasion, a *guajero* girl told Petra that her father lived and worked in the United States and that one day he would return to Guatemala City and bring her north. Surprised, Petra told Hanley the story that evening. Hanley explained that the girl's father was an alcoholic who lived somewhere in the dump and couldn't take care of his family. "The kids invented their own story to break out of reality," Hanley told Petra. On other occasions, Hanley would play on that childish imagination and use it as a force for good. Petra remembered a young girl one day in the church who had a headache and was beside herself crying. Hanley suddenly appeared, gave her a hug and calmed her down. Hanley told the girl about a magic cake that washes away all kinds of headaches (and heartaches). Someone on staff must have had a birthday that day, because a cake magically appeared. Hanley cut a piece for the girl, and her headache disappeared.

Despite the active compassion in her work, most volunteers never grew particularly close to Hanley, who worked constantly and kept an emotional distance from most on her team. But all felt deep admiration for her commitment to the community and awe for her work ethic. Some, including Petra, expressed concern with Hanley that she wasn't taking care of herself. She neither slept nor ate much. (A notable exception were the chocolate muffins that Hanley would sometimes buy at a "tienda" *shop* located between the bus stop and the church. The *gringa* loved chocolate; to some it seemed her only vice.) She was thin and rarely rested, the German woman remembered. Petra approached her and said she looked exhausted, and asked Hanley if she took any vacation days or holidays to fly home to see her family. "I have just started the project," Hanley said, surprised. The German woman observed that, no matter how busy she was, Hanley shared her time with everybody who needed attention. When she walked through the dump, people always asked her for help. Hanley always stopped walking—even if she was in a big hurry. "Hablamos más tarde," she would say. *We'll talk later.* Everybody knew that she meant it. She would always come back later to listen and help.

A MAY 2000 STORY in Guatemala's English-language *Revue Magazine* about Hanley and her new project in the garbage dump caught the eye of a Northern California native named Rachel Meyn, who was learning Spanish and interning in the western highland city of Xela. Her curiosity piqued by a *Revue* photo of Hanley hugging children, Rachel reached out to her while she was finishing her semester at American University in Washington, D.C., and then visited during her spring break in 2001 with the intention of volunteering at *Camino Seguro* that Fall.

Rachel, who was 20 years old at the time, distinctly remembers the day she met Hanley, who would transform her life and become like a sister to her. She was given directions to Padre Pérez Bamaca's local *parroquia*, by a French volunteer named Pierre, and expected to meet Hanley there. But no one was at the parish. Nor did it feel like a church, as trash bags and a few plastic chairs lined the wall of the otherwise empty space. Eventually a local woman gave her complicated directions to La Iglesia which required walking through part of the garbage dump, alone, under a beating sun down and through the light stench of trash. But what worried her most was getting lost. Rachel eventually spotted an old, red Toyota Corolla taxi in the street. A driver named Dono Loro looked up and shouted, "Mira, la hermana de Hanley!" *Look, it's Hanley's sister!* Once Rachel heard that name, she exhaled. She asked Don Loro to take her to Hanley.

Don Loro's taxi snaked through several winding streets in the *colonia* and then descended down a narrow, steep path that reminded Rachel of the hilly roads of San Francisco. At the bottom they turned left onto another narrow street, marked by black bags of garbage stacked on either side, an overwhelming smell of garbage, and dust billowing around them. The cab crept forward, careful not to hit the stacked tires and garbage bags, which Rachel later learned contained the spoils of this morning's hard labor in the dump. The *guajeros* would stack their picks in front of and inside their homes to guard them before hauling the bags to a center down the road where their spoils would be weighed and they'd get their earnings.

At the end of the narrow street was the chapel. Rachel could hear happy children's voices and squeals reverberating off the tin ceilings. Her mood shifted. Just as she hopped out of the car, she saw Hanley approach from the opposite direction, the sun in her hair, a backpack around her shoulders, and surrounded by mothers asking her questions about their children. Hanley responded to each of their questions and then turned and said, "Hi, you must be Rachel. Let's go inside!"

"It was one of those moments in life where my senses were on overdrive," Rachel remembered. "My eyes felt like they were going to pop out from all that I was taking in." Hanley's hair was pulled back in a big braid, which was the way she sported it in those days. She wore little gold hoop earrings and, Rachel thought that she seemed to be glowing from the heat and from being so darn on track. "She was radiant."

As soon as the two women sat down on an old wooden church pew, a 4-year-old *guajero* girl nicknamed "Chayito" climbed onto Hanley's lap and played with her earrings. She listened intently as Rachel offered that she would like to return in the fall to volunteer or work for the project, and potentially teach photography or film to the children. Hanley nodded "yes" to everything the college student proposed. By this time Chayito was climbing all over Rachel, too.

Their meeting was quick as Hanley had to hustle to her next

engagement, but she encouraged Rachel to come with her to meet several other volunteers. They walked with a group of kids ranging in age from 5–13 who, Rachel thought, seemed to be their protection as they moved from La Iglesia to a little school where some of the children in the project were enrolled to study. Dust flew all around them, as kids seemed to run up from all directions to give Hanley hugs and join the impromptu parade of people. Hanley joyfully greeted each child, and knew each child's name.

"I took note in that very first interaction that Hanley meant business," Rachel reflected. "She cared about each child deeply. She wasn't on her own schedule, she was on *their* schedule." The visit also left Rachel feeling exhausted. Hanley was constantly on the move, and keeping up with her, physically and emotionally, was difficult. "But I felt deeply that I had to return," she said. "I had to work with her."

RACHEL ARRIVED THAT FALL as a long-term volunteer, settled into a hostel in Antigua and made her way to Safe Passage's office, which was next to the room Hanley rented in the home of Doña Alicia de Reyes on Calle del Hermano Pedro. To access the office, volunteers walked through a side door next to the family's *tienda*, through their dining room—often pausing to say "*buen provecho*" as the Reyes family ate—and through an outdoor courtyard. On the left side of the office was a tiny room with its own entrance where Hanley slept on a small bed. On the desk or tacked to the wall in her room were framed pictures of her baby niece Layla, who was Seth's child; a CD player plugged into the wall and a stack of CDs (including Enigma's "Return to Innocence"); and a couple watercolor paintings that every backpacker and traveler in Antigua seemed to buy at Café Condesa next to the Parque Central.

Hanley had tried to divide the space into several work stations, but the office was only about 10 feet x 25 feet. A table supported Hanley's old desktop computer and stacks of papers and makeshift filing systems with folders and plastic "inboxes" and "outboxes" were strewn around the room. A reddish tweed loveseat faced a small television with a VCR mounted on a coffee table, which she turned into the "volunteer intake section."

Rachel eventually moved with three other volunteers—a Dane, a Swede, and a fellow American—into a rented house that Safe Passage paid for. Volunteers who committed to 6 months or more also rented rooms at Henry's place on the outskirts of Antigua. That house featured a large patio which hosted Tuesday night volunteer pizza nights—Tuesdays because that was the day Domino's offered a 2-for-1 deal—often washed down with Fanta soda pop. Hanley attended many of these volunteer nights, which Rachel believed was important because it helped her "get to know us and trust in our intentions to help the project grow." Hanley sometimes elated over a hot slice of pizza and a soft drink. "Yay, we have Fanta," she squealed with joy.

The young woman from California's primary job was to assist in a second-grade classroom and offer lessons in photography and creative storytelling to a small group of students of various ages. Children in grades 1–6 spent their time in the *escuelita*, an empty cinderblock house that *Camino Seguro* rented about 3–5-minutes on foot from the church. The *escuelita* had a dark, unlit hallway that opened to five simply constructed classrooms, each of which hosted about 20 children, a couple teachers and 2-–3 volunteer assistants. Natural light came from the central outdoor patio, which also had a *pila* water cistern and a table where lunch was served. Volunteers made wheelbarrow trips between the church and the *escuelita* to haul a massive pot full of soup, which was cooked by a few hired mothers. The soups were broth-heavy and contained vegetables and a few chunks of meat or chicken feet—whatever Hanley could get donated to the project.

To reach the *escuelita* from the church, a *Camino Seguro* team that included Maribel, Claudio, teachers, social workers and volunteers would walk along the edge of the garbage dump entrance where yellow trucks lined up to enter. The walk often included stepping over men laying on the ground, high from sniffing glue. Then the group would wait outside the school while one of them unlocked the massive door, all while the children arrived and rushed in with the staff.

The daily reinforcement sessions included singing, stretching and exercises, checking homework assignments, and helping children complete and understand their school lessons. The staff employed crafty activities, such as using plastecine modeling clay, and encouraged painting and drawing. But volunteering at the *escuelita* was a rugged experience in many ways. The building had two bathrooms, both with light switches in the hallway, so children frequently turned the lights off while their classmates were using the restroom. The toilets themselves suffered near constant plumbing issues. Flushing them required crossing the patio to get a bowl of water from the tank and manually pouring the water into the toilet. Rachel said that most of the children would skip that step and return to their classroom instead. "You could imagine after use of 40–50 children, the bathroom was a bit of a horror."

Rachel floated the idea of making a documentary film about Safe Passage that would feature Hanley. She connected with a documentary filmmaker back in the United States, but as soon as he suggested a timeline and grew eager to push ahead with the project, Hanley had second thoughts. She seemed uncomfortable being cast in the spotlight. "I shared that this could be big for her and inspire others to get involved, but she began to avoid the subject when I would bring it up," said Rachel. "Hanley finally answered, 'No.'"

Each morning the volunteers would arrive in the church by 8 in the morning, one of the *guajero* mothers would open the gate, and the youngest children would enter and sit on the laps of the volunteers and play quietly. "I believe this was modeled by Hanley," reflected Rachel. "In the early days we saw her leaning into the children, brushing their hair out of their eyes, giving them unabashed hugs, and listening to all they had to say. The modeling of this quickly grew to how Safe Passage became Safe Passage: a nonjudgmental safe space to be seen and validated. This was the essence of the program."

Word of mouth traveling through Guatemala brought more crucial people into Hanley's orbit. One of those was Ed Mahoney, a tall, stoic and soft-spoken New Englander with a thick Boston accent and a logical approach for solving problems. Like Rachel, ED WAS ALSO STUdying Spanish in the western highland city of Xela. On a weekend getaway to Lake Atitlán, the stunning volcanic lake which has been called "the most beautiful lake in the world," Ed met a couple Dutch women at his hotel in the village of Santa Cruz. One day while sitting on lawn chairs at the lake's edge, looking south at the twin peaks of Volcán San Pedro and Volcán de Atitlán, they told him about a project in the Guatemala City garbage dump where they were volunteering—a project that was just getting off the ground and could use the help of someone with an accounting background.

Ed was no fan of Antigua, which had already become a major tourist draw. Nevertheless, he agreed to come and meet Hanley, learn about the project and how he could help her. The Dutch women introduced Ed to Hanley in the room she rented from Doña Alicia de Reyes on Calle del Hermano Pedro which doubled as her office. Though not one to show his emotions, Ed said later that he was impressed with Hanley because "I felt that she was doing something that was worthwhile. On the other hand, I had been doing pretty much nothing for over a year in Xela. It was time to do something rather than just sitting around."

Ed agreed to help Hanley straighten out the project's muddled finances, though he promised that he wouldn't stay there longer than six months. The Bostonian organized Hanley's administrative books, her accounting systems and tracked, for the first time, how the small amount of money that arrived was spent. *Camino Seguro's* major expenses were school supplies, tuition, and food for the kids and their families. Because Ed still rented a room in Xela, and because he disliked the glitz of Antigua, he would commute four hours by bus on Monday mornings, return to the western highlands on Thursday afternoons, and stay in a $15 a night hotel in Antigua during the work week.

Word of a project in the garbage dump also reached Mary Jo Amani, the founder and director of a Nicaragua nonprofit called *Libros Para Niños* and a Montessori-trained teacher who moved to Guatemala City in 2001 with her husband Todd, an employee of USAID. Mary Jo had read a poetry and photography book about children scavenging in the garbage dump, which included mention of a woman who had started a school for the *guajeros* (possibly *Out of the Dump*, by Kristine Franklin and Nancy McGirr). Within weeks of her arrival, she and a friend hopped in a cab and drove to the *basurero* to locate that project. Mary Jo's search eventually led her to the drop-in center in the tiny church where she met Hanley. She later learned that this wasn't the same project she had read about in the book. Nevertheless, Hanley welcomed Mary Jo's offer to come three days a week and read to the children.

"The need of the kids was so great," said Mary Jo. "We were going to be in Guatemala for 5–6 years, and I wanted to get connected to the community. This was a wonderful way for me to do so—Todd was working for the foreign service at the U.S. embassy, and I would share my love for books with the community." Mary Jo eventually introduced Montessori materials to *Camino Seguro* and launched an expansive library and reading program.

In April 2001, an ambitious and no-nonsense, bilingual young Guatemalan woman named Lety Mendez saw fliers around Antigua that the new organization, *Camino Seguro*, was hiring a secretary. The job looked easy enough. It was based here in the tranquil town where Lety lived, and required her only to answer the telephones, open the door, respond to queries. Muy fácil. *Very simple.* So, she visited the office on the Calle del Hermano Pedro, met Hanley, and was immediately given the job. "You can start tomorrow," Hanley told her. The promise of the ease of the job was a trap, Lety later realized.

A couple days later, Hanley shifted gears and told Lety in English, "OK, you can train the volunteers."

"But how? I just started working here."

"I'll show you," the *gringa* responded. And Hanley began to tell Lety the story of her seeing the dump for the first time, calling home and asking her parents to sell her things, and devoting herself to educating the children in the garbage dump. "You can tell this story to the volunteers," she added. "On the way into Guatemala City on the *camioneta*."

Lety grimaced. This felt way over her head. She had grown up outside of Antigua, and before applying for the job with *Camino Seguro* she had never even heard of the Guatemala City garbage dump—not even on television. She hardly knew the capital city, and she didn't feel safe there. She wasn't ready for this.

Then, two months into the job, Hanley upped the ante on her. "You can give tours of the dump to the volunteers."

"What? But I don't know the capital at all ..."

"I'll show you, Lety. It's easy. Tú puedes, tú puedes. *You can do it.* Just pay attention. I'll take you there. I'll show you the *basurero*."

"Eeeh, OK, vamos a ver," Lety responded tentatively. *Let's see.*

The middle-class Guatemalan was shocked when she arrived in Zone 3 and saw the people scavenging through trash and living in homes made of cardboard.

"My whole life I thought that I was poor," she thought to herself. "But this is extreme!"

At La Iglesia they were mobbed by children yelling *"Hola, Hanley! Hola Hanley!"* and jumping into her arms. Lety couldn't believe how many *guajero* kids kept showing up to greet Hanley. This was insane, loco, she thought, *crazy*. For the first two months on the job she had hung fliers around Antigua to recruit volunteers to the project, and shown them an orientation video about *Camino Seguro*. That work was in her comfort zone. And now here she was, cast into a setting she didn't understood. It scared her.

What Lety hadn't shared with her new colleagues at first,

and what she eventually confided in Hanley, was that she had recently lost a baby three months before starting at *Camino Seguro*. She had been eight months pregnant and expected to give birth to her first child. Lety had thought she was out of the danger zone and the child would be OK. People she knew in her neighborhood who had seen her pregnant would ask about her child. "Donde está el niño?" *Where's the child?* The questions drilled into her heart, and Lety knew she needed a change of scenery. Something different.

She was still very much mourning the loss of her baby when she walked through the garbage dump for the first time two months after starting at *Camino Seguro*. There she saw children running around and playing, helping their mothers sift through the mounds of trash. They were filthy, and yet they shouted, they laughed, they frolicked as kids do. She saw teenage girls breastfeeding their newborns. She heard Hanley's stories of babies abandoned in cardboard boxes in the dump because their mothers weren't able to watch them.

"Why wasn't I able to have my child and feed it and give it a loving place to live," Lety asked herself, tormented by the irony. "It's not fair that I'm not able to have one—and here are 13-year-old girls in the dump, having children already."

Over the course of the next year working with Hanley and the project, Lety would come to understand that this was all a process, perhaps one that would help heal her own wounds. "You can't understand what it's like for these girls to lose a child, to give away a child, if you haven't lost one yourself," she rationalized her own process to Hanley.

"You weathered all that pain in order to be able to talk to these girls and mothers about overcoming their own pain," Hanley offered Lety. "You have to be a woman who overcomes all that pain in order to pull children out of that situation."

"What is the pain?" asked Lety "Why do we have to endure it?"

"It's bravery," answered Hanley. "It makes us brave."

Before working for *Camino Seguro*, Lety was a bilingual secretary with no interest in social work, or teaching, or psychology. Now she was practicing all those skills—without a degree or certificate from a school, but with her own empathy, her own human experience. She was providing emotional support for children who had been abused. She was counseling teenage girls who were pregnant. Years later, Lety would reflect that she was doing the exact opposite of what she thought she'd do with her life.

"Tú puedes. Tú puedes," Hanley encouraged her. *You can do it.*

Lety's first impression of Hanley, when she was talked into working with volunteers and giving tours of the garbage dump just two months after taking the job, was that the *gringa* was crazy. Totally *loca*. These *guajeros* were beyond help, she had initially thought. In Guatemala, "no nos cambiamos." *We don't change.* In Guatemala, "la gente no ayuda." *Here we don't have a culture of helping each other.* Pobre es pobre. *Poverty is poverty.* She told Hanley as much.

"No," said Hanley with a smile. "If we can change just one life, then we'll make a difference ... If we change the lives of 50 kids, we'll change the world forever. We'll help them study. We'll give them food, shoes, and medicine."

Hanley's plan was audacious. It was madness. But as the mission began to consume Lety's life, she realized that she, too, was becoming *loca*.

Together they would commute early in the morning from Antigua, spend all day in La Iglesia with the children, or visiting families in the shanty villages around the dump, or in the *basurero* itself. Around dinner time, the *guajeros* would all approach Hanley and ask her for help, or advice, or just wanted five minutes of her presence. Not until 7 p.m., or later, would she board the chicken bus from El Trébol and return to Antigua in the dark.

"Hanley, es peligroso! *This is dangerous.* They're going to rob us on the bus," warned Lety.

"No, it's OK. The driver and the passengers on the bus know me." Exhausted, Hanley would hunch over her backpack and notebook full of information about the families, and she would fall into a deep sleep as the *camioneta* left Guatemala City and headed into the hills on the hour-long ride home to Antigua.

"*Seño*, we have arrived. We're in Antigua," a fellow passenger would wake her as the bus pulled into the terminal behind Antigua's marketplace, a few blocks west of the Parque Central. Half awake, Hanley would walk home, sit on her bed and write notes and draft letters to potential funders until the wee hours of the morning. A few hours later she would rise, throw on the same clothes and board the chicken bus again for Guatemala City.

Where Will the Money Come From?

"COME PLAY *FÚTBOL* WITH US!" the local kids invited Ryan Mick, who was visiting *Camino Seguro* together with his parents, Cathy and Mark. The offer was a kind one, for the 9-year-old from Oregon loved the game they called "soccer" back in the States. It was also a reciprocal offer. The Mick family had brought real, round *pelotas* with them to donate to the community. These were far superior to the foam bladders of old soccer balls that *guajero* kids typically used as they ran, kicked and tumbled on the dusty *campo* in the Colonia Landivar on land claimed by the squatters, about five blocks from the church. The field was about half the regulation size of a soccer field. Two pipes on either end, probably reclaimed from the garbage dump, stuck out of the ground to mark the goals. There was no crossbar and no netting.

The only catch was that the Mick family had to walk through the shanty village, the *colonia*, to reach the soccer fields. Hanley insisted that a Guatemalan teacher from *Camino Seguro* accompany them. Before they left the safety of the church, Claudio, who spoke only broken English, pointed to the American guests and held one raised fist in front of the other, then shrugged his shoulders as if to ask them, "Will you fight? If we get jumped during this walk, will you fight?" Cathy and Mark, Ryan, and his 5-year-old sister Jennifer nodded, hesitantly. Claudio was able to explain that no one in the *colonia* would harm Hanley or mess with anyone walking with her, because of the trust she had established with the *guajero* community. But without Hanley, who knew what might happen?

They made it to the soccer field unscathed. On the walk back to the drop-in center at the church, following the match, Claudio and the Micks detoured a couple alleyways when they saw a few rough-looking, strung-out men sniffing glue in the street.

Early that evening, as they hopped into a taxi to return to their hotel in Antigua, Hanley suddenly appeared with a sobbing young girl who had been bitten by a street dog—a *chucho*. Hanley insisted that she and the girl join the Micks, diverge from their hour-long route and look for a health clinic that could treat the girl. A comical sequence followed, remembered Mark. One clinic after another had already closed for the day. The taxi then stopped at a hospital, where Hanley learned that treating the girl for the dog bite would cost more than $100. Mark offered to pay on the spot. But conscious of her project's meager finances, Hanley politely refused. A clinic near the dump that would open the following morning would charge only $10, she said. Their last stop on this odyssey through Guatemala City took them to a pharmacy, where Hanley got cough syrup for the girl before dropping her off at her home in the *colonia*. The Micks didn't arrive in Antigua until late that night, which worried Cathy. She had traveled enough in Guatemala to know that, as a foreigner, she should avoid traveling at night.

During the futile nighttime search for a health clinic, Cathy Mick was paying close attention to *Camino Seguro*, the value of the program, and how it was run. She was studying Hanley, her commitment, her approach, and how much the children adored her. Cathy was impressed. On that trip together with her family, she met the Micks' sponsor child, a 10-year-old girl named Leslie, who lived with her parents in a one-room cement-walled house with dirt floors near the garbage dump that the government provided for *guajeros*. Leslie beamed that she wanted to be a secretary when she grew up. "This girl had absolutely nothing, but Hanley was giving her hope. She was giving these kids a chance," said Cathy. "The life of those kids outside the walls of the school had to be horrific. But within those walls they could be children who were loved and supported and nurtured—what we privileged Americans would consider a 'normal' childhood."

On Cathy's first trip to Guatemala in January 2001 together with her boss Arthur Berg, Hanley had impressed them and convinced them that *Camino Seguro* was worth supporting financially. This was an enormous breakthrough for the project. Arthur Berg owned Oregon-based Berg Wholesale, one of the nation's largest distributors of door and bath hardware. Arthur traveled extensively throughout Central America looking for products and business partners. While walking around Antigua one day in the spring or summer of 2000, he happened to read the story about Hanley in *Revue*, Guatemala's English-language magazine which catered to tourists and ex-pats in Guatemala. The story, by Kara J. Ward in *Revue*'s May 2000 edition, was titled "Dreaming Beyond the Dump: Project Safe Passage is getting disadvantaged children into the classroom." It was the same story that caught the eyes of Rachel Meyn. Berg emailed Hanley after he returned to Oregon, they corresponded electronically for a time, and he asked Cathy to fly down and check out the project for him.

At the time, *Camino Seguro* was supporting approximately 100 kids but Hanley wouldn't turn a single child away. She constantly ran the risk of taking in more children than she had the money to support. According to Cathy's notes from conversations with Hanley, the project had a budget of $35,000—a third of which was a one-time grant from an organization of nuns. Hanley had a small, devoted staff and passionate volunteers who would work for several months at a time, but no real long-term sustainable path forward. No individual donors were yet writing checks with more than three zeroes. Hanley continued to work 18-hour days and slept on a cot in the corner of her home office in the apartment she rented in Antigua. Her pillow lay close enough to the desk that she could pop out of bed at 2 a.m. if she suddenly remembered and felt the urge to write down the name of a potential donor in the United States or a language school in Antigua she should approach for volunteers or to hang fliers.

Cathy recognized Hanley's innate warmth, love, and genuine confidence. She could also see that Hanley sometimes struggled with logistics and operations. "She was all about the kids, recognizing the need, and doing what had to be done. But the money side of things wasn't her strength." She needed to think about where the money would come from for Safe Passage to survive and grow. Still, she and Arthur both saw Hanley's ability to make hard decisions, work on a shoestring budget, and get the most out of what little she had. "If someone didn't go to school, she would have to cut them out of the program because she had limited resources," said Arthur. Her ability to persevere despite so many hurdles attracted him.

"I had assumed that the locals would be happy and supportive (of Hanley), but they actually fought her hard in the beginning. They didn't want the 'dirty little dump kids' going to their schools." Other organizations, many religious, came to the garbage dump and gave a speech or a sermon, handed out toys to the kids, then left. "But Hanley got these kids and families on a path that would change the next generation," observed Arthur. "One of her biggest strengths was also getting people committed to helping in whatever way they could."

Cathy wrote in her journal:

I believe strongly in the philosophy of the Safe Passage program. Where most programs simply give away necessary items to needy people, Safe Passage teaches responsibility, self-reliance and independence, requires school attendance, and provides a safe, supportive place for the children away from the disease and dangers of the dump and abusive, neglectful parents. The program provides much needed vitamins, hot lunches, tutoring, medical attention, school supplies and tuition, counseling, and arts and sports activities." And yet, Safe Passage's resources at the time seemed minuscule. Cathy's journal entry continued: *"Lunches and snacks are supported by a very small budget, but the results are more than these children would ever otherwise eat in their lifetime at the dump. The lunch that was served the day we visited the project was ramen noodles with a few cooked vegetables, a tortilla, and juice. Each child ate all of their meal without prompting!*

Help and small favors seemed to come from a hundred different sources. A flight attendant whom Hanley had befriended would bring bags of extra clothing for the children on return flights from the United States. A foundation covered the cost for large shipments of supplies to be mailed to Guatemala City. "The project needs children's chewable vitamins, clothes, kids paint brushes, construction paper, pencils, scissors, big glue, erasers, paints, crayons, markers, used children's shoes and jeans and pants," wrote Cathy. "Toys would include used Barbies, checkers, chess, thinking games, memory games, teaching materials,

Spanish reading books, playground equipment—soccer balls, basketballs, jump rope...." Children who missed no more than three days of school in a month were "rewarded with 40 points." With these points, the children could "purchase" pants, shoes, and backpacks from the Safe Passage "Reward Store." Favors came from within Guatemala City, too. The Marriott Hotel in wealthy Zone 1 of the capital hosted a Christmas party in 2000 for *guajero* children who had dutifully attended school. Even Santa Claus appeared with his bag of gifts.

Cathy, Arthur, and Hanley shared dinner one night at a classic old hotel in Antigua that had been converted from a monastery. They ate a delicious chicken soup, Cathy remembered, almost certainly served with fresh, warm tortillas, as per local tradition. The Oregonians asked how they could support her from the United States, and the conversation led to them offering to take much of the clerical work off Hanley's hands. From the office at Berg Wholesale they would send newsletters and donation requests to supporters, child sponsors and prospective donors. At first, the list of recipients totaled no more than a few hundred. One of Hanley's volunteers would email program updates and scanned photos of the children from Guatemala to Oregon, and then send artwork and "thank you" cards in bulk, either through the mail or sometimes with a volunteer who was flying back to the United States. The arrangement was laborious and could be clunky, but it worked.

ON JUNE 10, 2001, Hanley emailed Cathy to outline her needs for a sponsorship office based in Oregon. Hanley's written tone, like her oratory style, was deliberate, articulate and polite.

*I have read the notes you sent me from our initial conversation
and have given careful consideration to what our organizational needs are at this time," Hanley wrote. "I am including
the following information for your consideration in hopes that
it will serve as a shared starting point as we move forward with
the Safe Passage office." Her email was also honest and sincere:
"I appreciate your willingness to help very, very much! For a
long time, I was trying to do most of the office work alone and
as a result, fell terribly behind.*

Hanley asked for someone in Cathy's office to print and
mail a quarterly newsletter to supporters in the United States
and England that was written and produced by her staff in
Guatemala; the liaison in Oregon would also mail videos, brochures and photos of sponsor children. If a child left Safe Passage, Hanley wanted Cathy's staff to inform the sponsor, and
also call sponsors who weren't responding to emails. Any checks
sent to the Oregon office would be forwarded to a PO Box in
Hanley's hometown of Yarmouth, Maine. A retiree named Stan
Sylvester, a friend of Hanley's father Michael, would visit the
post office once a week, process checks and inform her of new
donors, and give the checks to Michael to be deposited at People's Heritage Bank in Maine. Stan also provided the fax address
for Safe Passage. Rachel Meyn remembered Stan as a "no fuss
kind of guy" who took the job seriously. The voicemail on his
service emphatically pronounced each syllable in the message:
"You have reached the facsimile for Safe Passage."

"It seems to be working very well as he just sends me a pho-
tocopy image via internet of each check received and we enter
the data here. He then files the copy of the check in Maine,"
Hanley wrote to Cathy.

Hanley alluded to the need for speaking engagements so she

could build more support for the nascent program. It seems she was overcoming her own reticence to leave the project in the hands of her staff and go on fundraising trips. "It is my hope that as things get more established, I will be able to visit the states periodically to do some fundraising ... speaking about the project." She also mentioned the need for an eventual Board of Directors and asked if Cathy would be willing to serve on a board.

> *It is my hope that with a solid, active board we can begin to address some of the following areas: Recruitment of long-term volunteers; Speakers bureau ... setting up speaking engagements by members of the board or regional volunteers; Fundraising; Long term planning; Grants and Foundations; Capital campaigns; Connections with corporate sponsors.*

But a followup email six months later, on December 4, 2001—this one to Cathy, Arthur, and to her father Michael in Maine—was more direct and belied a tone of frustration and immediacy. The email's concluding paragraph suggested that the project was in dire straits, just two years after Hanley had launched it. December 2001 was a time of global unease. The 9/11 terrorist attacks had put the western world on edge, the United States was at war, and global markets were nervous about the path ahead.

> *The situation could be described as critical," confided Hanley. "If Safe Passage is to avoid closure, I think it's important I take a more active role stateside at this time. However, I cannot do this alone and greatly appreciate your collaboration and assistance in planning and implementing this proposal.*

Hanley proposed an immediate fundraising effort in the United States between December 7–30, while her project next to the garbage dump was closed December 21–January 3. She would target Oregon, Maine, and New Hampshire. She would go on the road with brochures, videos, slides, mailings, and a Christmas letter. She asked Cathy, Arthur, and her father to help find funding for her flight home from Guatemala, money for lodging and transportation while in the States, assistance in scheduling speaking engagements at churches, women's groups, clubs, and libraries and meetings with potential big donors, and help to cover phone expenses so she could check in frequently with Lety and Claudio, whom she would leave in charge of the program while she was away.

Also, Cathy and dad," wrote Hanley, *"What do you think the odds are of setting up a Christmas luncheon in Maine and Oregon for current sponsors and friends? We could charge them a small entrance fee to cover the cost of the food and I could talk about the project. Dad, you could invite people who are currently sponsors and we could tap into people in the area who are on our mailing list but don't sponsor, etc. It could be a question & answer session.... The objective is to hit as many people and places as we can in the time I will have available. I can work very hard so don't hesitate to book me as much as you can. There is always time for one more. For every reach out ... we just might get the hit we need to keep this thing afloat this month, January and beyond.*

Hanley's comfort zone may have been playing the role of social worker, talking with children and families in the little church next to the garbage dump. But she now realized that, if Safe Passage were to survive, she would need to take on more roles—ambassador to the project and fundraiser. Through her storytelling, through photos, videos and artwork, she would need to introduce the Guatemala City garbage dump to Americans and their pocketbooks—and fast.

I have given this a great deal of thought," Hanley's December 2001 letter concluded. "I don't think trying to coordinate things from here is the best use of my time in this current situation.

ONCE HANLEY COMMITTED to travel more frequently to Maine and become an ambassador for Safe Passage, word of her project in the garbage dump spread. In June 2002, her alma mater Bowdoin College awarded her with its annual Common Good Award, which honors alumni who have "demonstrated an extraordinary, profound, and sustained commitment to the common good, in the interest and for the benefit of society, with conspicuous disregard for personal gains in wealth or status." The concept of "the common good" as a guiding principle was framed by Bowdoin College's first president Joseph McKeen, who said in his inaugural address 200 years earlier: *"... It ought always to be remembered, that literary institutions are founded and endowed for the common good, and not for the private advantage of those who resort to them for education."*

Bowdoin's commitment to idealism, liberal education, and the common good had endured even through times when those ideals seemed to clash with the conflict of the moment, such as the United States' nationwide mobilization during the Second World War, when the military draft reduced the college's enrollment to fewer than 200 students. Nevertheless, during a 1944 address by Eleanor Roosevelt titled "English Youth in the War," Bowdoin's McKeen Center for the Common Good reported that the nation's First Lady "reaffirmed the value of a liberal arts education, emphasized college students' responsibility for understanding America's goals in the war, and encouraged students to actively participate in restoring the peace that would follow."

Hanley graduated from Bowdoin College in 1992, at a moment of great optimism for the western world and for democracy. The Soviet Union's Iron Curtain had fallen, the United States had emerged from the Cold War as the world superpower, walls between peoples were being dismantled, and new nations were being born. It seemed that a Bowdoin graduate need only spin a globe and pick a spot to move to and make a difference. The Common Good Award she received on June 1, 2002, read:

> Hanley Graham Denning, you have dedicated your life to helping the children of the world, particularly those suffering the ravages of disease and poverty. You have exemplified the Common Good in your tireless service to those children most in need, whether as an outreach worker for Shoreline, a Brunswick mental health center, or as a teacher with Head Start in North Carolina or the Foundation for Children with AIDS in Roxbury, Massachusetts. Working amid the filth of Guatemala City's garbage dump, you have brought dignity to the daily lives of countless families and provided an education to students under your care and inspiration to those who know you.
>
> A native of Yarmouth, you were a track champion at Bowdoin while excelling in the classroom as a psychology major. At Wheelock College, you earned a master's degree in early childhood education. In 1997, you sold all your possessions and moved to Guatemala despite knowing little Spanish. You immersed yourself in the language and culture of the country, working with 90 children for a church-based teaching program there. You have said that working with these children 'captured your heart' and prompted you to continue your work for three years. In

December 1999, you hesitantly agreed to visit the Guatemala City garbage dump. Despite your years of work with those in need, you said recently that 'nothing prepared [you] for the horrors [you] saw' there—families living in cardboard houses and digging through the filth for food; few families with running, let along potable, water; scores of children with no formal education; rampant drug abuse.

A visit turned into a calling, and you soon founded Safe Passage, a nonprofit agency providing education, food, and a drop-in center for the children who live in the garbage dump. Your leadership has created an empowerment program that teaches children the value of education, gives them a safe place to play and study, and provides them with much-needed hope. You have become a passionate advocate for the children, securing donations to provide them with the books, uniforms, and fees needed to attend the Guatemalan public schools. In an abandoned church at the dump's edge, you work as Safe Passage's executive director, training volunteers and staff, and overseeing the hundreds of children in the program. Your work has made a difference in the lives of countless individuals and your selfless devotion has become an inspiration for many.

Hanley Denning, it is with great pride and an even greater sense of admiration for your commitment to the children of Guatemala that we present to you the 2002 Common Good Award.

IT WAS A LATE SUMMER MORNING in 2002 at the youth soccer fields in Yarmouth, several weeks before the colors of the majestic New England forests would burn campfire red, orange, and yellow. Parents stood on the sidelines cheering their children as a battle for control of the ball ensued at midfield. Jane Gallagher, a 42-year-old gregarious and sociable litigating attorney, whose 11-year-old son Jake played for the Yarmouth Colts soccer club, walked over to say hello to Mike Denning, whose youngest son Luke—a year older than Jake—suited up for the opposing team during this friendly scrimmage. Another soccer parent approached them, too, and mentioned that she had read a story in her husband's alumni magazine from Bowdoin College about a young woman named Hanley who had started a project in Guatemala. "Is she related to you?" the parent asked Mike.

A smile spread across his face. "Yes, that's my daughter," the elder Denning beamed with fatherly pride. He talked briefly about the project, and how Hanley had seen the garbage dump just before she was to return home and how she had decided to help the children living in those squalid conditions. But, he added, "she really never knows from month to month if she can keep the doors open." The words hung in the crisp air.

Jane's ears perked. Loath to easily accept defeat, her lawyerly drive for success kicked in and she told Mike she wanted to help. She had no experience in the nonprofit world or in fundraising, and she had little desire to go to Guatemala to "work in the trenches," but Jane was staying home raising young kids in those days and she had extra time. She was acutely aware that her family enjoyed excess material possessions—a stark contrast with families in the garbage dump. "My kids don't have three puzzles; they have a stack of puzzles," Jane told Mike. "They have Legos coming out the ying-yang.... Please put me in touch with your daughter."

Jane began to correspond via email with Hanley, who was 10 years her junior, but they instantly developed a strong rapport. "I hear you're doing this amazing thing in Guatemala," wrote Jane. "I hear that you don't have the resources you need for it. What can I do to help? You know that we live in a place where we have so much. If we just skim the surface, then we can help you keep your doors open." Jane eventually convinced

Hanley that she could become an ambassador, too, and help raise awareness about Safe Passage. "Tell me what you need in terms of project and school supplies," Jane implored. "I'm really good at telling stories and having dinner parties. I can use those skills."

Later in the fall when Hanley returned to Maine on a fundraising trip, Jane hosted her for breakfast and remembered that she felt like she had met a long-lost sister. At the Gallagher family's dining room table, Hanley described combing the head lice from the hair of the children who played in the dump. Jane's children—Jake, in particular—piped up. "We have to go to Guatemala," said her soccer-loving son. But Jane made it known that she still preferred to help Safe Passage by networking her connections in the Yarmouth area. She would hold a lunch at her friend Joan's house, and a dinner party at her friend Laurie's, to tell the guests about Hanley's work, and to bring them on board as child sponsors.

Meanwhile, Jake invited Hanley to visit his middle school class and used her appearance to launch a drive for Safe Passage school supplies. Hanley left a lasting impression on his classmates when she told them stories and showed impactful photos of the *guajero* children toiling in the dump—photos of a baby sleeping in a cardboard box while workers and vultures scavenged for food in the background, photos of children receiving after-school snacks in the little church next to the dump. One parent of a fellow student would later contact the *Portland Press Herald* and suggest that Maine's largest newspaper cover this unique fundraising effort by local students. Just as the *Revue* story in May 2000 had done in Guatemala, stories in the *Herald* in August and November 2003 by reporter Tess Nacelewicz immediately introduced Hanley and her mission to a much larger New England audience.

This was a major spark, Jane remembered. She and a few other Mainers who became Hanley's hand-picked, informal advisory group would schedule speaking appearances for Hanley at area churches, schools and Rotary clubs. "Hanley would go from meeting to meeting with these images of the garbage dump on a poster board, and she would tell her stories," said Jane. "You couldn't look at these photos and not have a heart and not get attached."

Formal presentations made Hanley nervous, Jane observed. And she didn't love fundraising or going around the table asking for money. Cold calls for money she abhorred even more. But this 32-year-old local woman turned international nonprofit leader was a natural storyteller. The photos and tales of life in the garbage dump could warm even the coldest person in the room and prompt them to open their pocket book to sponsor a child. "For someone who didn't have a master's degree in development work, she was a natural," said Jane. Some supporters immediately recognized that what Hanley was doing was community-based development. She had gone into the community and asked what they needed, instead of forcing her ideas on them.

Jane also witnessed Hanley getting frustrated at times. She remembered a high school student asking Hanley, "Why Guatemala? Why are you going to another country when there's a need right here?"

"This is what *I'm* passionate about," Hanley responded. "You don't have to support Safe Passage if you don't want to. Just figure out where you can help instead. Take your energy and skill and put it toward anything that's going to make a difference in the world."

Hanley's frustration wasn't with people who wouldn't support Safe Passage, Jane explained. "It was more a frustration because people would use that question—'why Guatemala?'—as an excuse to do nothing."

Jane, and others in Yarmouth, offered themselves and their time almost completely to help Hanley. Jane would put her kids on the school bus in the morning, return to her house on Boxwood Drive and sit down in front of her desktop computer to correspond via email with Hanley, set up meetings for her next visit to Maine, and research potential funders or grant sources. "Whatever she needed, I would do," said Jane. "Literally, I would hear the bus come back at three in the afternoon, and I realized that I hadn't moved from that computer all day."

OTHERS ON HANLEY'S ADVISORY COUNCIL leant crucial resources from their places of work. John Coleman, who ran an advertising agency, designed the initial logo for Safe Passage and donated tens of thousands of envelopes and stationary for mailings. Jim Highland, founder and owner of the Portland-based healthcare consulting firm Compass Health Analytics, leant a space in his office for the project—before Safe Passage had enough resources to afford its own lease. Hanley convinced Rachel Meyn, the woman from northern California who was back living with her family in Sonoma County, to move to Yarmouth in November 2003 with an eye toward opening a U.S.-based office. At first, Rachel had no car in Maine. Hanley's mom, Marina, would drive her to Jim's office each day, and she or Jane would pick her up. All material donations to Safe Passage, bound for Guatemala City, were stored either in Jane's living room or in Jim's basement. "We were flying by the seat of our pants," laughed Jane.

Rachel had seen the twinkle in Hanley's eye in Guatemala

as her vision formed and she grew the project. Now Rachel saw that same twinkle, as they worked to get Hanley's beloved Maine community hooked on helping children in Guatemala City. She saw it as Hanley and Marina gave her driving tours through Yarmouth and proudly pointed out the local attractions. Here was Pat's Pizza; there was Cousins Island, and there was the home of Meg, who had just adopted a young Guatemalan girl and was "a firecracker" ready to help the project. The Maine support network was coming at Rachel a million miles per hour, and she would quickly become Hanley's right-hand person in the United States. Jim Highland agreed to pay Rachel a salary of $19,000 for the first year—a modest amount for a college graduate who worked long days and nights, but Rachel had learned to live frugally during her time in Guatemala. The afternoon that Jim committed to pay her salary, she and Hanley celebrated by going to Pat's for pizza and popcorn chicken baskets. "Food never tasted so good!" beamed Rachel.

Hanley joined Rachel for the first three weeks as they drove up and down the coast of Maine in a rental car—they called it their "Maine roadshow"—giving presentations at three or four churches, schools, and senior homes each day with little more than a stack of large photos, many taken by Maine photojournalist John Santerre, and stories from the garbage dump. Hanley wore business work outfits that her mom, Marina, gave her, remembered Rachel. Sometimes they didn't fit quite right, because Hanley was taller than Marina. Rachel also remembered Hanley wearing 1990s women blazers. These "power outfits" were a far cry from the short-sleeved pink polo shirt, faded blue jeans and white tennis shoes that Hanley wore at the Guatemala City garbage dump. Since Rachel had volunteered and worked at nearly every Safe Passage site in Guatemala City and knew *Camino Seguro* children and families by name, she could draw from her own stories. In the years that followed, she would later stand in for Hanley at presentations across Maine.

In December 2003, Hanley and Rachel wrote and sent the first big end-of-year appeal letter to donors. While Compass Health Analytics employees worked quietly on their phones during workday hours, crunching insurance data with clients, Rachel fielded calls from across the United States and Europe about inquiries to present about Safe Passage, sponsor questions about financial commitments and about sponsor children, and from groups that wanted to visit Guatemala on a service trip. Jim Highland's office in Maine suddenly felt like a little international hub. When his staff left for the evening, Hanley and Rachel went to work. They printed hundreds of appeal letters, which benefited from Hanley's persuasive writing and editing and meticulous attention to grammar. Rachel figured out how to run a mail merge and print labels and envelopes on Compass Health Analytics' office equipment. At about 1 in the morning they spread out and assembled all the pieces on the company floor, and kept their energy levels charged by eating chocolate bonbons and joking about whether this was how nonprofits typically got their fundraising materials out the door. They did their best to wipe the occasional chocolate smears off envelopes. By 6 in the morning the envelopes were boxed and ready for delivery, and they transformed the space so Jim's staff would know nothing of the nighttime operation. It was the first of many such all-nighters.

TIME AND TIME AGAIN, anonymous angel investors—probably friends and business contacts of Mike Denning, whom he knew through the investment banking world—would come through with big checks when Hanley needed them most. Jane, Rachel and Marina occasionally witnessed those breakthrough moments. "Hanley was at my house for breakfast when the call came through from a donor in New York that she was going to get the money to build an educational reinforcement center at Safe Passage," Jane remembered. "She took the call on her cell phone, went outside and then came back shouting, 'You're not going to believe what just happened!'"

Early afternoon on a bright, sunny weekday in 2005—probably the springtime, after Charlie and Theresa Gendron returned from Florida where they waited for Maine's frigid winter to end, it happened. Rachel and Marina both recall they were in the car with Hanley as they approached the Gendrons' long, curvy driveway and parked in front of the house, large but not opulent, in a wealthy neighborhood of Yarmouth near the ocean.

This particular visit to court a potentially lucrative Safe Passage supporter would show Hanley's innate ability to win the hearts and attention of people who had otherwise not felt a connection to Guatemala. This story would reveal her talent to connect on a deeply human level with people from all backgrounds—from the slums of the garbage dump to the gilded offices of wealthy CEOs.

Charlie, a multi-millionaire who made his fortune as a low-income housing real estate investor, had invited Hanley to stop by as a favor to her father Mike, with whom he played basketball on Saturday mornings, and briefly meet him and his wife Theresa. Their conversation wouldn't last long, Charlie figured. He was a busy man, with business conference calls filling the afternoon. He would shake her hand, offer her a coffee, chat for a few minutes, wish her the best with her project in Guatemala, hand her the check they'd already written for $250, and return to his office. This would be easy. A small contribution to a faraway cause.

"Those days, my wife and I were more focused on support-ing basic needs in the greater Portland area like food kitchens," Charlie Gendron reflected. Many charities asked the Gendrons for money. "When her Dad brought it up to me what she was doing in Guatemala, I told him 'I really want to help people *here.*' But Mike, as good as he is, he kept coming." The elder Denning dropped off a video at the Gendron house that showed Hanley in the dump, narrating why she was drawn to help this commu-nity, as mournful, melancholy music played, and garbage trucks dropped their payloads in the background.

"Mike said he'd like her to stop by our house, just so we could meet her," said Charlie. "So she called and set up a time."

Hanley felt jittery and anxious. She told Rachel and Marina to remain in the car for the visit, which none of them expected would take longer than a few minutes. "Stay here. Don't show yourself!" she half yelled. Then she walked up to the house wearing one of those dark "power outfits" that Marina had leant her, and carrying her large posterboard with photos of *guajeros* working and playing in the garbage dump. This was the primary tool she used during her month-long trips back to Maine to court people like the Gendrons.

Charlie and Theresa both greeted Hanley at the door and took seats in the dining room, with Hanley at the head of the table and the Gendrons on either side of her. Hanley declined a coffee, though she may have drunk water, and began narrat-ing how she had found herself in Guatemala to learn Spanish, how the nun showed her the garbage dump, and how she called home and asked her parents to sell her car and her computer and decided to stay and devote herself to help the children and families break the cycle of poverty.

"This is not what people usually do," Charlie thought to himself as he remembered Mike describing Hanley as an all-American girl with bachelor's and master's degrees from two prestigious schools. "They take paths in the United States and follow them."

Then Hanley asked if she could show them pictures of the project. She pushed back her chair, stood up and showed the Gendrons her poster board with photos of the garbage dump, the children, the mothers, the *guajeros* digging through piles of trash, the little church they used for the drop-in center. But she never explicitly asked for money, Charlie keenly observed. Never once. The real estate tycoon used words like "crazy, nutty, spiritual" to describe what happened next, and the effect it had on the Gendrons.

Five or ten minutes into Hanley's poster board presentation, Charlie looked across the table and gauged an expression of awe on his wife's face. "Theresa was absolutely blown away," he recalled. "She hadn't wanted to be a part of this, but I had asked her as a favor to meet with me and Hanley. We have a philanthropic foundation, but she isn't the primary driver." Charlie described the look on Theresa's face as one of both dismay and amazement as she studied Hanley and the poster board.

"Can you give Theresa and me a second?" he asked Hanley. The Gendrons left the dining room and made a righthand turn to enter the kitchen for two minutes of privacy.

"Oh my God! Can you believe what she's done?" Theresa said to Charlie. On the spot, the Gendrons decided to help her. Charlie confessed that he felt embarrassed for treating this meeting as a mere obligation to Mike. He tore up the $250 check and wrote a new one, for $5,000. (Checks with even more zeroes would follow in the years to come.) Then he wiped clean his slate of upcoming conference calls for the next couple hours.

They returned to the kitchen and presented the check to Hanley, whose face lit up with surprise. "I didn't come here to ask for money," she said. "I just wanted to tell you about the project, and how we're trying to get a piece of land to build an educational reinforcement center."

Then Hanley upped the ante and *did* put the Gendrons in an unfamiliar position.

"I'd love to have you come down and visit the project, and see it for yourself," said Hanley. "You can help in whatever way feels right, but the children and families of the garbage dump need to see and know that people value them and care about their education."

Charlie and Theresa Gendron—like Jane Gallagher, like the Oregonians Arthur Berg and Cathy Mick, like Rachel Meyn, like Joan Anderson the Danish woman, like so many other privileged Americans and Europeans—had never considered visiting a destination so foreign, so desperate, so physically and emotionally dangerous, as the Guatemala City garbage dump. They could write checks, they could make phone calls and hold benefit dinners, they could organize donation drives—wouldn't that be enough? Why did they also have to spend money to fly to Guatemala—money that could have been donated directly to Safe Passage?

That was Hanley's bold if unconscious brilliance, of course. For once they visited and saw the project with their own eyes, they would be committed—both emotionally and financially. And the children of the garbage dump would know they were valued, not just by Hanley, not just by foreign volunteers, not just by their Guatemala teachers and social workers, but by their sponsor families—their "*padrinos*." Hanley was building a reciprocal relationship.

"I wouldn't say we're religious," reflected Charlie, "But

Theresa and I said that she is the closest thing for us to someone's description of God. There was something about her cher-
ishing those kids, her love for them.... I never felt I was being
sold an idea. She had nothing to fabricate. This feeling of wanting to help her was overwhelming."

The 10 minutes Charlie and Theresa Gendron expected to
spend with Hanley on that spring afternoon in 2005 turned
into a moment suspended in time for them. Rachel and Marina,
waiting in the car outside, both remember that Hanley was
inside their house for more than 30 minutes. Charlie suspected
that 90 minutes could have elapsed.

A beaming smile covered Hanley's face once she finally
emerged from the Gendron home and rushed to the car. She
was grinning and laughing about the successful visit. "You won't
believe what they gave!" Marina remembers Hanley saying. "I
hardly even needed to use the poster board."

"I think she had a presentation ready, but flew by the seat of
her pants once she got inside," reflected Marina. "She just had a
magic touch with people. Her charisma was amazing. She never
asked for money directly. She had a way that wasn't purposeful.
It wasn't planned."

Whenever she made subsequent trips back to Maine,
Hanley would visit the Gendrons, who would write more and
more checks. Each time, she would encourage them to also visit
Guatemala.

Hanley was rarely seen in the garbage dump community without her blue jeans, tennis shoes, and backpack, in which she carried a notebook and files on the children she was enrolling in the program. She would update her notes on the bus ride back to Antigua. (JOHN SANTERRE)

PART II

It was said that Hanley knew the name of every child enrolled in Safe Passage—even when her program grew to serve more than 500 children. (JOE DELCONZO)

For many children of the garbage dump, the lunch they ate at the project was the only balanced meal they received all day. (JOHN SANTERRE)

She Sees Them

THEY STOOD AT THE TRAFFIC LIGHTS of Guatemala City's busiest boulevards, their tiny feet barely filling flimsy sandals or old used tennis shoes they found in the garbage dump. On a good day they found a safe spot on the sidewalk to hawk their wares, on other days their movements blended with the capital's chaotic automobile traffic.

"Chiclets, chiclets," one child yelled as he held packets of bubble gum over his head for the drivers to see.

"Bananos, bananos," shouted another. They sold fruit, candy, cigarettes, old clothing, whatever would pocket them a few coins and earn them the right to walk back to their *barrio* that night.

Red *camioneta* city buses rolled by them, their exhaust pipes belching thick, black smoke. Taxis, too, with holes in their floorboards and windows that no longer rolled up. Even in front of the Marriott Hotel, the Radisson, and the Westin, in Guatemala City's wealthy Zone 1 or Zone 9, this mobile market scene played out. Occasionally a sports car with dark tinted windows zoomed through the intersection, the driver oblivious to the children standing just inches away from the road. To them, these *niños* of the street, of the dump, of the capital's regrettable underbelly were invisible.

"We're allowed to come home once we have earned 20 quet-zales," Mamá Forunda's daughter Gloria told Juanita Anderson, Hanley's first international volunteer, as they worked on art projects one afternoon at the drop-in center in the church next to the dump.

"You sell things after you've been at school?" the Danish woman asked.

"Yeah, first we go to school, then we come here, and then we have to sell things on the street," answered Claudia Roque. The children proudly showed Joan and Hanley the crafts they had made out of egg trays, crepe paper and popsicle sticks. They were also excited about the possibility of selling them.

"Sometimes we have to walk all the way home after the buses have stopped running late at night," said Angel David Roque. "All kinds of strange people are out on the streets when it gets dark." The approximately 3-mile walk from the Marriott back to the *colonia* near the dump would lead them across the Avenida La Reforma, up Calle 10 or 11, then along the busy Panamerican Highway to the Fifth or Sixth Avenida. The Danish woman shuddered at the thought of these tiny children walking through the streets of Guatemala City at night.

"But it's better than working down in the dump," said Angel David.

THE TOUGH GIRL SELLING SWEETS on the street at first ignored the voice coming from the tall *gringa* in the pink shirt, jeans, and tennis shoes with a backpack slung over her shoulder.

"Amiga. ¿Cómo estás?" *How are you?*

She couldn't be talking to me, thought the tough girl. Why would she talk to me?

But the *gringa* persisted. "¿Tienes familia? ¿Tienes casa? ¿Porqué no te vas a la escuela?" *Do you have a family? Do you have a home? Why aren't you in school?*

Perplexed, annoyed, the tough girl refused to engage with this stranger, this foreigner. "What does she want from me? Why won't she leave me alone?" she thought. The tough girl was used to sticking up for herself and not taking crap from anyone. She and her older sister, Monica, had learned their street smarts in a hurry after their parents died four years earlier—their father in a traffic accident, their mother by drinking herself to death. The tough girl was nine years old when she was orphaned. She and her sister left El Porvenir, a shanty town on the eastern outskirts of Guatemala City, and moved to the *colonia* next to the garbage dump, where Monica found work. Independent and strong-willed, she sold sweets on the street instead.

Hanley had probably passed by the tough girl many times after hopping off the bus from Antigua at El Trebol and walking to the garbage dump. She recognized her. Indeed, the *gringa* was said to know the names of every child in the neighborhood, every child in her project. When it came to the *guajero niños*, she apparently had a photographic memory.

"I'd like to help you." She approached Nancy Gudiel, who finally turned and acknowledged that Hanley was speaking to her. The tough girl was no longer invisible.

"I have a program called *Camino Seguro* that helps children near the *basurero* go to school," Hanley said. "Would you like to go to school and learn?"

Nancy wasn't sure. She had heard about this mysterious *gringa* through the gossip of the garbage dump community. She figured she could hold her ground and stand up to the other kids and a teacher, just as she stood her ground when a driver only offered her half the money she charged for sweets. She tentatively nodded her head. *"Sí,"* Nancy said.

NANCY GUDIEL, 13 YEARS OLD when she started *Camino Seguro*, was no easy student. Lety Mendez, Hanley's right-hand Guatemalan employee, said that she fought, hit other students, and created problems. Nancy would be kicked out of one school after another, and Hanley kept apologizing to teachers and kept asking the *Camino Seguro* staff to find her a new class. "She was angry and never opened her heart, never said 'thank you,'" said Lety. "She couldn't show love because no one had shown her love before. Her life on the street had been very hard."

Hanley moved Nancy to a dormitory in the Santa Ines neighborhood of Antigua that the program established for street kids or those who came from violent, broken homes. That dormitory eventually expanded and became known as the "Casa Hogar." But Nancy caused fights with other kids, and she sometimes hopped the fence and ran away back to Guatemala City. Nancy couldn't be controlled or contained. Lety and other Safe Passage staff grew weary of getting calls from Hanley, late at night, requesting that they go search the streets of Antigua to look for children who had snuck away from the Casa Hogar. By the end of 2001, her first year in the program, Nancy had failed four of her classes at her school in Antigua—English, music, programming and computing. She was sent to the office, where Lety adopted the role of disciplinarian and told her, "You don't want to study. You're throwing away your opportunity. Go back home." But Nancy had little in the way of a home to return to.

About a week later, Hanley found her and brought her to the church next to the dump. "Do you want to try again? You don't have to throw it all away. Do you want to try school again?" Nancy agreed that she would return to the program and repeat those four classes she had failed. Eventually, she was placed with a host family who lived on the highway between Antigua and the capital. In that home, the Vásquez family had three younger girls and a boy, but no one Nancy's age for her to compete with. Hanley found a private tutor to help her manage her classes. She stuck with it.

Nancy found an important ally in Vilma Garcia, a Safe Passage staff member who joined in 2001 and worked at the Casa Hogar in Antigua. Vilma would sometimes accompany Nancy on visits to her school, the Tecnologico Moderno, and help sort out her problems there. Nancy gained trust in Vilma and even called her "mamá" on occasion. "Each kid in the Casa Hogar had a difficult life story," said Vilma. "They needed to build confidence."

Vilma was a native of Antigua who, like Lety, knew little about the garbage dump in the capital before she took the job. She was hired as a receptionist, but when Hanley discovered she spoke English, Vilma was tapped to give tours of the dump to visiting child sponsors and service learning teams—even though Zone 3 in Guatemala City seemed foreign and intimidating to her. The first visit to the *basurero* profoundly affected Vilma. "I had never before seen people living like that, next to the dump, like that," she remembered. "That day it was raining. There were rats and cockroaches running around all the people. It hurt me to see people in Guatemala living like that."

"It was an important initiation for me that I'll never forget. I think Hanley knew that my impression would help me do a better job at *Camino Seguro*. She said you can no longer sit behind a desk answering phones."

Vilma soon developed an allergy from the smell of the garbage dump—which she described as a mix of dead animals and rotting fruit. The allergy was especially acute during the rainy season. For a time, she convinced herself she could handle it. "I have to remind myself that I'm only here for a few moments or hours, but these people who live in the *colonia* and work in the dump are here all the time."

The generosity and solidarity of some of the *guajeros* also left an impression on Vilma. One morning she had arrived early to *Camino Seguro* to conduct a tour of foreign visitors. While she waited in the reception area, she remarked that she had missed breakfast that morning but couldn't leave to pick something up because the guests might arrive at any moment. A small boy seated there whose family worked in the garbage dump asked her "You're hungry?" She nodded. "Espérame un momento." *Wait just one second.* The boy returned minutes later with a hamburger, which he had clearly retrieved from the dump. "Please eat this," the boy said. "I had saved it for my lunch, but I want to share it with you."

IRIS RAMÍREZ AND HER MOTHER worked as paper sorters in the garbage dump. They would find paper and nylon, separate it from the trash, and transport it to a factory where it was recycled. The work was filthy and dangerous. Sometimes they'd find bloody syringes amid the paper. And Iris panicked when she saw rats scurrying around the *basurero*. She and her mother sometimes worked from five in the morning until eight at night in the dump, returning to their home in Zone 12 only to sleep. Her father, an abusive alcoholic since she was born, and who once tried to kill her and her mother, was rarely in the picture.

Iris was six when she met Hanley for the first time. The *gringa* approached them in the dump with a smile across her face and asked if she and her siblings wanted to join Safe Passage. Hanley explained that she wanted her program to help all kids who worked in or near the dump, not just those who lived in that community. Safe Passage would help them get a free education, despite the prohibitive costs of books or notebooks. Iris's mother could bring her to the drop-in center in the church when she arrived to work in the dump each morning. Her mother was thrilled and accepted the opportunity on the spot. Even from the first encounter, Iris remembered that Hanley used affirmative, loving language. "Hola cariño. Hola nena!" *Hello dear. Hello girl.* And she gave each child strong, reassuring hugs.

The church didn't yet have tables for all the students when Iris started a year later, so they sat on the floor. Lety remembered that a cook named Doña Isabel would prepare rice, beans, and a cornmeal mush called *atole* for the kids. Guatemala's national newspaper, the *Prensa Libre*, donated some learning materials for the classroom. Hanley's crew of volunteers from the language schools in Antigua—or visitors flying in from the United States or Europe on "service learning" trips—were encouraged to be creative and initiate games and activities with the kids. Fredy Maldonado, the soccer player who helped Hanley on a volunteer basis before he joined the staff, remembers that she purchased a blackboard and then cut it into many smaller pieces—one for each kid. Fredy remembers that the children would sit on the floor or on benches and lean over their tiny blackboards as if prostrating themselves in prayer.

DANIÉL OSORIO'S MOTHER attended services at the church next to the garbage dump in 2000 when Hanley started Safe Passage. She asked the priest whether the *gringa* could be trusted and if the project was legitimate, and he affirmed that it was. Daniél, who was five at the time, joined along with one older brother, Alejandro, and one younger brother, Manuel. Their family's decision to embrace school may have saved the boys' lives. Alejandro had gotten involved with a dangerous gang, Mara Salvatrucha, who controlled territory in the *barrio* in Zone 3. "I could have gone down that path and followed my big brother," Daniél reflected years later. "In the conditions where we lived, eating and safety seemed more important than studying books."

In 2002, a couple years after they joined *Camino Seguro*, their stepdad began selling cocaine in front of the Osorios' home in the *colonia*. He was executed by rival drug dealers. Hanley hid Daniél and his brothers in a safehouse before moving them to the Casa Hogar in Antigua, where Nancy Gudiel, the tough girl, also lived. For some, this dormitory located in a tranquil neighborhood an hour's drive from the bustle and violence of Guatemala City was more than a place to receive three balanced meals a day and go to school—it literally separated them from the dark forces that would have forced them into gangs and potentially killed them.

Gustavo Lias tells a similar story. The 13-year-old recycled aluminum, paper, cans, copper, and plastic in the garbage dump when Hanley showed up in the *basurero* carrying sandwiches and a bucket filled with juice for the children. "She hugged us and promised us better opportunities if we chose to go to school instead of working in the dump," said Gustavo. He enrolled in the program the following day. Gustavo helped the youngest kids walk through the dump by holding a line of rope for them to use as a guide. Later, he spent three years living at the Casa Hogar. Years later, Gustavo reflected that he'd be dead, either killed by the gangs, or overdosed on drugs, if it weren't for Hanley helping him.

Hanley had a soft spot for every child and a famous ability to forgive and give them another chance—even those who stole from the project. One day the Safe Passage checkbook went missing and a local bank began to cash checks forged with Hanley's signature, as money drained in small increments from the project's account. Hanley's staff coordinated with the bank to set a trap in order to catch the thief the next time he tried to cash a stolen check. The plan worked, but when the culprit was revealed to be a local teenage boy, Hanley refused to call the police on him. "Pobrecito, él tiene mucha necesidad," she reasoned. *The poor boy is in dire need.* Lety thought Hanley was crazy for not involving the law, but the *gringa* instead insisted that the boy's parents pay back the amount he had stolen from Safe Passage, bit by bit.

HANLEY NOT ONLY *SAW* THE INVISIBLE *niños* of the garbage dump, she chose to imagine them as children who deserved to play, laugh, celebrate, and enjoy a carefree existence independent of their hard-luck parents and their depressed community. Her staff couldn't believe the vast connections Hanley made and the schemes she concocted. Sometimes they shook their heads in wonder at the *gringa's* far-fetched ideas.

There was a Christmas party for approximately 100 children of Safe Passage to visit the upscale Marriot Hotel in Zone 9, where international businessmen and well-to-do tourists stayed. Ironically, this was also the neighborhood where some of these children, like Nancy Gudiel, sold chewing gum and candy in the street after school. Hanley apparently knew someone at the hotel who offered to host a party for the children from her project. American Airlines bought Christmas gifts for the children. The Marriott also supplied cakes for birthdays at Safe Passage.

Several days before the event, a truck full of party clothes arrived at the project for the kids to wear, Juanita wrote in her memoir, *Garbage Dump of Dreams*. The invitation to the Marriott for these kids from the garbage dump reminded her of Cinderella's invitation to the ball. "But I almost can't bear to think about how they'll be transformed back into poor children in rags, recognized by no one, once the party is over," she wrote.

Nevertheless, at the Christmas party, the children sat in their new clothes and ate fried chicken and French fries. The boys' hair was combed and they had so much gel that their hair stood up on its own. The girls wore braids and shiny shoes. Their small bags with packed lunches sat in a big pile in the corner.

"You can literally see the Christmas tree lights shining in their eyes," Hanley told the Danish woman.

Juanita conceded she was right. Before them on the ground lay long carpets, chandeliers hung above, and carved wooden figures graced the hotel's lobby. When they first entered "the ball" the children suddenly fell silent. But then they immediately began running around planting their fingers all over the gold mirrors. Joan wrote that the elegantly dressed women who greeted them at the door looked completely startled. And that was before Santa Claus showed up to greet the children.

"I want a bicycle! And four bunnies!" yelled one.

"I think my mom should get a new dress!" yelled another.

Juanita told a friend later that, while it saddened her that the children returned home to their slums afterward, she could see in their radiant eyes that they couldn't wait to tell their parents and everyone they met along the way about their remarkable Christmas party experience at the Marriott.

Those Christmas parties became annual events for a time. The wealthy class occasionally regaled the children of Safe Passage with other lavish gifts, some of which bordered on comical and frivolous. For example, on December 23, 2005, American Airlines invited students from the project to sit in seats on a passenger airplane and meet the captain while it rested on the tarmac. Most *guajeros* would never experience flying on a plane.

Lety Mendez remembered that Hanley would spontaneously come up with an idea, and despite how complicated or illogical it sounded at first, the *gringa* would make phone calls all evening, and by morning, plans were in place.

"I want to take the kids on a day trip to the beach," Hanley once said, seemingly out of the blue. The children of the garbage dump had probably never visited Guatemala's black sand Pacific coast, with its hatching turtles and mangroves. Transporting dozens of kids out of the capital on a daylong trip on buses the project didn't own seemed like a logistical nightmare. But on numerous occasions Hanley pulled it off.

"Her imagination was enormous," said Lety.

Those trips out of the capital could also be dangerous.

A *Camino Seguro* foreign volunteer once secured permission from *guajero* parents to take their children on an overnight

trip to Lake Atitlán on a public bus. But while in transit, the
children accidentally pushed on the backdoor of the bus, and a
girl fell out onto the highway, causing a closed head injury and
putting her in a coma.

Though the trip wasn't officially a Safe Passage trip, Hanley
made sure the girl, Garcia Barrios, was sent to the best hospital in Guatemala and no costs were spared to help her recover
from the accident. Lety remembered that Hanley visited the
girl every day for a week straight.

"Without being her actual mom, you wouldn't believe
how much she cried and cared for the girl," said Lety. "She felt
responsible for her."

Hanley stayed with Garcia until she recovered well enough
to leave the hospital. From that point on, *Camino Seguro* man-
dated that children wear seatbelts when they traveled by bus,
and volunteers were no longer allowed to take them on trips.

One More Step

LET'S IMAGINE SHE STRIDES FORWARD, her determined legs constantly alternating the burden as the balls of her feet absorb each impact with the ground. Her arms, locked at each elbow in a 90-degree angle, move in unison with strong, but tired legs. She pushes on though her body is exhausted, her brain fatigued from a lack of consistent sleep. But her legs and lungs operate on autopilot. She's been running for two decades; the feet know the drill. Her trusty feet land, spring, and push the body up again as her lungs inhale and exhale. In and out. In and out. Her mind drifts as ever back to the garbage dump, back to the children. In her brain, constantly working, the questions nag.

Did Angel Roque attend school today? Did Nancy Gudiel sneak out of the Casa Hogar again last night? Is Daniél Osorio and his family safe? Will there be enough food for the families this month? More and more children want to sign up for the project and attend school. How will we care for them all? Can we attract more sponsors? Will the money come through to build the educational reinforcement center so we can move out of the dark little escuelita? How will our children leave the garbage dump for good if we can't teach them useful trades? Do we need a board of directors to help me run the organization? Do we need more media exposure? We must grow. We must grow the project. We must share the story with more people.

121

Each question she asks herself creates 10 more goals. With each step she thinks of another task to share with Maribel, Claudio, Lety, Ed, and Rachel.

Her mother and her father, Jane Gallagher and Rachel, her supporters here in Yarmouth have all insisted that she forget about work for the afternoon, leave the computer and cell phone behind, clear her head and relax. Or run. Oh, but she has so much to do, she tells herself. So many emails to send to court donors, so many phone calls to tie up loose ends. But she knows her body and mind will break down if she doesn't rest. With her limited time, it's either nap or run. She opts to run.

HANLEY'S MIND DRIFTS into easy meditation as she moves. As her brother Jordan recognized, this is her time to organize her thoughts without 100 different voices coming at her. Her time to mentally lay out the tasks of the day. Her running also lets her travel in time, back to those carefree days before she saw the garbage dump. During her first months in Antigua when she volunteered for God's Child Project she often climbed Cerro de la Cruz, *the hill of the cross*, which looks south across town and toward the majestic Volcán de Agua. Or back to a time before she knew Guatemala, before Wheelock and Bowdoin, before she wanted to be a social worker, when her mind focused on winning races.

Her mind drifts back to the 1987 state championship race during her junior year, which Hanley entered despite having suffered a stress fracture. Before the race, Coach Danny Paul shares with Hanley the inspirational story of fellow Maine native, and Bowdoin alum, Joan Benoit, who began running to recover from a broken leg suffered while downhill skiing. Joan severely injured her knee during a training run and underwent arthroscopic surgery 17 days before the 1984 United States Olympic Women's Marathon Trials, but won that race by a whopping 30 seconds. Three months later she won gold at the first Olympic Women's Marathon in Los Angeles—in less than 2 hours and 24 minutes, and several hundred meters ahead of the competition. Hanley listens to the story of Joan. And she wins the state championship that day, even as onlookers gawk in wonder at the cast on her leg.

Let's imagine that improbable victory on the track as a high school junior is an important instrument Hanley keeps in her emotional toolbox. Whenever she needs to dig deep to find the stamina, strength and resilience to push forward, her mind returns to the 1987 state championship meet.

Joan Benoit follows Hanley's running accomplishments at Greely High School, and later at Bowdoin College. Though the Olympic gold medalist never visits Guatemala, and meets Hanley only on a few occasions, she is aware that this competitive young runner chooses to devote her life to the health and education of the children of the Guatemala City garbage dump. It's an extreme commitment, like long-distance running, and one that requires both selflessness and committing one's whole self. In Hanley's case, it also requires a dash of spontaneity.

"Marathoning is a metaphor for life, when you don't know what's going to meet you around the next corner," Joan reflects years later. "Did she know what would happen when she had this calling? Maybe she didn't know what would meet her in the dump, but when she saw it, she wanted to meet the challenge head on. Nobody ever wants to drop out of a race. She had skills that she took with her to Guatemala that she had learned through her accomplishments as a runner. She didn't want to give up."

Now let's imagine she's home in Maine on one of her month-long trips to visit schools, churches, Rotary clubs, and wealthy philanthropists to share stories and raise money for Safe Passage. Let's imagine it's early 2004, a few short weeks before the massive yellow educational reinforcement center—which her *Camino Seguro* staff also called the "edificio," or *building*—is supposed to open. Without it, there's no way to increase the number of children clamoring to join her program. Will her family travel south and attend the opening of the *edificio*? She hopes so, this is a big deal to her. But Jordan is planning a destination wedding in Mexico around the same time, and her father Michael is reticent about traveling to Guatemala. Will they make it?

Her mind focuses on her project in the garbage dump, on whether she can inspire another 10, or 15, or 20 Mainers to sponsor a Guatemalan child, on whether she can keep it alive for another six months, on whether any of these children will one day make it through the program and graduate high school. There are so many more families in the *basurero* who want to join. They represent a never-ending ocean of need. She can't say 'no.' She refuses to say 'no'. But each child needs a corresponding donor who will contribute $25 per month. Can she raise the money? With each step, with each footfall, she tells herself, "I need to work harder. Sí, yo puedo. Sí, yo puedo." *I can do it.*

Let's imagine she jogs at Mackworth Island State Park, accessible from the Andrews Avenue causeway off Route 1, between downtown Portland and Yarmouth. She runs a 1.5-mile loop on the trail that hugs the perimeter of the island, once, twice, maybe three times. She probably ran this route as a high schooler in the 1980s with Coach Danny. The trail moves south from the parking lot, up a slight hill and across a meadow, then down into deep forest. If she looked to the right, she would observe seagulls perching on nests in the coastline trees, seaweed lapping in the surf as it washes over rocky beaches, and sea ducks bobbing their heads into the ocean water to look for insects. Further south sits Halfway Rock, whose 1870s era lighthouse once guided ships through Casco Bay and helped them avoid smaller rock islands that resemble whales' backs. As she runs, Hanley's feet don't need to be reminded to tread carefully over the icy path still covered in part with snow. They know the way.

As the island trail turns north, let's imagine she pauses for a moment and drinks from her water bottle at Governor Percival Baxter's pet cemetery, where crude gravestones mark the spots where the former Maine governor buried 14 of his beloved Irish Setters and one horse. Two bronze markers accompany the gravestones, which are enclosed by a circular stone wall. Further north, she passes a spot in the woods where visitors have built tiny "fairy houses" using rocks, sticks, branches, leaves and other natural materials found on Mackworth Island. She is running through the beauty, the tranquility of coastal Maine. These are her roots, and perhaps they bring her a moment of nostalgia, to her running days at Greely.

But Hanley doesn't dwell long on nostalgia or peaceful beauty. She cannot rest. Let's imagine that, when she sees the gulls swooping over Casco Bay, she sees the vultures stalking the garbage dump. The animal graveyard calls forth the Guatemala City cemetery above the landfill, from which bodies are dumped into the ravine. The stick village morphs into the fragile homes of posts and sheet metal in the *barrio* around the dump, where Safe Passage's families live. Her mind never strays far from the project. The trail turns west, rounds the island, and leads her back to the parking lot. Her feet carry her all the way to the car. It's time to go. She has work to do.

"The Life You Change Might Be Your Own"

JANE GALLAGHER HEARD HANLEY field the question over and over again at speaking events throughout southern Maine. The query went something like this: "I want to support your project, but why should I come to Guatemala? I'd have to raise money for the trip, so why don't I just give that money directly to you?"

Hanley was very clear about the need to bring supporters to Guatemala, even if it meant drawing them out of their comfort zones. Her answer was always the same: "These kids need to know that they matter. I need people to look them in their eyes, hold their hands, wipe their noses, and sit with them. If we don't do that, then all the other things we do to reinforce their education and support their nutrition and hygiene ... none of that will have the same impact if we don't let them know that they matter. Only then can they start to feel like human beings and begin to dream about a life beyond the garbage dump."

For someone who didn't have a background in fundraising or international development, Jane saw in Hanley an innate understanding of how to connect with people. "That was a big part of her brilliance. She didn't read it in a textbook. I'm not sure she heard it in a lecture," said Jane. "I think she just knew that if she could get people to look (the children and families) in the eye, they'd connect with the garbage dump.... Hanley saw angels in everybody."

Each supporter who traveled to Guatemala and met the child they sponsored would become an ambassador for the project. They would return home and share Hanley's story—the story of those toiling in the Guatemala City garbage dump—with their friends, their family, their school, their coworkers, their fellow soccer moms and dads, their church, their Rotary club. Each conversation led to more supporters. And more and more North Americans and Europeans boarded airplanes for Guatemala City. Nothing could prepare them for what they would experience once they saw the dump. Nothing could change them like the real thing changed them. Hanley knew that. But could she convince Jane, herself, to visit Safe Passage? Jane was inspired, but reticent. Central America felt way out of her comfort zone.

The service-learning volunteers came from North Carolina, they came from Maine, they came from Michigan. Soon they would come from everywhere.

Dean DeBoer, who met Hanley in the late 1990s when he volunteered at God's Child Project and built one-room houses for families outside Antigua, recommended her project to fellow North Carolinians, including Leah Katz, an idealistic 18-year-old who wanted to volunteer at Safe Passage in February 2002 during her gap year after graduating from high school. She had already spent time volunteering at an orphanage in Nicaragua during a school trip, and wanted another experience in Central America working with kids.

Hanley had given Dean a tour of the garbage dump in 2000, soon after she launched Safe Passage. "When I saw the dump and the way people were living there, I said to myself 'Hanley's walking right into the lion's den. She has no fear of the lions,'"

Dean reflected. "I would have expected any young white woman from the U.S. to have some fear of what she was getting into. Or at least be a little anxious. This was her calling. If she was afraid, she didn't show it."

Hanley initially resisted Leah's offer because she hadn't yet worked with any volunteers who weren't college graduates or at least in their 20s. "Get back in touch in a few years," Hanley wrote. But Leah persisted. As her dad, Arnie Katz, tells it, Hanley eventually recognized his daughter's kindred and determined spirit—perhaps not unlike her own—and gave Leah and her friend Katie Weber the green light to volunteer at Safe Passage. Each woman worked various part-time jobs to save money for their upcoming adventure in Guatemala. For 10 weeks they served as volunteers in a second-grade classroom, helping the kids with homework, playing games, leading activities and lessons, handing out snacks, and supervising on the playground.

"We had just come from a month at an orphanage in Nicaragua. The kids there didn't have much and most of them had come from situations of extreme poverty, but their current setting was a rural mango farm, where they were safe, fed, and clean," Leah reflected. "Coming to this project was a very different scene and a different feeling. It was definitely the most extreme poverty I had witnessed in person."

Though he encouraged his daughter's adventures and humanitarian work, and supported how the experience would contribute to her global awareness, Arnie nonetheless felt nervous about these 18-year-olds working in Guatemala City. So, he joined them. After flying to Guatemala City in February 2002 and catching a cab to Antigua, Arnie visited Hanley's office in the room she rented on the Calle Hermano Pedro. Arnie noticed a cot in the back corner of the office.

"Sometimes you pull all-nighters?" he asked.

"No, that's where I sleep every night," she responded, a touch embarrassed.

The next day Arnie visited the capital and got a tour of the garbage dump and the surrounding neighborhood. He was struck by the poverty and the need, but he was also amazed by watching Hanley walk through the *basurero* and the *colonia*, connecting with people, no matter who they were, on a warm, emotional level. "She connected with the 4-year-olds running up and hugging her, or their mothers working in the dump, in the same way she connected with me," Arnie reflected. "For a lot of people, she connected with your heart and made you want to help her. She made you want to be your best self."

When Arnie returned to North Carolina he helped organize fundraisers to support Safe Passage. He networked with the Church of Reconciliation in Chapel Hill—Dean DeBoer's church—which already had a connection to Guatemala through a missionary project working with the Mam indigenous Mayans in the western highlands. Thus, a devoted and passionate support network in North Carolina's research triangle was born.

Marilyn and Tom Alexander, who had walked into the Church of Reconciliation looking for organizations to support, traveled to *Camino Seguro* for the first time in July 2002. Each morning during their two-week "service learning" trip they took a chicken bus from Antigua to Guatemala City, and walked the 4–5 blocks to the garbage dump. The Alexanders met Hanley for the first time at the *escuelita*, where they painted pictures with the children and assisted at a carpentry workshop which had recently been set up to teach the *guajeros* practical skills.

"She was open, kind and welcoming," said Tom. "She seemed perfectly at ease surrounded by the children, who loved her so much. They each wanted to touch her, to talk to her. That was part of Hanley's magic. The kids instinctively knew who to go to, and who to avoid. They would flock to her."

The Alexanders were deeply moved by the stories they had heard of Hanley's courage and dedication to sell what she owned and remain in Guatemala. During their trip, Marilyn and Tom took part in the weekly hair-washing and delousing activities. One day in the classroom, Hanley grew emotional, and so did the visitors from North Carolina, as she told them about seeing a little girl in the garbage dump who picked up a chicken drumstick from the ground and ate it. "I couldn't leave," Hanley told them. "I had to stay."

HANLEY UNDERSTOOD that donors visiting Safe Passage on service learning trips would change the lives of the *guajero* children and families, not just by financially supporting the project, but by being present and affirming that they mattered. She also understood that the experience at the garbage dump would change the lives of the first-world travelers, too. For some, it would shake their very core.

In airplanes they came, from cities all across North America and Europe. They represented high schools, colleges, churches, and organizations that sought to do good. They forsook typical "spring breaks" and comfortable, indulgent vacations to spend a week supporting those less fortunate than themselves. In their checked luggage they carried shorts, t-shirts, and suntan lotion for those warm days in the Parque Central in Antigua and the *lancha* boat ride on Lake Atitlán. As per the request of Hanley, or their contact at Safe Passage, they also carried a laundry list of supplies for the children of the garbage dump community:

children's chewable vitamins, clothes, kids paint brushes, construction paper, pencils, scissors, glue, erasers, paints, crayons, markers, used children's shoes and jeans and pants. An extra checked bag included used dolls, checkers sets, memory games, teaching materials, Spanish reading books, and playground equipment such as soccer balls, basketballs, and a jump rope.

Many had met Hanley before on her fundraising trips in Maine, in Boston, in New York, in North Carolina, in Oregon, in Michigan. Others had heard stories about her—stories that seemed larger than life. They had seen her poster board with photos of the garbage dump; they had heard her describe the *guajero* families and their daily struggles; they understood the need to donate and sponsor these children. Hanley had also convinced them to come and witness this scene for themselves. Perhaps they had an inclination that these journeys to Guatemala would change them, too.

Mainer Chip Griffin put this to words. After visiting *Camino Seguro* for the first time in 2004 together with his wife and two teenage children, the attorney wrote, "Beware, the life you change may be your own." He used that quote again and again with his rotary club in Boothbay Harbor, a 90-minute drive northeast of Yarmouth, as a call-to-action to encourage acts of service among the club's members. Chip had met Hanley during one of her frequent speaking engagements at churches and coffee shops in Boothbay. Hanley's poise and knowledge of the project immediately inspired, but also reassured Chip. "She was grounded. She could relay any depth of detail about the dump," he said.

Seeing the teaming *basurero* for the first time, with its gases and odors wafting from the trash, and *guajeros* crawling like ants through the mounds of refuse, reminded Chip of Ground Zero in Lower Manhattan after the 9/11 terrorist attacks. In a passage titled "Vacation with a Mission" that appeared in *Our Daily Tread: thoughts for an inspired life*—a book that Hanley's Bowdoin classmate Lisa Belisle published in 2008—Chip recounted meeting their sponsor child, a four-year-old boy named Marco Tulio, who he hugged and with whom he tossed a Frisbee on the lawn as Hanley watched from inside her office at the project.

Hanley knew Marco Tulio, as she personally understood each and every one of the 500 impoverished dump children in her program. She and I visited Marco Tulio's home, about 10 feet by 12 feet of makeshift materials with a dirt floor of reclaimed dump land where the methane fumes seep up through the ground. No power, no lights, no bathroom, no stove or fridge, no running water, and no windows or doors. Only one mattress was cast in the corner, where Marco Tulio's mom told me that seven of their family members lived and slept in this tiny, grimy, and dark place.

Prior to the 2004 trip, Chip's daughter Betsy, who he called his "princess daughter" acted picky about things around her being neat and clean. By the end of the first week, she had relaxed. When they helped wash the children's hair at the church, the 17-year-old saw a small tick on someone's shirt, flicked it away and kept going. During that first trip to Safe Passage, Chip watched the realities of the garbage dump, and the work they were doing, have a transformative effect on his teenage daughter. "Beware, the life you change may be your own."

Many volunteers and supporters brought their teenage children with them to Guatemala, thus opening more sets of eyes. Christine Slader had met Hanley in the bleachers at a basketball game in Yarmouth, where her son Wilson and Hanley's younger brother Lucas played on the same team. Christine was invited to a luncheon in November 2004 organized by Jane Gallagher, where Hanley presented her poster board of photos and someone passed the hat to collect donations for Safe Passage. In her pocketbook Christine carried a check for $50 that one of her parents had recently given her. She decided on the spot she didn't need that money, and gave it to Hanley.

The following year, Christine and Wilson, then 15, took their very first international trip to Guatemala to volunteer at Safe Passage. On their first morning in the country they took a shuttle bus from Antigua directly to the project. They parked in front of the church next to the dump, and suddenly the two big metal doors opened and out walked Hanley as the sun peaked through the clouds. "It was like a shaft of light hit her at that moment," said Christine. "She was an angel coming out of the dump." Later that day Hanley led the Sladers by a huge pile of garbage, with someone sleeping in it. Christine broke down and cried and asked Hanley, "How do you do this every single day?"

"This is just what I do," Hanley responded nonchalantly. In the ensuing years, Christine typically saw the Safe Passage founder smile, laugh or giggle—even in the face of this despair she saw every day in the dump.

Some visitors were struck most by the contrast between the wholesome oasis Hanley was creating in Zone 3 and the grimy, overwhelming hopelessness that surrounded *Camino Seguro*. Phil Kirchner first met Hanley in 2003 when she visited First Congregational Church in Yarmouth with her poster board featuring photos of the garbage dump. The church often featured speakers who visited to talk about world topics. But Hanley's charisma was unique, he remembered. Phil described her as a Mother Teresa-like figure who, in the moment she saw the dump, decided "this is my mission, and my life will forever be different now." First Congregational Church organized drives for school supplies, clothes, tennis shoes and soccer balls and shipped the products to Guatemala or sent with a group that was traveling there from Maine. "We were the mules bringing the goods," joked Phil, who took his first mission trip to the project in 2004.

His first time seeing the dump seared visceral and emotional memories into his mind. One day Phil and a group of volunteers were asked to cook soup for the kids' lunch and transport the covered pot in a wheelbarrow to the *escuelita*. Their path took them along the entrance to the dump, where they passed a dead dog lying in a trash heap with flies swarming above it. The contrast between the soup they had prepared and the filth of the dump stuck with him. So did a fieldtrip to a courtyard of freshly planted green grass where Safe Passage's educational reinforcement center was being built. The children on the fieldtrip fell on their hands and knees and rolled in the grass as though it were a bed of feathers. How novel the lawn seemed to these kids of the garbage dump, who knew only dirt paths interrupted by the occasional stretch of pavement.

Hanley understood that these experiences would turn supporters into ambassadors back home to support this project.

EVEN AS SHE EMBRACED VOLUNTEERS helping at the project, Hanley remained cautious about letting journalists and photographers document the children and *guajero* families, or casting her in the spotlight. She had turned down the documentary film that Rachel sought to organize. Was Hanley worried about objectifying the community and using photos of destitute children to raise money for Safe Passage? Would she strike a balance between exploitation and the publicity that would help her expand *Camino Seguro* and serve more children?

A New Jersey photojournalist named Joseph Delconzo, whose lens had captured war orphans, heavy metal bands, and famous musicians and actors, witnessed that evolution in Hanley between when he first met her in 2000 and subsequent trips to Guatemala. On that first day, Joe, Hanley and a Canadian volunteer took a diesel fume-belching *camioneta* from Antigua to Guatemala City, then disembarked and walked for what felt like half an hour to reach the garbage dump. Joe, who carried 15 pounds of camera gear on his back, asked her several times if they could stop and take a water break. "I'm dying here," he told her. But Hanley pushed on. "Let's keep moving."

Joe had traveled in 2000 to neighboring El Salvador to pursue a follow-up photo story about the war orphans he had documented during that country's 12-year civil war, which ended in 1992, four years before Guatemala signed its peace accords. Conflict photography inspired him: there was the Bang Bang club in South Africa during the violent transition from apartheid to democracy; there was Eugene Richards and his intimate look at the lives of addicts, drug dealers and sex workers in *Cocaine True, Cocaine Blue*. Joe's heroes were those who had the charisma, the intimacy to gain the trust of the subject and get close enough to photograph them putting a needle in their arm. But Lena Johanesen, editor of the El Salvador version of *Revue* magazine, discouraged him from photographing the war orphans. "These kids have been exploited to death down here," she told him. "Every photographer in the world has been down here to shoot these kids.... But there's this girl from Maine who's in Guatemala getting kids out of the garbage dump and into school. It's a story that hasn't been told before."

The conflict photographer's interest piqued. He found a copy of the same story in *Revue* Guatemala that lead Rachel and Arthur Berg the Oregon businessman to Hanley. But when he tracked her down, the *gringa's* initial reaction toward Joe was curt and suggested mistrust. "Hanley didn't like the whole press thing," he remembered. "She was very tough and difficult to work with in the beginning. She was protective of the children. She did not like people taking their picture; she didn't want them to be exploited."

Joe slowly convinced Hanley, during conversations over meals in Antigua, that she could trust him. He told her he had enough scruples to know when to photograph children, and when to cap the lens and point the camera toward the ground. They reached an agreement. Joe could join Hanley in the garbage dump community, at the church and the *escuelita*, but she had veto power over what he could and couldn't shoot. This was a bitter pill for a photojournalist to swallow, but he agreed. Now he just had to keep up with the ambitious runner.

He shot inside the church as she made her rounds, making sure that snacks awaited each child after school, that volunteers had enough art supplies, paper plates and cups ready, that bags of rice, beans, and vegetable oil were being prepared for the families. He shot her crouching next to a child as she pointed to a piece of paper and a book. Then he followed her outside into the teeming *basurero*, which baked and stank under the late morning sun. Maribel Cholotio joined them and held a parasol over Hanley's head so she wouldn't get sunburned. Into the dump they walked. *Into the pits of hell*, Joe said to himself.

"Keep the camera down, don't pull it out yet," Hanley told him. Over and over again, he would see an opportunity for a powerful photograph, and she would say "No, not yet. Put your camera away." ... And then ... "Now you can have your camera out." He snapped a photo of her climbing a steep embankment with huts of corrugated tin sheet walls on one side and a ravine on the other. A street dog approached Hanley; *guajero* women in flimsy sandals walked behind her. Her eyes focused on the foot path ahead, intent on accomplishing the next goal on her list. Joe said that his photos of Hanley in 2000—the early days of *Camino Seguro*—showed a determined and rail-thin young woman who didn't smile, except when she was with the children. Her eyes always looked forward, as if she stared through the camera.

That first day with her stretched into late afternoon, then evening. They hardly ate. They hardly drank water. One child after another, one family after another they visited. More than once Joe looked around to see if any police patrolled the dump, anyone who could protect them if something went awry. No, it was just Hanley, Maribel and himself, and kids, running to them from all directions. He found himself frightened.

The second day scared the photographer even more. One of "Hanley's kids" was sick, and she insisted that they hop on a red city bus—the kind that, in later years, Hanley would *never* permit her staff or volunteers to ride—and visit him in the gang-infested neighborhood of El Mezquital. They walked to the young man's house and found him in bed, Joe remembered. Through his lens this photographer had seen blood, he had seen trauma, but he recalled this as the most dangerous situation he had ever experienced.

They left El Mezquital unscathed as night fell on Guatemala City, and Joe offered to pay for an expensive cab ride back to Antigua. "What a treat!" said Hanley, suddenly chipper. The photographer would have paid a thousand dollars for a cab ride at that moment. He was tired, he was hungry, and most of all he was scared. "I wasn't just doing it for her, I was doing it for me," he reasoned.

Joe spent 3–4 days trailing and photographing Hanley on his first visit to *Camino Seguro*. She began to trust him, just as the *guajeros* had begun to trust her. During their conversations over meals at Doña Luisa's, he observed that Hanley began to understand the attention that photographs and media coverage could bring to her program in the garbage dump. Over the ensuing years, Joe would sell his photographs to newspapers in Maine, to the Catholic News Service, to *The Washington Post* magazine. Wire services would carry his images from the garbage dump to newspapers all over Europe. The press attention led to more checks and more child sponsorships.

He returned in 2004 for another assignment to photograph Hanley, the project, and the dump. Her eyes still showed that determined focus, but she was no longer rail-thin, and Joe's lens now caught her smiling on occasion. This time, because the photographer had gained Hanley's trust, he had free reign to shoot all *Camino Seguro* activities. "I'd go to the garden and introduce myself to the teachers," he said. "I'd shoot the teachers, the kids, and the hallways. It was great."

Joe Delconzo paved the way for other photographers and filmmakers to come and capture Hanley's story. Their work would elevate Safe Passage's exposure and lead to more volunteers, more donors, and more sponsor parents. There was John Santerre from Maine, whose striking photos of Hanley walking through the garbage dump and standing inside the cramped little church where the program started were used by Rachel and Hanley on their Maine "roadshow" and later featured in *Our Daily Tread*; there was Beth Price from Michigan, who took the now often-used portrait of Hanley smiling in the foreground and wearing a pink blouse, juxtaposed against a blurry background of *guajero* kids huddled in the back of a room; and there were filmmakers Mike Glad and Leslie Iwerks who shot interviews with Hanley that they would use in a short documentary they created about the garbage dump. On camera, Hanley smiled and laughed on occasion, as she told them about Safe Passage's origin story and how she "couldn't turn away" after seeing the children playing in the *basurero*.

As PART OF HANLEY'S EVOLUTION, she came to recognize that each volunteer, each visitor from a wealthy country who was inspired by Safe Passage had a particular role to play. Some of those volunteers brought their own projects and sought to build on what *Camino Seguro* was already doing. Hanley, who wanted to give the *guajero* children as many tools as possible to leave the garbage dump and break the cycle of poverty through education, rarely said "no" to any project. That impulsive instinct was both a strength but also a weakness.

North Carolinian Susan Attermeier, who traveled to Guatemala with her daughter Julia in July 2003, met Hanley for the first time at the *escuelita* where food was being prepared as the children sat on the floor coloring in an adjacent room. Susan spent no more than 3-5 minutes that day with Hanley, who always seemed to be on the go. "You never had long conversations with her," she said. "There were always 'Hanley alerts, or Hanley sightings' around the project.... I probably spent a total of 30 minutes with her in all the years I knew her." Nevertheless, "she was shiny and present for every single person she met."

Susan, who ran a physical therapy company back home and would visit *Camino Seguro* for a week at a time, sometimes multiple times a year, one day caught up with Hanley during a lunchtime break during a trip in 2004. "I'm interested in working with the moms of the project and helping them learn how to read," said Susan, who explained that she had worked with adult literacy for many years back in the United States. "When adults become literate, their children become literate, too."

"Yes! I've always wanted to do that, but I've never had the money or time," Hanley responded with an enthusiastic tone. "But go for it!"

Over the next five days before she returned home, Susan teamed up with a fellow volunteer, Sarah Hightower from Bowdoin College, who spoke excellent Spanish but didn't have a background in adult literacy. Together, they translated Susan's curriculum, and the project's social workers sought out and found seven mothers of *Camino Seguro* children who wanted to learn to read and write. Without much planning, the adult literacy program launched. However, one hurdle that emerged was that several of the women were indigenous Mayan and didn't speak Spanish, the national language. They had grown up in Guatemala's rural *aldeas* and had fled to Guatemala City during the civil war after their husbands or fathers were murdered or disappeared. Without an education, without connections, the only work they found in the capital was in the garbage dump.

Back in North Carolina, Susan raised about $5,000 each year to pay the salary of Lorena, the project's first Guatemalan head adult literacy teacher. The group eventually expanded to 12 women, all of whom faced incredible personal challenges. They struggled to find enough money to feed their children, they coped with abusive husbands, many nursed babies or carried them on their laps when they came to class. Susan fondly remembered a tiny little woman named Petronilla, who spoke no Spanish, had five kids and a husband who beat her. "She was my special woman, my hero," Susan said. "We'd spend every morning trying to teach her Spanish and using black beans lined up on the table to count. She carried a baby on her lap and a baby on her back."

At first, the other women didn't relate to Petronilla because she was shy and had trouble communicating with them. But as time passed, said Susan, she found her way into the group, and the culture of the women's group changed completely. They became a cooperative that helped each other. Years later, Petronilla ultimately lost her vision and went blind, but only after she learned a basic level of Spanish and gained the acceptance of the other women.

"Hanley would just inspire people to do things," said Susan.

By 2006, thanks to the adult literacy program, Safe Passage had a full-fledged Family Nurturing, Adult Education and expanded Family Support program.

Doug Pride, a math teacher at Greely High School in Maine who knew of Hanley from her high school running days, had first learned of Safe Passage from Michael Denning, who told him about his daughter's daring endeavor when they ran into each other at the local YMCA locker room a few months after Hanley first set foot in the garbage dump. Doug remembered the sense of awe and distinct pride in Hanley's father's voice. Doug and his wife Becky, a fellow teacher, decided that in 2004 they would take a service learning trip to Guatemala in lieu of a typical vacation. "We wanted to do something more than just go to Paris," he said.

Hanley visited their home in Falmouth and addressed Becky's misgivings about traveling to a developing, and potentially dangerous, country like Guatemala. She also fended off the question she'd heard many times before: "Why don't we just write a check and hand it to you?" asked the Prides. "No,"

Hanley countered with a smile across her face. "I want you to see the program and be a witness, so you know what your donation is funding."

She explained the precautions they took at the project and when they walked around or into the garbage dump: walk with a Guatemalan guide, don't flaunt signs of wealth like cameras, phones or jewelry. The risk of getting mugged could happen in any American city, she added. "You'll be with a group of volunteers at all times, and you'll get dropped off the bus in a relatively safe part of the city. When you're inside the project you'll be behind a locked door. At the end of the day you'll walk back as a group, get back on the bus, and return to Antigua, which is a quaint little touristy town." The reassuring tone put Becky at ease about their trip.

During their two weeks at Safe Passage, Doug and Becky both found themselves in their natural element, volunteering inside the classroom—Doug in a second-grade class, Becky in kindergarten. Rachel gave them tours of the *colonia* next to the dump where *guajeros* live, and the Prides met their sponsor child, a 6- or 7-year-old girl named Catarina. "Seeing where they lived and actually being able to tell them that we'd like to continue the relationship, it was great."

Before their trip ended, Doug told Hanley that he and Becky wanted to hold an annual 5K road race back in Maine to raise money for Safe Passage. As she had with Susan Attermeier's idea for an adult literacy program, as she had with countless other volunteers who came forward with great ideas, Hanley smiled and nodded her head. "Go for it!"

HANLEY WOULD INSPIRE prosperous Guatemalans to help her project, too.

On those airplanes flying south, across the Mexican isthmus and landing at La Aurora International Airport, less than three miles from the garbage dump, were native citizens, coming home to reconnect with their birthland and lend leadership to help move the nation forward. Juan Mini, Jr., a 1999 graduate of the University of California Berkeley's Haas School of Business and the heir to his family's real estate and civil engineering firm, decided in late 2002 to leave California and return home to work on the family business and to spearhead tech opportunities in Guatemala City. The landfill was part of the Mini family's portfolio. In the early 20th century, his grandfather bought the land that included the *basurero*. According to Juan, his grandfather's vision was one day to fill the ravine with trash and turn it into a park. But the *guajeros* complicated that dream when they began to arrive in the 1940s to live off the trash and "take advantage of the environment," said Juan.

When he returned to Guatemala on a visit in October 2002, Juan's father, Juan Mini, Sr., told him, "you have to meet this woman named Hanley who is helping the kids in the municipal dump." His father took him to the little church, and Juan, Jr., watched the *gringa* "kneel and hug and kiss these kids that were dirty and sick. She had this heart for them. She exuded goodness," he said. "This scene happened over and over again."

Juan told his father, "I'm going to help her when I move back here." He returned to stay in January 2003, and invited Hanley to visit his office, where she shared her hopes and dreams for the project, including having an educational reinforcement center more noble than the church next to the dump and someday also having a nursery. The conversation led to the Mini family giving Safe Passage a warehouse, which was used as a daycare center and where the mothers could learn to read, write, sew, and make crafts they could sell. Juan Mini, Sr., also secured land—owned half by his family, and half by a company which they partly owned—for Hanley to expand her project.

Juan's wife at the time, Amina LaCour, joined him on a visit to Safe Passage in the spring of 2003. Guatemala was in the middle of the rainy season, and they walked through huge mud puddles along the *Calle Sucia* near the garbage dump's main entrance with Hanley and Freddy Maldonado, and they talked about locations where *Camino Seguro* could grow. Hanley spoke excellent Spanish, but with a thick *gringa* accent, Amina remembered. In the distance, Hanley saw kids swimming in puddles in the *basurero* and began to shout, "peligroso!" *That's dangerous.* She ran toward them, hopping over garbage piles as her backpack swung from her shoulders. Juan, Amina, and Freddy hustled to keep up with Hanley. But the kids got scared when they saw four adults running toward them so they hopped a fence.

Amina, a native of Denmark who had lived all over the world including in Africa, the Middle East, Europe, and the United States, specialized in early childhood education. She was instantly drawn to Hanley. "Her charisma was amazing," said Amina. "She had this ability to be super genuine with people from the very first moment they met. She'd just reach out to people on the streets of Antigua, listen to their story and connect with them, and steer the conversation toward her project for at-risk kids in the city. It didn't matter who she was talking to, she always had on the forefront of her mind how she could turn this connection into an opportunity for people to help each other."

Amina offered to volunteer at the project two or three times a week. There she met Mary Jo Amani, the Montessori-trained teacher whose husband Todd worked with USAID and who would launch a library for the children at *Camino Seguro*. Together they read books to the children in the church, put meals together, and helped Hanley develop a program for the youngest kids. In the warehouse that Juan donated, Amina secured materials to partition the walls and make sure the project had running water and food.

"Once a week we'd set up plastic swimming pools or troughs," she said. "We'd bathe the kids there. For some this was tremendous fun; but for others who didn't like water, it was terrifying." Once a month they also cut the children's hair.

Juan and Amina opened doors for other important volunteers of privilege, too. When their Guatemalan friend Sandra González called Juan and said she wanted to dedicate her time and help people of need in the capital, he told her, "There's this lady from the U.S. working in the garbage dump area, but she hardly knows any local Guatemalans. Why don't you meet with her?"

Sandra had never visited the *basurero* community before, though she conceived of the idea to launch a soup kitchen in Zone 3. The first afternoon she visited *Camino Seguro* was a rainy and grey day, with noisy garbage trucks dropping their payloads. She met Hanley in the warehouse which was full of kids, flies buzzing around their shoulders, and shreds of cloth and old clothing hanging from the ceiling to create makeshift walls. They had painted welcome signs for her that read "Bienvenida a Sandra." *Welcome to Sandra.* She observed that some of the children were the same age as her then-18-month-old son, José Antonio. Sandra and her family lived in a wealthy neighborhood a mere 15-minute drive away from the garbage dump, and the contrast in lifestyle struck her hard. Despite the humble scene, Sandra recognized the kids were happy in this oasis surrounded by the garbage dump.

"It really hit me after my son was born," said Sandra. "My interest was in nutrition. I couldn't imagine my kid going hungry or crying."

Sandra came to supervise the nutrition program at the project, which included examining the kids to make sure they weren't malnourished, and helping choose their weekly menus at *Camino Seguro*. She went to the supermarket near her house, picked up meats, cheeses and vegetables, and sought out in-kind donations from grocery stores. The project now formally served breakfast, a mid-morning snack, and lunch. "A year and a half later we didn't have any malnourished kids," said Sandra.

IN JULY 2004 *Camino Seguro's* brand new Educational Reinforcement Center opened to provide after-school enrichment including tutoring and a mentoring program on land that the program purchased. The *edificio*, as Safe Passage staff called it, included two levels covered in a fresh coat of white paint and had classrooms, a library and a dining area. The program would later raise more money to build a third floor that would house a medical clinic and more classrooms. Children would no longer have to huddle on the floor of the church or the *escuelita* holding pieces of chalkboard to write on. Here in this immaculate space they used clean tables and ate lunch with real plates and glasses. The center's open-air courtyard featured a green lawn where the *guajero* kids could tumble and play.

"Hanley had told us it was her dream come true to be out of the church, out of the warehouse, and in the new *edificio*," said Lety. "She wanted happy kids doing their homework there. She imagined it being *grande* with lots of classrooms and green space, and a large area where the kids could eat. It was the building of Hanley's dreams."

The Denning family didn't make it for the opening of the *edificio*, but it was a grand affair nonetheless, as Hanley was surrounded by many long-term volunteers, donors and core staff who had stood with her since the early days of the project. On the day of the event, Rachel remembered that Hanley became unsettled and told her, "I have a wardrobe crisis, Rachel. Nothing fits!" She was no longer the bone-skinny long-distance runner who skipped meals in favor of constant work. She had begun to gain some weight as her lifestyle made it difficult to find the time to exercise. Sitting during long meetings and eating whatever was brought to her, Hanley was suddenly gaining weight for the first time as an adult. Rachel remembered she was devastated.

Only hours before the ribbon-cutting of the educational reinforcement center, Hanley's driver Oscar took her to clothing stores in Guatemala City to go shopping. When she appeared at the *edificio* she wore a dark blue blazer and matching skirt. "She looked amazing, and the part of a leader of a growing organization," said Rachel.

HANLEY'S PROGRAM HAD GROWN and upgraded from the rat-infested church to the attractive new reinforcement center. She was evolving, too, as the need to make her program financially sustainable competed with her impulse to give each child at *Camino Seguro* a daily hug. What didn't change was her innate ability to connect with people and inspire them to join her cause. It mattered not whether they were working-class American families who could afford little more than $25 per month to sponsor a child, or CEOs who could write bigger checks. It mattered not whether they were *guajero* families from the garbage dump or Guatemala's wealthy, landowning class. She sat down with them and told her story, and it touched them all.

Susanna Badgley Place was already interested in Guatemala when she heard Hanley give an interview on Maine Public Radio in 2003 about the challenges of her work with the garbage dump community and her drive to build support for Safe Passage in New England. Susanna was no stranger to service-focused international NGOs. She had traveled to Africa with the U.S. Peace Corps and worked there for a decade with small-scale enterprises and economic development. With degrees from Princeton University and an MBA in economics, finance, and marketing from Yale School of Management, Susanna was well-connected and motivated. But Africa felt too far from home, and Susanna wanted to explore Central America. She ventured for the first time to Guatemala in the early 1990s to study Maya textile traditions. In 2004, she trained her focus on the Ixil region in the northwestern highlands, where she was attracted by what she described as "the intricate tapestries of mythical figures on the Mayan Ixil backstrap-loom weavings that told stories of a culture in harmony with nature."

When Susanna heard Hanley on the air, she had just returned to Maine from a month-long trip to Guatemala with her teenage daughter Louise and her daughter's friend Colby to study Spanish in Antigua and tutor local Mayan children. Two days after the radio interview, Susanna met Hanley for lunch at a café called Scarlet Begonias across the street from the Bowdoin College campus. Hanley, who was on one of her fundraising trips home, brought her trusted poster board of photos from the dump to show this potential supporter. "She was captivating," remembered Susanna, who volunteered at Safe Passage the following summer together with her 15-year-old son Alex.

Most mornings Susanna and Alex would hop on the same *camioneta* with other volunteers in front of the marketplace in Antigua and disembark on Roosevelt Avenue in Guatemala City and walk five or six blocks to the garbage dump. But on one particular morning Hanley—who was so busy that she was hard to catch for more than a quick greeting—asked the mother and son to share a cab ride into the city with her. "I want some one-on-one time with you and Alex," she said. "Let's go together in my favorite taxi."

The vehicle had a hole in the floor, through which you could see the pavement below, and torn-up seats in the back. Nevertheless, Hanley called the cab driver a friend. She sat in the front passenger seat, turned around and, Susanna remembered, "talked a blue streak" all the way to the garbage dump about her future visions for the project. Alex's face was nearly turning green from all the exhaust coming up through the floor and nearly vomited in a paper bag. "Yeah, this happens all the time. Just breathe into the bag," said Hanley.

Though the setting couldn't be more different, this was the same Hanley that Susanna had met a year earlier at the café near Bowdoin College—in terms of her intensity, her desire to connect personally and directly with each person she met. This was her gift. Susanna would later hear about donors who met Hanley during a chance encounter at an Antigua bar or restaurant and would come to Guatemala City the following day because they were captivated by her entrepreneurship and her purpose. "She was totally engaged as she told the story of these kids and shared her vision."

At the end of her two-week trip, Hanley walked with

Susanna down a dusty street near the dump entrance, hopping over mud puddles, and stopped to show her an open area that Juan Mini had offered to give Safe Passage. Hanley explained that she had a donor who was willing to contribute a $5,000 matching grant to build a wall there that would keep out squatters and preserve the area for a future project. "Would you be the other half? Or help me find the other half?" she asked.

"She barely knows me," Susanna thought to herself, though she already felt solidly committed to this project, both with her time and her money. "She knew I was a former Peace Corps volunteer, she knew that I'd been to Guatemala numerous times before. She knew I didn't mind flies buzzing about me during lunchtime.... She could read people well."

The other donors who had agreed to help fund the wall and preserve the land for Safe Passage were Marty and Frank Helman, Boothbay Rotarians and principals in a family foundation who had learned about Hanley through Chip Griffin. When Chip returned with his wife Denise from leading a school group trip to Safe Passage in 2004, they carried a list of needs that Hanley had written on the back of an envelope. The Griffins were quickly becoming ambassadors for the project.

Marty and Frank stepped up and wrote a check to help fund the wall. When they traveled to visit Safe Passage the following year, the Helmans met Hanley for the first time. Since they had contributed, they felt a sense of ownership about what would be built inside that wall and how she was stewarding the funds for that project. Then, in January 2005, a cloud of methane gas hovering over the garbage dump ignited and caused a massive fire which burned for days, prompting the city to temporarily close the *basurero*, build a wall around the dump and post armed guards there to keep *guajeros* out during nighttime hours. The fire suddenly changed Hanley's priorities, and she told the

Helmans she needed to build a nursery school—a *guarderia*—where the *guajeros* could bring their toddlers during the day.

"How much will the nursery cost?" the Helmans asked Hanley during that visit in June 2005. She turned to an itemized list that accountant Ed Mahoney had given her and she had written, once again, on the back of an envelope. Hanley read the list verbatim. "We'll need $5,000 for this ... and $2,000 for that ... and $10,000 for that...." Marty remembered she would add the numbers up and just as quickly try to push the final tally down—like a used car salesman hawking a deal. Perhaps Hanley thought the Helmans would be more likely to help if she lowered the figure.

"Hanley was very naive in terms of working with a foundation," Marty chuckled later.

"She didn't realize that when you're dealing with a foundation, an ask for $180,000 is the same as asking for $200,000. The answer will be the same," said Frank.

"You're gonna need more than that," Frank ultimately told Hanley during their meeting. "Let's make it $220,000."

Hanley nearly fell out of her chair. The Helmans' contribution eventually reached $250,000.

"And that's how the *guarderia* got funded," smiled Marty.

What impressed Marty and Frank most about Safe Passage wasn't just that their donations helped poor children—it was that they knew the names of the kids they were sponsoring. Marty remembered that one day they and other volunteers took preschool-age *guajero* children to the Guatemala City zoo. "There were two kids for each adult. Our hands reached down, the kids' hands reached up." Somehow the Helmans got separated from the rest of the group. The kids whose hands they held cared not about the animals in the zoo, they were more excited about novelties like green grass on the lawn, or wallpaper, or big trees, or park benches. "We gelled there at the zoo with these tiny, vulnerable people. This was probably the first time they had been outside the dump community before."

"That's the key thing about Safe Passage," said Marty. "We've traveled plenty in third-world countries. We've seen dump communities before. But in other places we've never gotten out of the car, never asked children their names, never asked if the children had goals, or wants or needs. Hanley's project was the first time we had that experience."

JANE GALLAGHER, THE ATTORNEY and soccer mom who helped Hanley organize fundraisers and events in Maine, initially swore that she would not visit Guatemala, even though her son Jake insisted they go after Hanley regaled them with stories of delousing the children from the garbage dump. Jane said she preferred to help Safe Passage by networking her connections in the Yarmouth area and organizing lunches at people's homes to recruit more donors. But after three years of pressure from Hanley, she finally relented.

Jane and Jake flew down for the first time in June 2005 on a trip together with other Mainers including Doug and Becky Pride. They were exhausted from the long journey after waking at three o'clock in the morning in Yarmouth and traveling through airports in Boston and Miami, and were nestled in their pajamas at a homestay in Antigua when Hanley and Rachel knocked on their door late that evening to welcome them to Guatemala. Hanley was giddy as a child that Jane had finally come. That message that Jane had heard Hanley deliver so often at fundraisers in Maine—"You can't just give money, you have to visit the project and see it for yourself, and show your commitment directly to the children"—had finally rubbed off on her friend.

The next morning, when their shuttle bus pulled up at the garbage dump, Jane disembarked, looked around the scene about which she had heard so much since she learned of the project from Michael Denning on the soccer field in 2002, and promptly burst into tears.

"I had been hearing about this for years. But this was the first time I'd seen Hanley in this context, in this environment," she said.

Hanley and Claudio, the project's lead social worker, led a tour through the *barrio* next to the garbage dump. As they walked, an elderly Guatemalan approached Hanley and explained that he had grandchildren who needed to go to school and pleaded for her help. Though she didn't speak Spanish and couldn't understand each exchange, Jane watched, mesmerized, as Hanley engaged in the same conversation she had with so many hundreds of *guajeros* since launching Safe Passage in early 2000. "Will you support the children in going to school, not just once in a while, but every day?" Hanley asked the *viejo*. "Is there an adult in the children's household who can take responsibility for making sure they get to school? ... The food bags we hand out to families are a reward when the children attend school."

Through his tone and mannerisms, Jane perceived this man was earnest and full of hope while he asked for Hanley's help. "It was like everything in his family rested on this moment. If only he could get his grandkids into the program, then his job would be fulfilled," Jane said. "It was a beautiful scene to witness."

But Jane also knew the dilemma confronting Hanley each time a new *guajero* family courted her. She could almost hear her friend's internal dialogue going back and forth. "We can't take any more kids," Hanley had told Jane many times. "We need to stabilize the number." While Hanley was able to say 'no' on occasion, it was also common for her to suddenly accept 25 more kids into the project—sometimes to the chagrin of her staff.

"She knew she had to stabilize things. But instead, like 100 people would apply for 20 spots in the project, and she'd take 30," said Jane. "She knew she couldn't take all 100, so she reached a compromise.... She always said the hardest part of her job was figuring out which kids to take and which ones to turn away."

Jane shared a memory in the book *Our Daily Tread* that revealed how one life she changed by visiting Safe Passage with Jake was indeed her own:

> I was hoping against hope that I would not get assigned to the lice shampoo station. I'd been hugging and playing with kids all week long and had enjoyed the contact and the closeness, but for some reason, thinking about that lice station caused me great anxiety. Of course, when assignments were given out, not only was I assigned to combing head lice, I was put in charge of it! I resigned myself to the task. It wouldn't be that bad. I could deal with this. All morning I worked on combing head lice from the hair of these beautiful children who literally lived down in the dumps. At lunch I was so tired I wanted to curl up in a corner and go to sleep. After lunch I paced myself, knowing that in a few hours, I would be on a plane heading to comfort and cleanliness and peace—leaving this place of grime, garbage, smells and sights so sad I couldn't process them all at once. Every time I heard a plane overhead I welled up with tears, thinking that I can go home but these kids, my sponsored kid and the ones I'd come to love during that week, would be still here tomorrow and tomorrow and tomorrow.

> At last it was time to clean up and leave. It was about 4:15, and we were supposed to pack up our station at 4. A young girl came

over and asked for a lice shampoo and combing. Every shred of my being wanted to say, "sorry, it's too late," but for some reason, all of us who were still working at that station smiled and said, "It's OK, come on over." I was done, cooked, spent, hollowed out at that point and seriously questioned whether or not I could do it. I felt so frail and vulnerable. As I looked at this beautiful young girl, I knew that I could do this: I could comb her long, tangled, lice-riddled hair. I could do it by starting very small and working my way through one bit at a time. Another volunteer from Maine was working with me, and as we began to untangle the little girl's hair, I began to feel something inside me untangle, too. With each stroke, I felt a bit more relaxed and a bit less empty, a bit more filled up. What was filling me up was love. As I cared for this child, this stranger to me a few minutes before, I was getting back this amazing, overwhelming sense of peace. I knew that few things I'd done in my life were as important as what I was doing at that moment.

"Which Child Am I Supposed to Send Back to the Dump?"

YEARS LATER, FREDDY MALDONADO, the soccer star would reflect on what Hanley meant to those touched by her work with *Camino Seguro*: "For the poor people and the *guajeros*, she was a saint," he said. "For the workers, she was an example. And for the *gringos*, she was an inspiration."

But there was a price to Hanley's drive and work ethic.

Jane Gallagher observed that her friend wanted to play a hand in every aspect of Safe Passage, even as it grew. She micromanaged. "That worked for a little while, then things got so big that, at a certain point, she just couldn't do that anymore," said Jane. "Things were getting too big for her to run in her vertical management way. You could see the toll the stress was taking on her."

Safe Passage was falling into a classic pattern that dooms many small nonprofits, Jane observed. Hanley asked too much from her volunteers, too much from her paid staff, and she wasn't taking the steps necessary to develop a robust fundraising program, which would have helped the project achieve sustainability. With each new building, Safe Passage's physical footprint expanded, but the long-term maintenance budget didn't grow along with it. "It was a battle to get Hanley to spend one dime on a building, or on the systems and structure that she needed in order to have a bigger, more robust and sustainable organization," said Jane.

Worse, the founder wasn't paying herself a salary, and her frenetic lifestyle was talked about all over town. Local Guatemalans still had the sense that she worked nearly 24 hours a day, 7 days a week.

"What if something ever happened to you?" Jane once asked Hanley. "Who's going to step into this? You have to make this sustainable. You have to make it a job someone else could do, or Safe Passage goes down with you."

Hanley would smile and thank Jane for the advice. But her friend observed that Hanley had a way of tuning out if she didn't like what she heard.

Lety Mendez soon found that she struggled to keep up with her boss. Some days Lety worked as many hours as Hanley, tracking down missing kids in the *colonia* or the streets of Antigua if they ran away from the Casa Hogar, corresponding with volunteers and donors at the project's new *edificio*, and often arriving long after dark in her home village of Jocotenango. "Hanley was *loca*," Lety smiled. "She was crazy. Trying to accomplish what seemed impossible."

Lety remembered once when lice were found in Hanley's hair after she worked in the delousing station in the church. It was obvious the *gringa* had it because of the color of her light blonde hair, whereas the kids working in the dump all sported black hair. "It mattered little to her," said Lety. "She wanted to be just like the families in the dump." When it came to uplifting the families of the garbage dump, Hanley often asked the same herculean commitment from her employees as she herself put forward. One particular story illustrates the extent to which she pushed her staff—sometimes to a fault. About a year after she began working at *Camino Seguro*, Lety gave birth via Caesarian section to her son, Pablo Manuel, at two o'clock in the afternoon on December 3, 2002. No more than 90 minutes later, Hanley called Lety on her cell phone to ask if she could coordinate a task in the office. "No, I can't," Lety replied. Hanley knew she had just given birth, and they had arranged that Lety would take three months off from the project.

"Please, Ústed puede," the excited *gringa* pushed. "You can bring the baby into the office with you. Please."

The following day, while recuperating in the hospital with her newborn son, Lety made a few work-related phone calls. Less than a week later, mother and baby took a taxi to the office so Lety could arrange monthly meetings and food pickup for parents who worked in the garbage dump and whose children were enrolled in the project. Meanwhile, Pablo Manuel napped in a cardboard box in the office, just as Hanley had seen babies sleeping in boxes in the dump so the vultures and street dogs wouldn't hurt them.

"Suddenly there were dos locas," said Lety. *Two crazy people.*

FOR ONE *CAMINO SEGURO* EMPLOYEE, in particular, Hanley was nuanced and could be more challenging than the saint the *guajeros* saw in her. To Ed Mahoney, the tall and stoic accountant from Boston who promised in 2001 to help Hanley clean up the project's muddled finances, she was inspiring and tenacious, but she could also be exasperating and stubborn. Balancing the books and convincing Hanley not to overcommit, overspend, and grow Safe Passage too fast became an exercise in futility, Ed learned.

Having committed to volunteer for Hanley for no longer than six months, Ed hired Carlos Quisquina, who had a background in Guatemalan accounting, to reconcile the new project's financial discrepancies. Expense lists were often written on the backs of envelopes. Cash flew around without being recorded. Money trails stretched from the Banco Agromercantil in Guatemala City, to Oregon, to Maine. Once they came within $10,000 of balancing the checkbook, Ed told Carlos, "This is good enough. This is as close as we're going to get."

In the early years, Safe Passage's budget neared a quarter million dollars and was funded mostly by donations from supporters in Maine and also the Sisters of Notre Dame, with whom Hanley probably connected through Sister Regina Palacios, the nun who first showed her the garbage dump in 1999. That budget funded lunches, uniforms, school supplies and tuition for the children, monthly food bags for their families, and salaries for Hanley's staff, once the project began to grow. Safe Passage had two accounts with the Banco Agromercantil, one in U.S. dollars and one in the local currency, quetzales. The bank generously waived the wait time to withdraw cash once money was transferred, Ed remembered. Despite the favors from Guatemalans and more and more donations from the United States and Europe, money always seemed tight.

"She was optimistic," Ed remembered about Hanley. "She told me, 'Don't worry, I'll find the money'. And she always did. Or somebody did. We never went bankrupt."

Ed also took it upon himself to make sure that Safe Passage didn't run afoul of Guatemalan law. Here on the periphery of the city garbage dump, foreigners were caring for disadvantaged local children, sometimes taking them on field trips to the Pacific Coast, sometimes hiding them from dangerous family members or neighborhood gangs, sometimes finding new accommodations for them an hour away at the Casa Hogar. Mothers and caretakers of the children would sign their consent—when they could be located, and when they could write their names. Hanley's project was growing at a time when alarmist rumors of baby thefts at the hands of *extranjeros* continued to sound throughout Guatemala—both a fallout from the recent civil war, and a reaction to a growing, unregulated international child adoption industry, which peaked in 2006 when American couples adopted, and left the country with, approximately one percent of all babies born in Guatemala that year.

Ed also worried about Hanley cutting corners paying health and retirement benefits to her staff: social security payments represented a significant 14 percent of Guatemalan salaries.

"Everything you're doing is fabulous. You're paying the children's school fees, you're feeding them lunch," Ed told her. "But you're doing it at the expense of your employees. You're not treating them fairly. For some reason, you expect that just because you self-sacrifice...."

"It's going to catch up with you, and you're going to be in big trouble. The government could come and shut the whole thing down," Ed said. "Then what will you do?"

Following a heated argument, Hanley would turn a cold shoulder and avoid talking with Ed about financial issues for a week at a time. "That's just the way she is. She'll get over it," he thought to himself. Eventually the conversation between the two of them resumed as though nothing had happened. Despite the bluster and the fights, it's clear that Hanley deeply respected and cared for Ed. Indeed, she and her project needed him. In a conversation with Susanna Place, Hanley once referred to Ed as "like my uncle." Her father, Michael Denning, also developed a bond with Ed, his fellow New Englander, and would call him if he couldn't contact Hanley or get a level, straightforward analysis of his daughter's project.

ED TRIED TO LEAVE THE PROJECT in 2002, when his six months were up, but Hanley wouldn't let him. "You can't leave. You can't go," she pleaded. Ed wasn't yet on her payroll. He was living on savings and almost broke. He had no subsequent plans, but halfheartedly figured he would move to Florida where his parents lived and get a "real job." Instead Hanley convinced him to stay as a paid employee of Safe Passage. At the time, the project was still relatively small and consisted only of the church and the *escuelita*.

But when the *edificio* reinforcement center—Hanley's dream—opened in 2004, the project's student body suddenly ballooned from 250 to 500 children. With this large new building firmly under its control, now Safe Passage had electrical bills, water bills, maintenance costs, and more staff to worry about. Expenses skyrocketed.

"The problem with money wasn't when we were in the church or in the little school that the municipality gave us. There was only so much space there," said Ed. "Costs didn't become a big issue until we built the *edificio*, and the school population doubled almost overnight."

"My advice at the time was to take it little by little. But that's not the way Hanley was. When she had a goal in mind she always just went for it. She wanted to have a self-sustained project that did everything that everyone needed."

With operational costs soaring out of control, Hanley was

forced to launch a major campaign to find more child sponsors, each of whom paid $25 per month in support. In 2006, that monthly sponsorship amount increased to $50. The project also made the decision to increase the number of sponsors each child at Safe Passage could have.

"The money came from different donors. It just came," said Ed.

Despite her innate ability to connect with people, the glad-handing and courting of supporters didn't interest Hanley in the least. If she met them in the United States on a fundraising trip she would show her poster boards and tell stories of children eating chicken drumsticks pulled from the garbage dump. If she met them in Guatemala she might lead them on a tour of the *basurero*. Unless they were personal friends from Maine, like Jane Gallagher or Susanna Place, Hanley didn't usually have time to schmooze with them in Antigua's fancy restaurants. Instead, the wining and dining of supporters fell to Ed. When donors and child sponsors showed up, particularly if they were wealthy, he would take them around Antigua's colonial streets, which were filling up with more and more high-end restaurants, music venues, and bars.

"Hanley didn't like raising money," Ed said. Or at least she didn't like to be the one grooming lucrative donors so they would give. "She wanted to do her job and let someone else worry about where money came from. I often suggested to her to do kamikaze hits in the U.S. Fly to Boston, fly to Philadelphia, get donors in those areas to set up meetings in churches or wherever ... But that wasn't her thing. She didn't do a lot of direct, face-to-face fundraising. She would meet people who came to Guatemala, but I was the one who would take them around and hold their hand."

"I can't tell you how many people I met. Some panned out, some didn't. Some wanted to give money with strings attached. Some had pet projects or felt they knew what was needed. But they weren't from here and had never been here before."

As an example, Ed remembered one donor who wanted to produce a glossy coffee table book full of everyday photographs shot by the *guajero* children with cameras they would take home to their *colonias* each evening. The donor suggested that Safe Passage help distribute the cameras.

"That's not in the cards," Ed told him straight up. "The cameras will get stolen."

When certain projects didn't pan out, or when the money grew tight and Ed pushed Hanley to slow down or cap the number of kids she was admitting, their conversations devolved into arguments.

"She would get very exasperated and angry," said Ed. "She'd say to me, 'I didn't hire you for advice. I hired you to run the finances!'"

One evening during a tense period between the two of them, Hanley asked Ed to meet her for coffee. He doesn't remember what they talked about, but the conversation must not have gone well, because she called him again at five in the morning. "I just sent you an email. But don't open it. Delete it," she said. "I'm afraid if you open it, it will adversely affect our relationship."

"Alright," Ed said, and deleted the email in his inbox.

"I can imagine what (the email) said," he reflected later. "She must have gone home and stewed about what we talked about, then woke up and sent the email early.... I never opened that email. But had I done so, I probably would have quit the project.

"By that point in time, I was pretty committed [to Safe

Passage] myself. I didn't want to up and leave, but I would have done so.... I don't know what Hanley wrote, but she could be pretty nasty when she wanted to be."

WITH THE *EDIFICIO* TO MAINTAIN and 500 children to serve, Hanley understood that she needed a board of directors, to better organize the project, to help her navigate difficult decisions, and also to write checks. An informal advisory council, which consisted of Jane and family friends in Maine, wasn't enough. She had told several confidants that she needed a board, even if that meant giving up some control of the project which she had created and of which she still hovered over almost every detail. But who would lead the board?

In January 2004, a clinical psychologist and author from Traverse City, Michigan, Marilyn Fitzgerald, traveled to Guatemala looking for a project to support. She and fellow Michigander Paul Sutherland, a financial investment adviser and founder of Financial & Investment Management (FIM) Group, were launching a philanthropic foundation called Children of the World, which would later morph into Paul's "Utopia Foundation." Marilyn, who was particularly interested in microlending and projects like it, initially visited Common Hope, a family-run nonprofit, founded in St. Paul, Minnesota, which supported the underserved and was based near Antigua. But she found that Common Hope was already large and well established. "My heart was in something smaller," Marilyn said. John Huebsch, the son of Common Hope's founders, told her about Hanley and Safe Passage, an organization very much in flux and nowhere near financial sustainability.

Marilyn met Hanley for the first time in the bed of John's

old, rusty pickup truck as they drove the switchback mountainous roads from Antigua into Guatemala City, stopping on occasion to pick up Guatemalan hitchhikers who needed a ride. Hanley's hair billowed in the breeze and she struggled to hold onto her loose files, while explaining her project to Marilyn as they braced themselves against the back of the truck's cab. Once they arrived in Zone 3, Hanley gave Marilyn a personal tour of the garbage dump.

"It was amazing, and so was her dream for the project. The story about the nun, and how she sold her computer and stuff to stay in Guatemala," said Marilyn. "You look at Hanley and say, 'of course I'll do whatever I can to help.'"

Marilyn called Paul Sutherland back in Michigan and told him she wanted this to be the first project they would support. It was midday, and Paul was eating lunch in a FIM Group conference room with his brother Michael, a couple blocks from West Grand Traverse Bay. The reception on the international call was spotty, and Paul repeated out loud what Marilyn told him, just to be sure he understood. "Why don't we just buy the project," Paul initially suggested. Then he learned that someone had offered to donate a couple run-down hotels in Guatemala City's red-light district to Hanley. She wanted to know if she should accept the offer, if they could be repurposed to serve Safe Passage. Michael was a builder and small business owner in nearby Glen Arbor. True to his impulsive nature, he said to Paul, "Let's just fly down there and check it out." Within two weeks, the Sutherland brothers arrived in Guatemala City. A tall tale would later materialize that Paul spontaneously met Hanley sitting next to him on an airplane. The true story wasn't quite as dramatic, but Paul soon played an enormous role in changing Hanley's life and the fortunes of her floundering project in the garbage dump.

The Sutherland brothers concluded that the hotels were poorly constructed and of little value, but Paul quickly turned his attention to Hanley, whom he wanted to understand before financially supporting her work. "I've met a lot of remarkable people in my life, so I like to get to know them first before I say 'wow,'" he said. "I've heard many stories, so I take everything with two bags of salt."

Paul quickly realized that, while an inspiring leader, Hanley was in some ways naive, and she didn't have a background in finance or business. Nor had she articulated her long-term vision for the project. Those skills would be necessary for Safe Passage's future. Could she resist "shiny new thing" distractions? Could she move beyond "working out of the back pocket?" Paul concluded that her charisma and manic work schedule alone were driving the project.

"She was holding up the world with the power of her own energy," said Paul. "But that's not sustainable. That's burnout stuff."

Hanley and Paul walked around the garbage dump community and talked heart-to-heart. Though Paul made his money as a financial adviser, he related to people on a spiritually Zen level. "What's she all about," he wanted to know. "What place inside was she coming from?" Paul remembered that Hanley did most of the talking during that first encounter.

"The more she talked, I realized she really could make a change, a difference in the world," he concluded. "This wasn't about her, or about stroking the ego. I felt like she was coming from a very unselfish place. She didn't blog, she didn't journal, she didn't leave etches in the sand about what she was doing. This work was never about her. It was about the children."

That evening, the Sutherland brothers took Hanley out for dinner at a restaurant in Antigua. Paul sat across the table from her and began to recite his laundry list of things that needed to change for Safe Passage to survive and become sustainable: "We've gotta have a board of directors; gotta have systems in place; you can't work 20 hours each day; you can't have meetings with the entire staff every week, you have to delegate...." Hanley's face must have turned red because Michael started kicking Paul's feet under the table as if to say, "Shut up, you're making her mad!" Paul just wanted to help, but realizing he was being too assertive, he pulled back.

"Can we talk privately?" Hanley asked, clearly flustered. The two retreated to the hallway of the restaurant.

"Hanley, I'd like to help," Paul said, trying not to be overbearing. "But if I get involved, I don't do things half-ass."

She nodded. "I understand."

"You have a great thing. I think it will change lives," Paul said, reinforcing everything about the project he thought was positive and impactful. "But if we work together, things will change a lot. So don't get me involved unless you're ready for that."

Hanley and Paul agreed that she would think about his offer overnight and she would tell him over breakfast the following morning if she would allow him to mentor her and help her establish a board of directors.

That night, Hanley called Marilyn, who had introduced her to Paul and who had become a trusted confidant, and asked her for advice. Hanley confided that she felt overwhelmed by the situation, and perhaps a bit intimidated by the power dynamic, but she understood how beneficial Paul's resources would be to her—not just his money, but his leadership and knowledge.

The following morning maybe they met at Doña Luisa's, Hanley's favorite spot in Antigua for breakfast—she and Paul met alone. "I want your help," she told him.

The money adviser Buddhist initiated a "pinky finger shake."

"Hanley, you can ask anything of me, and I can ask anything of you, but we have to keep it all confidential. That's what I want our relationship to be. We should never worry about asking each other anything."

Thus began a mentorship and friendship that Paul described as the bond of siblings.

After their meeting, and before they returned to the United States, Michael asked Paul what had transpired over breakfast. "We made a pinky swear we wouldn't talk about it," Paul told his brother.

"THE PROJECT WASN'T SUSTAINABLE, but it was marvelous," said Marty Helman, the Rotarian from Boothbay, Maine, who with her husband Frank would fund the nursery. "She was learning how to deal with donors. She did everything wrong according to the book about how to fundraise, but it worked for her."

At the time, donors received no regular Safe Passage newsletter. Instead, from time to time the Helmans got postcards in the mail from Hanley. Marty understood what was happening: Hanley would be on an airplane flying between Guatemala and the United States. She would have four hours to spare, and she'd write postcards to donors.

"We got these individualized, handwritten notes from Hanley every few months," said Marty. "Maybe she wrote them every time she flew on a plane.... She did the fundraising all wrong, but it absolutely worked."

Marty remembered that when they first met, Hanley asked her how boards of directors work and what role they play. She wanted to know about an executive director's relationship to the board and what advice the Helmans could offer her.

HANLEY VISITED PAUL early in the summer of 2005 and spoke to a core group of potential new supporters at his FIM Group conference room in Traverse City. Members of the Sutherland family attended, as did Sharon and Wayne Workman, who like everyone before them were struck by Hanley and her work in the garbage dump. Hanley didn't bring her poster board of photos with her to Michigan, but her extemporaneous stories of children in the *basurero*, and of her calling to launch the project, were powerful enough, remembered Sharon. Meanwhile, Paul encouraged Hanley to write a strategic plan for Safe Passage. He was pushing her to think long-term in ways she hadn't done before.

She returned to Traverse City in August to present to Paul's local Rotary Club and to speak at the newly formed Great Lakes Friends of Safe Passage's first annual fundraiser at the sleek Hagerty Center with glass walls that looked out onto West Grand Traverse Bay. But at a subsequent meeting in Paul's conference room attended by Sharon and other advisors, Hanley broke down in tears when her new mentor pressed her hard about a strategic plan for her project. That echoed what Susanna Place had told her in conversations the previous year, "Hanley you can't do everything yourself." She knew she needed a board that could help her think long-term. The survival of her project depended on it.

But beyond the children, the mothers, the needs she saw every day and which drove her, she couldn't articulate the concepts of purpose in ways that boards of directors used. In this, her soul was uncertain and perhaps, frightened. Still she pressed forward.

Hanley's first Safe Passage board of directors officially formed in 2005 and held their first board meeting in Portland, Maine, on August 8 with Paul Sutherland as its chairman, Sharon Workman as vice chair, and Susanna, Arnie Katz from North Carolina, Chip Griffin from Boothbay Harbor, Jim Highland who had opened his Yarmouth office for Rachel Meyn to use as the project's U.S. base of operations, as well as financial advisor Betsey Anderson, and several others. Comically, Sharon didn't know that she was to be vice chair until Paul told her when she arrived in Maine.

Susanna observed that Paul had become not only Hanley's mentor but her partner in running the board. The board wanted to establish processes for how Safe Passage would move forward; it wanted the facts, the financial outlook, and a detailed plan for the coming year. Hanley sometimes pushed back, remembered Susanna. "Does it really matter what the plan is?" Hanley would ask rhetorically. "This is what we need to do. I've thought it through, and I'll provide the details later." Sharon remembered that the board never learned the identities of some of Hanley's most lucrative angel investors.

The board learned that Hanley, this young rebel, could be guarded. Sharing the responsibility of running Safe Passage didn't come easily to Hanley. Ed perceived that she viewed the board as "a necessary evil." She was respectful to them. But didn't always agree with them." Hanley had launched her project almost on an impulsive whim, and she had improvised each step of the way. Now she struggled to spell out an intentional, organized plan with a long-term vision. Nevertheless, these board members were fully committed to her and the garbage dump community. They weren't going to let her down. "At some board meetings it was expressed directly, sometimes it was expressed indirectly, 'get out your checkbooks, we need to move ahead,'" said Susanna. "I think most board members, to the extent of their capacity, were happy to do that, and would have done that without her asking or without Paul asking."

But during one particularly tense moment at a board meeting in Maine, Hanley's relationship of convenience with the board nearly collapsed. There was a new board member who wasn't all that familiar with the project's history but who wanted to quantify all of Safe Passage's operations. According to Paul, he took a PhD white-paper approach to managing the nonprofit. The new board member may not have known what Paul and a few others knew—the organization wasn't going to fail, financially, because there was an anonymous donor who would step in and write checks that would keep Safe Passage afloat. The new board member heard Hanley say that she wanted to add more children to the student body the following January school year, which at that time totaled 500, with an annual cost of $3,000–$3,500 per child. The numbers were tight; overall, the financial situation looked untenable.

"Well you shouldn't take so many children. Maybe you should just send a few children back," he said. "We need to keep enrollment flat to balance the budget."

Paul sat across the table from Hanley and watched her reaction.

"Oh my God, she heard that," he said to himself as her fair skin turned beet red.

"Why don't we take a bathroom break," Paul interrupted the conversation. He convinced her to leave the conference room and join him privately in the hallway. Hanley's head was already spinning out of control.

"Who are we gonna send back!? Who's going back to the dump, Paul?" Hanley shouted. She began to name names of children in the project. "Angel ... Nancy ... Daniél ... who!?"

Rachel Meyn, Hanley's righthand employee in the Maine office, had just arrived to take photos of each board member. She came upon Hanley and Paul in the lobby. He listened with calm. But she was irate and advocating the way a mother would care for any of her own children. "What do you want me to do? How can I choose one child and not another?" she yelled at Paul. "I can't do that! I won't do that!"

"Hanley, I promise that as long as I'm involved, we're not gonna send anybody back," said Paul. He realized at that moment that the strength of what Hanley had built couldn't be quantified in one number. No, these were individuals—every one of those 500 kids was an individual. Each one as precious to her as though she had only one child to care for in the whole world. That was her strength, her magic, Paul understood at last. It had been said that she knew the names of every child in the garbage dump community. She knew their parents, too. And now he believed it. Only that kind of protectiveness would drive this defiance.

Paul thought of his late father, Dale Sutherland, the headmaster and principal at Glen Lake School near the Sleeping Bear Dunes National Lakeshore, west of Traverse City, who also knew the names of every student at his school. Paul had once asked his dad, "How do you know the names of all the kids?"

"It's not that hard," Dale replied. "If you meet them one at a time." Paul remembered his father standing outside on cold northern Michigan winter days and greeting every child as they stepped off the school bus. He met each of them as individuals over a long period of time. Hanley did the same.

"We're not gonna kick anyone out of the program," Paul

announced when he and Hanley returned to the meeting room. He knew that statement was the only way they could keep this visionary and her care for her people in line with the realities of the nonprofit world.

WHERE THERE HAD BEEN NO SYSTEM BEFORE, the board of directors began to create a structure and economic plan for Safe Passage. Some, like board member Chip Griffin, thought Hanley was naturally moving in that direction and accepting the necessity of the shift. But on the ground in Guatemala, change could be slow.

"Hanley would say, 'I have my own system.' We'd all roll our eyes," remembered Fredy Maldonado. "She always said there needed to be room for one more family, but there wasn't the money. It was difficult to convince her otherwise. She kept giving one more chance, then one more chance after that, to Francisco or whomever. Finally, people around her just said, 'It is what it is.'"

Even with an established board encouraging Hanley to mitigate the project's growth, she couldn't turn down new initiatives that funders or volunteers presented to her. "She never said, 'we don't have the money,'" remembered Arnie Katz. "Instead she said 'Go do it!' That's how Safe Passage grew organically in the early days. She would never say 'no.' It was both an incredible strength of the organization, and an incredible weakness."

When Arnie had first met Hanley, he observed over a conversation at lunch at Doña Luisa's that Hanley was trying to manage *Camino Seguro* through the force of her own willpower. She was the most extraordinary leader he'd ever known, he later told a fellow supporter. But she hadn't yet built an organizational structure to catch up with Safe Passage's explosive growth. Hanley possessed incredible leadership ability, said Arnie, but the management skills of a slug. "She wanted to run everything." Nevertheless, he was mesmerized by her mission and committed to support her.

Now Hanley wanted a bakery; she wanted a carpentry and metal workshop, she wanted a garden for the kids. She wanted lacrosse matches with teams visiting from the States; she wanted Christmas trips to the Marriott, she wanted kids to sit on an airplane on the tarmac. These ideas came from others and Hanley gave her blessing. Once kids finished their afternoon studies, they got to watch carpentry in action once a week. They learned woodworking, they learned baking. She wanted a hotel in Antigua where students interested in hospitality could train, and where volunteers and donors could stay during their service learning trips. And no matter what anyone said about the Casa Hogar dormitory for troubled youth—expensive, extralegal, and inconvenient because it was so far away from the garbage dump-centered project—she insisted that it remain open.

"Hanley didn't have much patience for bureaucratic things," said Susanna Place. "She called this 'a life-or-death situation.' Eventually she'd get to the legalities, but for now she felt she needed to rescue these kids. There were several dozen that she felt would disappear into the dump forever if they weren't rescued. She was a maverick in that sense, willing to crash through a few barriers, break a few rules, walk unchartered ground. She felt these things needed to be done." For Hanley, the dreams kept coming, the need to save the children was ever paramount.

Hanley wanted a beautiful garden in the nursery where the babies of the *guajero* families could be watched, remembered Lety. When she learned that workers from the garbage dump were about to invade the land that Juan Mini had promised her for the *guarderia* and build more shanty houses there, she asked the city government to move them and give them somewhere else to live. In the first years of the project, Hanley tried to create a nursery in a building next to the church that the municipality had given to *Camino Seguro*. But the babies and toddlers cried continuously. "They just cried and cried the entire day," Lety remembered. "'When is this going to stop, Hanley?' we asked. 'It's not working.'"

The entire board visited the project for the first time in January 2006, remembered Sharon Workman. For many who had not yet visited *Camino Seguro*, this was their first time actually seeing what they understood on paper and through meetings with Hanley.

"She had told us about all the programming, the educational reinforcement center, the adult literacy, her dream for an early childhood center," said Sharon. "I almost thought it was exaggerated how much she was doing, but then I saw it with my own eyes. It was unbelievable the number of programs she had put in place in such a short amount of time."

Hanley planned a visit for the board that included activities and experiences that Sharon described as so compelling that they were "blown away." They stayed at Lazos Fuertes, Safe Passage's new hotel in Antigua and saw the Casa Hogar dormitory for at-risk kids; they visited the early childhood center in its location in the huge warehouse where they sat on bleachers and met children enrolled in *Camino Seguro*; they smelled methane gas flames seeping up from the garbage dump. At lunchtime at the *edificio* educational reinforcement center, Hanley arranged for each board member to sit with a parent of a student in the project.

Sharon and Wayne Workman met a mother named Samara in the library; their translator was Mary Jo Amani, the volunteer who had helped establish the project's literacy program. Samara told them that *Camino Seguro* helped her after her husband was shot and killed in front of their kids. A social worker reached out and got her boys, Saul and Richard, enrolled in the project, which Samara described as a godsend. Nevertheless, Sharon asked her, "*Camino Seguro* has done this for your children. What about for you? What can it do for you?" Her answer was "Nothing, you've done so much already for my kids." The Workmans decided to sponsor Saul, who was then eight years old. He would eventually complete high school and get a job outside the garbage dump. They later sponsored Richard, the younger child, as well.

When the board members reconnected with each other after lunch in the *edificio*, they described feeling struck, almost numb from the experience. "It deepened our commitment to Safe Passage," said Sharon.

"Tranquila, Madre Teresa"

HANLEY POSSESSED THE TENACITY, bravery, and compassion of many world-changing philanthropists who came before her. Like Clara Barton, a hospital nurse during the American Civil War who founded the Red Cross, like Jane Addams, a settlement activist and women's suffragist who co-founded Chicago's Hull House, she refused to ignore poverty and suffering. Her dogged determination and manic work schedule earned her weighty, often unwanted analogies to Mother Teresa, the Albanian-Indian Roman Catholic nun who was considered one of the 20th century's greatest humanitarians for her work serving the poor in Calcutta and who would be canonized in 2016. Hanley was certainly aware of another privileged American, Dr. Paul Farmer of Boston, who brought medical aid to poor, rural communities in developing nations. Rachel Meyn remembered that Hanley read and found great inspiration in the book *Mountains Beyond Mountains*, which Tracy Kidder wrote in 2003 about Farmer and his work fighting tuberculosis in Haiti, Peru, and Russia.

Like Barton, like Addams, like Mother Teresa and Paul Farmer, Hanley would need help along the way, she would need to delegate responsibility to others to grow the capacity of her organization if Safe Passage were to survive and succeed. In essence, she would need help raising the child she had borne. Hanley was a visionary, but it was clear to some around her

177

that running the day-to-day operations of a growing organization wasn't her strong suit. Cathy Mick had noted that she had trouble with the operation's logistics; Arnie Katz was blunt when he said that she had the management skills of a slug; Paul Sutherland observed that "she was holding up the world with the power of her own energy."

Would Hanley adapt and evolve as a leader? Would she give up some control of Safe Passage and, when necessary, slow the project's growth? Would she listen to the advice of others? Would she take care of herself? These were the questions that weighed on Hanley when the project expanded both its physical footprint and the size of the community it served, and the board of directors formed.

To her team at *Camino Seguro*, Hanley's actions and priorities made clear that the children and families of the garbage dump and surrounding *barrio* always came first. Always. Their needs came before those of the staff, the volunteers, and the organization's founder herself. Even if that meant she skipped a meal or wore the same clothes for days on end. Staff often had to jockey for position to get five minutes of Hanley's attention, yet she tried to make herself available to every family the program served. If she could somehow hug each of "her" 500 kids every day, she would. The team watched and worked, sometimes in awe and sometimes in frustration.

Fredy Maldonado, who knew the network of nonprofits and Guatemalan aid organizations as well as he knew the cobblestone streets of Antigua, found it ironic that Hanley treated the children and families so well but could be demanding of her workers. "When someone is passionate about something, they don't eat," Fredy observed. "They expect that others won't eat either. That's what happens when you run for 10 hours straight and then realize you haven't eaten. She was in love with her work, so she thought everyone was in love with the work, too."

Hanley had three traits that made her unique, said Fredy: she had passion, compassion, and innocence. Her passion for the work, and her compassion for the *guajeros* she shared with everyone who worked for Safe Passage. But that innocence, like a bird flying to the window, may have blinded her, on occasion, to the needs of her flock.

Lety remembered one hectic day in the office—too busy to walk down the street to the *tienda* and pick up something for lunch—when Hanley announced they would eat hamburgers that had been found in the garbage dump. "We have to eat what they eat," she said. "If they're suitable for the *guajeros*, they're good enough for us."

Reluctant at first, Lety complied. She was hungry, and she didn't want to disobey her boss. "We didn't get sick," she beamed, surprised.

Encouraging Hanley to spend money on food for herself was a futile pursuit. Telling her to buy new clothes was even more hopeless, said Lety. "Hanley, la ropa!" *Your clothes*! But she always walked in old tennis shoes, wore khaki pants or jeans, and a simple shirt, with her hair in a ponytail. A pink blouse was her "dress-up" outfit. Instead, Hanley gave the kids clothing for school, she paid for teachers, she sometimes ordered them pizza or chicken, and gifted them with trips to the beach on the Pacific Ocean. Hanley never used money from the program to buy her own clothing or support her own wellbeing.

"We the workers thought Hanley was *loca*," Lety smiled as she reflected years later on her boss and friend. When she spoke of Hanley, she used the word "crazy" as a term of endearment. "We'd tell Hanley, 'Go buy some clothes, buy some food, go visit the dentist, go do something for yourself.' But instead, she invested money to make sure there were classes in English or computer literacy for the students. She always paid for the kids. She wouldn't let a kid go to school without food in their stomach or a notebook to write with."

And so, at Safe Passage there was always food for the children, seemingly by magic, even when the program grew to 500 kids. Hanley sent someone to the market to buy bread every day. She also made connections with the Hotel Marriott and convinced them to supply cakes every month to celebrate birthdays of her students. Each year the program received leftovers from the luxury hotel's "el Día de los Muertos"—*the Day of the Dead*—celebration on November 1, when Guatemalans prepared a "Fiambre" salad and shared it with the ancestors. One way or another, food materialized, and Hanley always found a way to pay tuition for each child and cover the cost of their uniforms, which included pants, shirts, sweaters, blouses, and shoes. Somewhere on the back of an envelope she wrote down the number of pens, books, and notebooks needed. An employee, or in the early days Hanley herself, trekked to the Mercado to buy those, too, and haul them back to be stored in a makeshift warehouse at the project.

"AHH, SANTA MARÍA, es mucho dinero," Lety gasped when she saw how much cash Hanley carried with her. *That's a lot of money*. "Es peligroso." *Dangerous*.

Ed the accountant would tell Hanley the same. "Slow down, *tranquila*. You're moving too much money. You can't give it all away!"

But Lety noticed that Hanley was happiest when she saw children who were supported by Safe Passage leaving the garbage dump community and walking to school wearing their new uniforms, carrying utensils in their pockets, and taking lighthearted steps that kids only make when they are fed and nourished. Hanley's program was a lifeline for them; it paid enrollment, gave them access to a computer station and English teachers, and afterschool access to a *panadería* where they learned to bake bread. Her dream, Hanley told Lety, was to see babies crawling in the new *guarderia* daycare, while older kids learned cooking or carpentry skills, or learned to type, or learned English. Next would come art, theatre, and music. Their parents, too, would learn to read and write. With approximately 525 students by 2006, the whole operation was ambitious, amazing, unsustainable, and *loca*.

As always, fulfilling Hanley's daily aspirations fell to the hard-working staff. Each month, Lety and other social workers and coordinators had to visit 25 different schools in order to supervise the children and ask the teachers how often they had missed school. Those with passable attendance records got to take home a bag of rice, beans, and cooking oil to their families in the *barrio* near the dump. The supplies usually lasted one month, though some families who had multiple kids in the program figured out ways to re-sell the contents.

If an employee ever disagreed with Hanley, they knew they would come out on the losing end. "She was stubborn. We all had to change our way of thinking and believe that her ideas, *loca* though they seemed, were possible," said Lety. "If she said something was red, it had to be red—even though chiles are green."

One day Lety overheard Hanley speaking on the phone with Marina, who now worked part-time as a volunteer coordinator in the Maine office. "You work like this every day, Monday through Friday?" her mother asked.

"Yes, and Saturday I work only half a day," Hanley replied.

"That's crazy, Han. You need to relax. Let Lety relax. She has a family."

But workdays that stretched into the evening and sometimes through the weekends continued—particularly if a service learning group arrived and only had a limited time to see the garbage dump and the project.

Hanley was incapable of relaxing and taking time off from the project. "Her preoccupation was, 'If we relax, how will they eat?'" said Lety. "We'd return to the project after *Semana Santa* (Easter week) and ask the kids, 'What have you eaten?' They'd say 'nothing.' There was nothing to eat inside their homes." That reality impacted Hanley's entire staff, who worked hard to serve the community even though they were exhausted.

LETY LOST TRACK of how many times a kid in the program would ditch school, or would escape from the Casa Hogar dormitory in Antigua, and she was ordered to find them. "You need to leave home, get a taxi, and find the child," Hanley called and issued the stern command at any hour of the day or night. Her word was final. This was part of her craziness, her *locura*. For Lety and other Guatemalan staff, the irony was that the Casa Hogar from which the kids escaped was nicer than their own homes. The dormitory complex outside Antigua had a swimming pool, a grass field, plants and flowers, a bed for each child, and a teacher for each room. And yet many of the 40–50 kids there—the tough kids, like Nancy Gudiel—couldn't be contained. They escaped over and over again.

"If the kids fell or got into a fight and hurt themselves, we had to take them to the hospital ourselves," said Lety, who carried serious pressure on her shoulders whenever a child got hurt or went missing. Because Hanley was a foreigner, she couldn't officially deal with the Guatemalan police authorities. In those cases, it was *Seño* Lety who took care of matters. Had something gone terribly wrong at the project, and had the police intervened, Hanley's deputy could have been taken away and put in jail. Yet she persisted.

Once, Lety and Hanley trekked three or four kilometers on foot to find a child who lived in a dangerous, gang-controlled neighborhood after their cab driver let them out and refused to drive any further. But they wore their green *"Camino Seguro"* shirts and nothing happened to them. Lety understood that the *maras*, the gang members, knew and respected Hanley. She could go practically anywhere in these tough neighborhoods of Guatemala City and not be robbed or hurt. They looked after her, even after dark.

Hanley remained fearless about where she would walk in the dangerous capital. But her safety standards evolved significantly when it came to public transportation in Guatemala City. Once the Safe Passage staff and volunteer core began to grow, she forbade anyone from riding in the capital's intracity red *"público"* buses which were notorious for both accidents and pick-pocketers. Taking a "chicken bus" *camioneta* between the capital and Antigua was fair game, but staff were required to travel by cab within Guatemala City. "She panicked in the *públicos*," Lety said of Hanley. "'No quiero morir en un accidente de carro,' we heard her say over and over again." *I don't want to die in a car accident.*

THROUGH HANLEY'S CHARISMA, her impassioned storytelling, and her brilliance in convincing people to come see the garbage dump project for themselves, she was able to attract donors like the Helmans who could write checks that would make a tangible impact on the lives of these children. But she struggled to visualize a sustainable, long-term plan for the project's infrastructure, she struggled to say "no" to smaller projects that may not have been central to the greater cause, she failed to establish a work-life balance for herself, and she was unwilling to take a hard look at what initiatives Safe Passage should cut. The new board of directors implored her to do both.

One of those costly and controversial ventures was the Casa Hogar dormitory in the San Pedro las Huertas neighborhood outside of Antigua, which housed 50–60 of the roughest kids in the program, including those who faced physical or sexual abuse, drug or alcohol issues, or outright homelessness if they returned to the capital. Students like Nancy Gudiel and Daniél Osorio. The self-contained compound included 10 houses and the place cost a fortune; Ed estimated the burden at a quarter million dollars a year to keep it open. With rumors of illegal adoptions and child trafficking sweeping through Guatemala during these years, the specter of foreigners housing poor children an hour's drive from the community where they grew up could have looked ominous.

"It wasn't legal," said Ed. "We didn't have the licenses from the government to run it. We didn't necessarily have the permission from parents to have their kids there. Originally the Casa Hogar was for children who were living in abusive situations to get them into safe environments. But it turned into something else. Basically it turned into, 'I've got too many kids, can you take two of them?'"

"As those kids got older, it was just a bad setup. They were teenagers who were virtually prisoners in there; they couldn't come and go as they pleased. You could imagine the rebelliousness. They'd climb the walls and run away, and we'd have to go looking for them."

"The Casa Hogar was clean, there was no monkey business," added Marc Wuthrich, a Swiss accountant who served as assistant to Ed. "But if you looked at it from the outside, here were small children with volunteers ... We needed to close it down for the good of the organization."

Meanwhile, a volunteer had helped Hanley raise money to open Posada Lazos Fuertes, a hotel where service-learning groups and short-term volunteers could pay to stay, and where Safe Passage students could learn hospitality management. The concept looked good on the surface. Indeed, Ed considered Lazos Fuertes to be a great marketing tool because the hotel was listed in tourist guidebooks everywhere and each guest would learn about the project. But Lazos Fuertes was located several blocks west of the Parque Central and the main tourist area of Antigua, on the Calzada Santa Lucia, the primary thoroughfare along which public buses rumbled as they honked horns and belched exhaust in route to Guatemala City or other destinations. The location on the outskirts of town was less than ideal. Young guests partying into the night clashed with older clients and businesspeople who wanted quiet. Things sometimes went missing from the hotel rooms. Even worse were rumors and threats of full-on assaults on the hotel, which could have led to hostage situations. Lazos Fuertes employed a lone security guard, and it was well known that *gringos* with money stayed in the hotel. Given its location on the route out of town, some worried that the hotel posed an easy target. For Hanley and Safe Passage, the security of guests and volunteers was penultimate. One murder or one kidnapping could have doomed the entire program.

"Lazos Fuertes was a financial drain, too," said Wuthrich.

"Even when the finances didn't allow us to do something, she'd say 'I'll get the money' and she would. She was like a hawk with the money. She started lots of projects that, if you analyzed them cold (from a cost-benefit analysis), you probably wouldn't do them."

The board pushed Hanley on the Casa Hogar and Lazos Fuertes, and other program expansions which they didn't consider central to the core mission of Safe Passage. And Hanley pushed back.

The board did convince her to ditch the tiny room she rented—with a bed several feet away from her computer so she could work into the wee hours—and move into her own Antigua apartment which had a lush courtyard draped with colorful bougainvillea flowers and a protective wall surrounding her home. They wanted Hanley to take care of herself and work less. Paul Sutherland sent her care packages from the United States with chocolate and popular magazines in order to convince her not to take her life so seriously. Hanley also got two dogs, C-Well and Lucha, to offer companionship. But the dogs must have upset a neighbor, or someone wanted to settle a score with her, because an intruder once used a mattress to scale the razor wire fence and throw rat poison into the courtyard to poison the dogs. They nearly died.

The board of directors also bought a used Jeep for Hanley to use, but she never drove it. Though she would walk into gang-ridden, dangerous neighborhoods of the capital, she was mortally afraid of driving in Guatemala. She told Ed, and others, on multiple occasions, "I'm afraid I'm going to die in a car accident here."

BETH KLOSER, A LONG-TERM VOLUNTEER from Indiana who arrived in the spring of 2005 and lived at the Casa Hogar, once stayed at Hanley's apartment for a week to watch the dogs while she was away on a fundraising trip. Hanley had left her several pages of typed and detailed instructions for how to care for C-Well and Lucha, whom Beth observed she loved "like her own children." Lucha, in particular, was a sickly-looking black lab who Hanley and Rachel bought in Guatemala City from a breeder. As a puppy, Lucha got sick and nearly died but rebounded and grew healthy, strong, and energetic. The dog's name, which means "fight" in Spanish, seems fitting. Hanley's instructions for watching the dogs included details on how much food to give them and how often to take them for walks, and to "make sure they get a lot of love.... Talk to them. Make sure they know you're paying attention to them."

Books and magazines were strewn about the room—leadership books about "how to be a good boss" scattered among rags like *People* and light-hearted girlie magazines. Perhaps there was also a copy of the Paul Farmer book *Mountains Beyond Mountains*, or maybe Hanley brought that on her trip. Beth saw no signs that Hanley cooked much for herself. She continued to work in the office from early in the morning until late at night. "Everybody always needed a piece of Hanley's time," said Beth. However, the volunteer may have seen Hershey's Kisses wrappers in the trash can. Hanley was known to love chocolate.

Beth's job at Safe Passage was to arrange itineraries for, and lead, the service learning teams who would arrive for 7–10 days. She would meet most groups at the airport when they arrived on a Sunday afternoon and accompany them to their hotel or homestay in Antigua. Each day during the following week they would take a chicken bus into the project in Guatemala City and play an assigned role at Safe Passage. By this time, Safe

Passage personnel were no longer able to go into the garbage dump, itself—not since the methane gas fire in January 2005 prompted the government to regulate access. Beth watched and listened to how the groups—particularly high school or college-aged groups, evolved over the course of that eye-opening week. "I could see the wheels turning in their minds as they engaged in a social analysis of the unjust structures in our world," she said.

Following their end-of-week *despedida* send-off dinner at a bohemian, hole-in-the-wall bar named Café No Se, located about three blocks southeast of the Parque Central, Beth would typically lead the groups on a weekend-long excursion to Lake Atitlán where they would take motorboat rides in a *lancha* across the lake from Panajachel to the traditional Tzutuhil Mayan town of Santiago. "Hanley wanted folks to see and experience not just the horrors and tragedies of the garbage dump, but she wanted them to experience the real beauty of the country, too, so they wouldn't leave with a skewed notion of what Guatemala is," said Beth.

Once, Hanley joined Beth and other long-term volunteers on a brief trip to the Pacific Coast. The volunteer from Indiana remembered the organization's founder sitting on the black sand beach reading a magazine with a cover over it because she was embarrassed that anyone would see her reading something fluffy. Beth remembered that it was a romance novel or a light-reading magazine. "Don't tell anyone," Hanley told Beth while laughing.

"Tranquila, Madre Teresa," Juan Mini, Sr., whose family owned the land around the garbage dump, once told Hanley as her face flushed with embarrassment. "*Take it easy, Mother Teresa.* Slow down a bit."

Was it the constructive but unsolicited criticism from a Guatemalan powerbroker that put her on the spot? Or was it his analogy comparing her to Mother Teresa? Hanley shied away from the spotlight, and she bristled at weighty comparisons to famous people. It was that genuine humility that had attracted Paul Sutherland to support the project and chair the first board of directors. Her fear of attention or self-promotion had also lured New Jersey photographer Joe Delconzo, who became more and more interested in "shooting" the dump and Hanley's mysterious project, even as she pulled back from the camera—initially, at least.

Tranquila. Relax. Slow down, everyone told her. But these were things she couldn't do. She needed to know every child. She needed to observe and take part in every aspect of her growing program.

"She wanted to be part of *everything*. She wanted to do everything herself," reflected Juan Mini, Jr., who followed in his father's footsteps to coach Hanley and offer her foundational support after he left California and moved home to Guatemala. "The one thing I tried most to convince her was to delegate responsibilities."

But how could she trust others with important tasks, and how could she wait patiently for her staff to address a crisis on Monday morning when tragedy and heartbreak didn't wait for the weekend to end? Hanley felt compelled to act each time she witnessed an injustice. Amina Lacour, who stepped back from Safe Passage but continued to meet her socially for a coffee or lunch at Doña Luisa's, recalled a harrowing story that prompted Hanley to jump into action immediately. She learned one evening that a *guajero* man had locked his wife and sick child in their tiny tin shack in the *barrio* near the dump. They had been confined there all weekend without water or food, and the child had died. The mother, a young indigenous woman from the *altiplano* highlands, had no resources. No one in the *barrio* would help her in this male-dominated, often misogynistic community. Hanley immediately caught a cab to Guatemala City and approached the home, which was four walls of laminated steel with a corrugated tin roof and a padlocked door. The man ran off when he realized Hanley intended to call the police. Inside the shack was a miserable, decrepit scene. Half of the one-room home was filled with trash and plastic bottles. A makeshift stove sat in the middle of the room, and next to it was a wooden bed where everyone slept. When the door was locked, no light whatsoever entered the home. Hanley insisted on helping the poor woman by bringing her food and finding her a better place to live.

Amina remembered visiting the home the following day with Hanley and Lety. She asked how such a tragedy could have happened. "They explained to me that, all too often, young women from the countryside are brought by their husbands to the city, where they have no family, no friends, and very often no Spanish to be able to communicate or connect with others," said Amina. "They suffer abuse, isolation, and abandonment. They are kept locked away with their children when the husband is not around 'for their own safety.' This can last for hours or days. Deep-seated mistrust and fear of others leads to mistrust of self, which is most probably why she was unable to call for help even from a windowless tin shack."

Such squalid stories happened over and over again. Just as the vultures circled overhead and the garbage trucks continued to drop their payloads into the dump. Little by little the *guajero* population grew, as the promise of easy work attracted those from even poorer parts of Guatemala. But beneath the mountain of trash, noxious methane gases ignited the massive fire in January 2005 that burned for nearly three days and prompted the Guatemalan government to evacuate 300 *guajeros*, build walls around the dump, enforce hours of operation between 6 in the morning and 6 at night, and regulate who could enter. The authorities created an identification system so that only *guajeros* age 16 or older could work in the dump. Children and pregnant women were banned from entering. But kids continued to enter the *basurero* through holes in the fence and loopholes in the system. Some would hide inside the dump after it "closed" and continue searching for trash.

The danger, the misery, and the endless, sometimes thankless toil drove some committed workers to leave Safe Passage. Maribel, who Hanley hired in 2000 as her first employee, developed health problems from her proximity to the garbage dump's toxic fumes. She also bore a child the year after she began working for the project and named her daughter "Hanley"—an unheard-of name in Guatemala—and an homage to her *gringa* friend and boss. Little Hanley Cholotio lived, for the most part, with her grandparents in San Juan La Laguna. Maribel made the long commute home to her indigenous village on weekends and returned to Guatemala City on the early morning bus each Monday. But by 2005—a pivotal year for the organization—she could no longer bear to be away from her now 4-year-old daughter. The massive fire in the dump may have been the final straw, and she said goodbye to Safe Passage.

Hanley Denning stayed. Each blow to the community, each story of misery, each death strengthened her resolve to help guide the children of the dump out of extreme poverty.

"Even though Hanley was from another country, she wasn't afraid to enter any shack made of cardboard or sheet metal. She didn't mind the flies, the garbage," said Maribel. "She'd go into homes. She'd go into the dump, all the way to the bottom, to talk with families. It was dangerous, but Hanley never took a camera or anything with her. She just wanted to talk with people."

AS HER PROJECT GREW, as the *barrios* around the dump grew, so grew the colonial, cobblestone street-pocked town of Antigua, where Hanley and nearly all foreigners working or volunteering for Safe Passage lived. Now firmly on the map of every tourism guidebook, restaurants and bars popped up on what seemed like every street corner. Antigua had been a mostly peaceful oasis during Guatemala's horrific civil war; now it seemed an international party town. Restaurants of all nationalities opened. Salsa and reggaetón music pumped until one or two in the morning, as whiny tuc-tuc three-wheeled taxis careened over the cobblestones, carrying tourists and wealthy Guatemalans at all hours.

A popular drinking destination for ex-pats half a block southwest of the Parque Central—in the direction of Volcán de Agua—was Monoloco, owned by Billy Burns, who had met Hanley in 1999 at the private school orientation week where they were settling in to teach wealthy Guatemalan kids. Hanley had quit the job and found her calling in the garbage dump instead. Soon after, Billy opened Monoloco, which became the place to get together with friends, watch sports, eat nachos, and drink margaritas or Gallo beer. Out of reverence for Hanley's mission, Billy and other restaurant owners who knew about Safe Passage would hold occasional benefit nights, where the proceeds would go directly to Hanley's project. For volunteers or groups visiting on week-long service learning trips, Monoloco and other Antigua establishments offered a welcome respite and sense of casual normalcy after an intense and emotional day working for Safe Passage in the extreme poverty of the garbage dump community.

But Billy noticed something profound about Hanley's workers and volunteers. Over and over again, they would leave the bar at 9 or 10 p.m. to prepare themselves, mentally and physically, for the following day at the project—even as others at Monoloco partied until one in the morning. Sure, they had to catch a chicken bus into the city at 7 or 8 a.m., but 20-somethings could survive on few hours of sleep. No, there was something else. Billy observed in them an absolute, unflinching devotion to Hanley and to the *guajero* children. "I remember there was an almost idolatry of Hanley," he said. "People were in awe of what she was doing, in awe of her dedication and determination." They could kick back and enjoy their trip to Guatemala, but they were principally there to work, to serve, and to be part of an effort that changed lives. In turn, the experience would change their lives, too.

Catching sight of Hanley out on the town was extremely rare. If she visited Monoloco, it was probably a semi-obligatory social meetup with an important donor or volunteer, or perhaps a goodbye party for someone who had worked for Safe Passage for more than a few weeks. Hanley didn't drink much alcohol. Her mom, Marina, half jokingly, half seriously owed that to having served her a small glass of champagne with broccoli at her daughter's first birthday party. Hanley also didn't want to give the impression that she was relaxing or having too much fun in Antigua, a small town of less than 50,000 inhabitants where word traveled fast.

Only once did Fredy see Hanley out dancing at the popular club, La Sala. When she saw him, she became flustered and said quickly, "Ústed no me ve." *You don't see me*, she said to him in

formal Spanish. Fredy laughed and responded, "A mí tampoco."
You didn't see me either. She called him a couple days later and
said, "I feel bad about being out on the town. Someone might
see me and think I'm not serious about the project." Was her
austere lifestyle linked to the pure discipline of commitment, or
fear of losing the respect of her colleagues and donors? Either
way, she was embarrassed enough to make that call.

So, then Fredy shared with her a story that once he was
relaxing at a bar in Antigua, when an acquaintance approached
and mockingly asked him, "Drinking beer, huh? Where's the
social work?"

"We have feelings, too. We have hunger. We have thirst,"
Fredy had consoled her.

Not typically a late-night person himself, Fredy once ran
into Hanley at 4 a.m. while he was walking home after leaving
a rare afterparty. "I'm looking for a kid that escaped from the
Casa Hogar," she told him.

Even if Hanley *did* seek nightlife, she didn't give herself the
time to enjoy it. She worked every available hour. Hanley's rare
social escapes were instead breakfast or lunch dates at Doña Luisa's, or a weekend trip to Lake Atitlán or the Pacific Coast—but
only if someone visiting Guatemala pried her loose from work
and insisted that she join them. Instead, the wining and dining
of donors fell to Ed. Organizing social events for volunteers or
service-learning groups fell to Lety or Vilma or Fredy.

Not long after Café No Se opened in 2003, Fredy asked the
owner, a New Yorker named John Rexer, if Safe Passage could
borrow their long, narrow back room which was lit only by can-
dles to conduct trainings and show movies to new volunteers.
One film they frequently showed was *La Hija del Puma*, narrated by a young indigenous woman who tells of human rights
abuses during the Guatemalan civil war. Café No Se became

well-known through the expat community for selling "illegal mezcal," for its dimly lit bookstore in the adjoining room, for live music most evenings, and for *La Cuadra*, a radical magazine that Rexer published together with his buddy Michael Tallon, a fellow refugee from New York City. As such, "people from all over the world made Café No Se their home," said Rexer. Safe Passage held *despedida* goodbye parties there for long-term volunteers and special dinners for donors. Ed attended most of those social events as a stand-in for Hanley.

"She wasn't social like that," he said. "Even the volunteer parties, she hardly ever went. I don't think it was a comfortable situation for her. She wasn't the small-talk kind of person.... In the years I worked at the project I probably drank more than I ever had in my life. You had to keep everybody happy and show appreciation. It was important to the volunteers that someone higher up in the organization showed up."

ONLY ON VERY SPECIAL OCCASIONS would Hanley join Ed for an evening on the town with particular supporters. When Marty and Frank Helman, the Rotarians from Boothbay, Maine, who were funding the new *guarderia* nursery school, visited Guatemala in 2006, the four of them dined together at a fancy, European-style restaurant called Meson Panza Verde, which is located inside a luxury boutique hotel in Antigua.

Hanley shared with them that several students in her program hoped to enroll in Kinal, a high-caliber, prestigious technical school conveniently located just around the corner from Safe Passage. The director of Kinal had been reluctant to take kids from the garbage dump, but according to Marty, she "did the Hanley thing." She cornered the director at a party and made him agree that if any one of her kids could pass Kinal's entrance exam, he would grant them admission. Just to get rid of Hanley, the director accepted the challenge. He probably figured the course posed an impossibly high hurdle. As it happened, all of the boys who graduated from middle school took Kinal's exam, and six passed it. Now Safe Passage had to find scholarship money for them to enroll in the technical school the following year, 2007.

As they gazed at the poolside reflection of the restaurant's stone walls bathed in a candlelit hue, Marty and Frank asked Hanley and Ed how much it would cost to sponsor one child to attend Kinal. The executive director and her accountant looked at each other dumbfounded. They hadn't totaled the math. On the back of an envelope they hastily and clumsily wrote down the cost of tuition, then added the cost of uniforms, books, and an academic support person. Finally, they reached a number. $2,200 per student per year. Frank took out his checkbook and wrote a check for that amount. Ed was so excited that he spilled the wine on the table.

"Next time I'm going to send you the check in the mail," laughed Frank.

Life Back Home

JANE GALLAGHER WAS WAITING in the checkout line at Hannaford Supermarket off Route 1 in Yarmouth, Maine, one day in 2005 when she overheard the customer in front of her ask the cashier if they had visited Safe Passage in Guatemala. The cashier wore a t-shirt that sported the nonprofit's unmistakable black and white logo which featured a rounded doorway leading to stairs, next to the words "Safe Passage" and below that "*Camino Seguro*" in smaller letters. The clerk smiled and nodded an emphatic "yes" as she handed the customer change. Jane was about to lean in and ask the strangers when they had visited Guatemala and if they were sponsoring any children. But before she could do so, three or four other Hannaford customers suddenly leaned their heads into the aisle and began to share their own Safe Passage stories.

"I just can't believe people live like that, in the garbage dump ... Can you believe a girl from Yarmouth started that project all on her own? ... That trip changed our lives. We can't wait to go back!" Each anecdote seemed to punctuate and amplify the conversation. An otherwise mundane trip to the grocery store had turned into a cascade of joyful sharing for these strangers.

Jane returned home and, before putting all her groceries away, she emailed Hanley. "Yes! We have made it. People now know what Safe Passage is," she wrote. To Jane, it seemed like the project had achieved an important milestone. It had already changed the lives of hundreds of families in the garbage dump, it had changed the lives of everyone who worked or volunteered at Safe Passage, and now it had changed the town of Yarmouth itself.

Doug and Becky Pride, who had overcome their fears and traveled to Safe Passage in 2004 to spend two weeks teaching inside the classroom, organized a 5K road race the following spring in nearby Cumberland with entry fees benefiting the project—just as they had promised Hanley they would. The race has since become an annual event. Doug estimates that the races in 2005 and 2006 each raised about $15,000–$20,000. Hanley returned to Maine both years on fundraising trips and to participate in the Safe Passage 5K Run & Walk. Each year the Prides gave her bib number 1, while Rachel Meyn—her righthand person in the United States—wore bib number 2. Hanley took a microphone and shared words about Safe Passage prior to the starting gun. The race attracted nearly 1,000 runners, some competitive, including Olympic marathon gold medalist Joan Benoit. At age 36, Hanley was no longer a champion runner, and her commitment to Safe Passage left her little time to train. Still, the sport was embedded in her DNA. During the 2006 race, Hanley was the 242nd to cross the finish line, with a time of 27 minutes and 48 seconds.

Safe Passage generated support not just in southern Maine, but in pockets throughout New England. "It's surprising how many people know about Safe Passage or know somebody that has been down there," said Barbara Davis, who worked with Rachel in the Yarmouth office, running the project's U.S. accounting and database work. When economist Jim Highland had seen Hanley give a presentation about Safe Passage in 2003 at a Yarmouth church and decided to lend her office space in Portland, he asked Barbara, his employee at the time, to help with Safe Passage's budget. Two years later, when Hanley opened her own office in Yarmouth, Barbara came with her, along with Rachel, who ran operations in the United States.

"There are regional soccer tournaments that send their proceeds to Safe Passage. There are schools that send down service-learning teams almost every single year. It's become part of their culture at that school," said Barbara. Like Jane Gallagher, she had also walked into Hannaford and other places in the Yarmouth area and realized that complete strangers knew about Safe Passage.

"People feel as though she's our hometown girl, our hometown hero," said Jenn McAdoo, a religious educator who met Hanley during a visit to her Unitarian church in Yarmouth.

DREW CASERTANO, THE HEADMASTER at Millbrook, a private school 100 miles north of New York City which enrolls some of the most economically privileged students in the world, first learned of Hanley from his friend, Mainer Bob Stuart, while playing in a lacrosse tournament in the summer of 2005. The following February, he and colleague Liz Morrison took his children and 14 Millbrook students on a service-learning trip to Safe Passage. Liz's brother, an investment banker with clients in Guatemala, used his connections to arrange a visit to the national stadium, the Estadio Nacional Doroteo Guamuch Flores—named after the winner of the 1952 Boston Marathon—which has a capacity of 26,000 seats.

"We got four or five school buses and took our kids and [Safe Passage] kids," said Drew. "We brought t-shirts and shorts, and thousands of dollars of lacrosse equipment. At the national stadium, the kids were going nuts; they had never seen grass in their lives. The kids had an absolute ball. They played lacrosse, they had water fights, they ran around the track. For the first time in the children's lives they had status, they had access to something that no Guatemalans except soccer players get to access."

In May 2006, Hanley delivered the high school commencement address at Millbrook School.

> As many of you might not know, several members of this senior class recently chose to spend their 'vacation' volunteering with Safe Passage at the Guatemala City dump helping some of Guatemala's poorest children. Imagine an enormous dump the size of several football fields ... vultures swarming overhead and thousands of people of all ages scavenging in the heat with their bare hands through garbage and toxins and dust. Thousands of people spend their days scavenging for cardboard, plastic, paper, anything they can sell for food. It is a daily struggle for survival. As you can imagine, it's extremely dangerous work. But what changed my life wasn't the squalor and the hopelessness. Quite the contrary ... what I sensed was opportunity. These children wanted to go to school so badly. There was a sparkle in their eyes which made me think ... what if?

Hanley then read from a long list of Safe Passage's accomplishments, including: 548 children in school, a residential home (the Casa Hogar), an early intervention program, a carpentry program, an adult literacy program, permanent facilities for the early intervention program and the educational reinforcement program, a hotel training program and Safe Passage-run hotel, "and thanks to Millbrook School, a lacrosse program."

> My message here to you, the graduating class, is simple ... do something ... do anything and put all of your heart and commitment behind it. Once I was at a local high school doing an assembly and some kid kept asking me, 'Why Guatemala, why

Guatemala, when there is so much need in so many other parts of the world?' And my reply was, 'You are so right. I challenge you to take that on.' And I challenge you as well, to do the same. Make a difference.

Drew and Bob Stuart also trained a Safe Passage teacher named Rodrigo Pascual to coach lacrosse, and he would later launch Maya Lacrosse, which expanded the sport to six Guatemalan communities.

HANLEY WAS KNOWN IN GUATEMALA for her insane work hours and sometimes manic energy. That drive didn't change much on fundraising and speaking engagement trips back in the States. She visited Chapel Hill a few times as the North Carolina support network grew. Marilyn and Tom Alexander, members of the Church of Reconciliation who visited Safe Passage for the first time in 2002, hosted Hanley on two occasions, in 2005 and 2006.

"Each time we met her she was the same person," said Marilyn. "She was open, friendly and gracious. She was excited about the work she was doing, and that excitement and dedication moved from her into you."

But once pleasantries were exchanged and Hanley moved into their guest bedroom, they rarely saw her. "We'd take her suitcase upstairs and she'd just disappear," said Tom. "We might not see her for the rest of the day.... We were told by Rachel that she didn't sleep much."

On her second trip to Chapel Hill, Hanley ran a fever and she suffered from a nasty cough. Marilyn offered her Benadryl cold medicine, but Hanley refused to take it because she planned to address a local Rotary club the next day and she wanted to be at the top of her game, despite the head cold. Once Tom peaked his head into the guestroom to check on her, but she was sitting on the floor looking through papers sprawled everywhere around her.

Hanley didn't eat much when she stayed with the Alexanders. They remember feeding her juice and toast. "I don't recall ever seeing her eat a heavy meal," said Marilyn. "She was preoccupied with what she was doing."

ANNUAL VISITS TO TRAVERSE CITY, Michigan—Paul Sutherland's home—also became a regular part of Hanley's agenda. The Great Lakes Friends of Safe Passage launched on August 7, 2005, with a "friendraiser" which attracted a banquet hall full of wealthy philanthropists and Michiganders who had traveled to Central America and wanted to help. Hanley had arrived in Traverse City three days prior to the "friendraiser," and Paul made sure that she spent time with his mom, Mary Sutherland, over lunch in nearby Glen Arbor, the town next to the Sleeping Bear Dunes National Lakeshore, so the former school teacher could help Hanley prepare for a midday presentation to Paul's local Rotary club the following day. He may have been worried that her off-the-cuff, somewhat spontaneous style of storytelling could fall flat, and she might miss a lucrative opportunity to gain the support of Traverse City Rotarians.

The Sutherlands persuaded Hanley to use audio visuals, and board member Sharon Workman remembered that her presentation wasn't as compelling as if she had simply told her story organically, perhaps without technology. Hanley was frustrated, and at his FIM Group office later that day, Paul leaned hard on her to develop a strategic plan and balance Safe Passage's budget. Hanley broke down in tears and briefly left the room to compose herself.

On that Michigan trip, Hanley paid a spontaneous visit to her friend Marilyn Fitzgerald, the clinical psychologist and author who had connected her with Paul Sutherland. Marilyn worked in an office above the Omelette Shoppe half a block from Paul's Traverse City office. "We stayed upstairs and talked for about three hours," said Marilyn. "We just laughed and cried and talked about the pressure, the realities of the situation she had created."

Nevertheless, the Traverse City region would become a lucrative source of donations and child sponsorships for years to come, as dozens of Michiganders, including many school groups, would travel to Guatemala on service-learning trips. The Great Lakes Friends would hold subsequent annual "fiesta" fundraisers, and their network raised between $20,000 and $30,000 a year for Safe Passage, Sharon estimated. When she returned for the "fiesta" in 2006, Hanley riveted the room with her presentation of the Guatemala City garbage dump, the children who toil in its despair, and how Safe Passage helps them get back on their feet.

Even when she visited beautiful places like the Sleeping Bear Dunes, Hanley never truly left Guatemala City. Her mind was always on the project. On their summer 2006 trip, she and Rachel stayed with Sharon and Wayne Workman at their house on Little Traverse Lake in Leelanau County. Northern Michiganders love to show off their majestic nature to visitors, and Sharon took Hanley on a walk to Lake Michigan. "I remember her commenting on how beautiful it was, but most of the time while we were walking, she just talked about Safe Passage and what was going on at the project. Her focus was constantly on her work."

Some in Traverse City, like John McCarthy, made a deeply personal connection with a Safe Passage child they would sponsor. As told in the Great Lakes Friends' newsletter, John and his wife Suzanne had an autistic child—a teenager at the time—and when they traveled to Guatemala in 2006, they learned about Gustavo, a three-and-a-half year old with Autism Spectrum Disorder. They met Gustavo in the back of a warehouse, where he was playing with water in a sink. "Right out of the textbook," John said. "All kids like to play in water, but an autistic kid will play with the water in a sink 10 hours a day, seven days a week if you let him." The McCarthys' financial support allowed Gustavo to get speech therapy lessons and to attend San Nicolás de Bari, the best special education private school in Guatemala. A small, special education school bus picked him up at his door in the *barrio* every morning since another Safe Passage student already attended the same school. John initially pushed for the boy to move into the Casa Hogar, Safe Passage's dormitory, but backed down when he learned that Gustavo had both a loving mother and father at home (the exception to the rule), as well as 10 siblings.

As THE NUMBER OF STUDENTS in Hanley's program grew toward 550, as child sponsors and financial supporters came from everywhere, so did unsolicited advice and suggestions to add new projects. As the board of directors called on her to develop a long-term strategic plan, the mood grew more intense. Hanley felt at times that she was losing control of the program. She also lamented that she wasn't able to find a steady love relationship. Infrequent dates came and went—both with Guatemalans and with ex-pats. Lety and other Safe Passage employees and board members sometimes tried to set up Hanley with someone.

"We all said she had to find a husband. But I'd love to find a husband who knows how to clean, knows how to cook, and look after the kids. They don't exist in Guatemala!" Lety laughed. "Every time a volunteer arrived who was handsome, we'd say, '*Mira*, Hanley. Check out this one!' Let's see if he likes to look after kids because Hanley has to go to work. We'd say, 'Aha!' and she'd get red in the face."

For a time, she dated an American volunteer named Matt, with whom she got her dog C-Well, but the relationship fell apart and a custody battle ensued over the rights to the pet. Hanley was looking for a soulmate, she told Susanna Place, whom she would sometimes visit at the board member's home in Boston or rural Maine. "She hoped to be a mother. Either an adoptive mother, or to have her own children. I think her own parents had been role models for that," said Susanna. "Sometimes I'd joke with her, 'That was a nice volunteer.' She'd say, 'No, I'm serious. I'm in my mid-30s, and I want my own family. My dogs aren't enough. I just want a partner, and at the end of the day I want to go home and laugh and relax ... I'm counting on Ed to take me to the beach this weekend. But he's like an uncle to me.'"

Juan Mini, Jr., joked that he wanted Hanley to meet a Guatemalan man so she could put down roots in the country. He tried to play matchmaker. But she worked around the clock. "There was no room for anything serious with her," he said. "Her family were the kids, the families, and the project's volunteers." Juan's wife Amina LaCour, who no longer volunteered for Safe Passage but had become friends with Hanley outside of work, remembered that she had a relationship at one point with a photographer, with whom she had connected through the project, but he lived in the United States. They met occasionally on her fundraising trips, but it was a fleeting moment. "The project was her life," said Amina. "That was the challenge. How do you find time for personal life?"

Marina Denning said her daughter could be self-conscious and believed herself too tall to date. Hanley had two serious relationships during college—one with a man at Bowdoin, and one with a guy from nearby Bates College. She was hurt badly by both, said Marina. "She was madly in love with one, but he fooled around. She told me once, 'I almost committed suicide over this guy ... What a jerk.'" Marina gave her a subscription to the international version of the dating website Match.com, but even though she badly wanted a partner, Hanley found something amiss with each person she met, said Marina. There was an American ex-pat living in Guatemala to get away from his ex-wife and three kids, for example. Hanley once called home at midnight to tell her mom that she had been stood up in mid-date by a Guatemalan when he realized that she wanted more than a one-night stand. "Guatemalan men are really rude," she told Marina. "If you're not going to have sex with them, they don't like you."

In Maine, Jane Gallagher tried to play the role of matchmaker, too. Her hopes were raised once when a dynamic young restaurant owner and artist in mid-Maine offered to do a fundraiser for Safe Passage. But when she and Hanley Googled him, they found less-than flattering images of a "wild man" with crazy hair. That wouldn't work for Hanley.

During her 2006 visit to Traverse City, Michigan, Hanley ate lunch with Rachel Meyn and Sharon Workman at a Glen

Arbor restaurant called the Good Harbor Grill, where Sharon overheard her speak frankly about her longing to be a mother.

"I really, really would love to have a child, but I don't know how I could ever do that with my life right now," Hanley shared. Sharon heard a tinge of regret in her voice, as though she understood what she had sacrificed for her project.

Hanley shared with Rachel on several occasions the personal pressure she felt of being single in her mid-30s. "Ed asked me if I'm going to freeze my eggs!" she shared with Rachel. "What if I never have children?"

New Horizons

SAFE PASSAGE NOW had a strong board of directors and Hanley recognized, to a degree, that she didn't have to run the race all by herself. Sometime in the summer of 2006, while on a fundraising trip, she visited Susanna Place and her husband Scott Stoll at their home in St. George, Maine, located a couple hours northeast of Portland on one of those rugged fingers of rock that reach into the Atlantic Ocean.

"I'm thinking about taking some time off. I'm really tired," Hanley confided in Susanna. "There's a lot going on at the project. I need to step back and get some perspective. Would you be open to the idea of me coming up and spending some time here?"

"Sure, that would be great," replied Susanna, who didn't consider herself one of Hanley's close friends but was nevertheless eager to listen and help in any way she could. "We're not here all the time. It would be fine if you want to come up."

"What about my dogs? Could I bring my dogs from Guatemala?" asked Hanley, to which Susanna answered she was open to the idea but that C-Well and Lucha would need to get along well with their two German Shepherds.

Hanley's overture to Susanna was clear. The founder of Safe Passage, the idealist who once worked 20 hours a day and expected the same from her staff, the *gringa* whom the *guajeros* considered nothing short of an angel, was burned out. She wanted a sabbatical, or at least time off.

"I don't want to live at home. I don't want to live in Yarmouth," said Hanley. "That's too close to the office. Too close to my family."

She asked if Susanna and Scott had Internet access at their remote home in St. George. Hanley was already thinking about logistics. She was serious. "We have dial-up access," replied Susanna. "We don't have really good Internet, but it's coming. You can always go to the St. George library and sit in the parking lot to get reliable e-mail."

"It's an occupational hazard for me on this job to have breakfast, lunch, and dinner with someone every day and always be working," Hanley said. "I never have any time to myself. I love being with people, but that's why I have to send e-mails at two in the morning. I don't have any other time to do it.... I need to step away."

Susanna chuckled when she thought about Hanley's email habits. She would always send the same email twice, to emphasize a point. Or she would email, then call to say "I emailed you and I need you to focus on this ..." Susanna concurred that this would be a healthy move.

Was Hanley's need to repeat herself part of an insistence and tenacious worry that she wouldn't be heard? That she wouldn't get someone's attention? Or was it a way to emphasize the importance of what she was asking. Either way, she kept the work going, even as she recognized a need to step back.

BACK IN ANTIGUA, the dogs meant a great deal to her, perhaps replacing the personal intimacy for which she had not time.

They grounded her. Both C-Well, whom she got together with Matt, and Lucha, the street dog runt, who grew healthy and strong after she adopted them.

Marina was visiting Guatemala and staying with Hanley in Antigua the night that someone in the neighborhood tried to poison Lucha by stuffing rat poison into a dead bird that they threw over the wall into the courtyard. Hanley wailed hysterically at three in the morning when she realized that Lucha might die. She begged her mom to do something to keep the dog alive. They took an emergency trip into Guatemala City and visited a pharmacy that was open around the clock and found a veterinarian who made Lucha vomit up the poison. Hanley was so frightened by the incident that she hired a kid who lived across the street to be her security guard at night.

Caring for the dogs was a small but important step toward domesticity for Hanley. They were stand-ins for a real relationship and perhaps for raising children. "But what five minutes did she have to give to a relationship?" Paul Sutherland wondered aloud years later. "She called me once and told me, 'I got a dog, and I moved into an actual house, so I'm living a balanced life now. I even took her for a walk this morning.'" Paul was happy to learn that, by mid-2006, Hanley was no longer working 20 hours each day. According to Ed Mahoney, she no longer went to Guatemala City every day but worked from the office in Antigua or sometimes from home. Sometimes she even slept in on Saturdays, then called Paul to proudly tell him so.

That July, for Rachel's 26th birthday, Hanley hosted a huge party at her house and invited volunteers, staff and friends from all over Antigua. She even tagged along to a late-night afterparty. Rachel was thrilled to see Hanley out and enjoying herself. It was one of several late nights that summer when they laid back and shed the heaviness of their work during the day. At one party Hanley met a man with whom she clicked, but learned he lived in Nicaragua. She asked Rachel to join her on a trip to the Central American nation to the south to track down the guy. "We can also check out the situation at the garbage dump there," joked Hanley.

Upon landing in Managua, they discovered that he was out of the country on business, so Hanley and Rachel visited the beach on the Pacific Ocean and relaxed. Then they hired a taxi to drive them to the capital city's dump. "The driver looked at us like a couple of crazy *gringas*," Rachel remembered. "We went to the city landfill, and it was muddy and the taxi got stuck. We couldn't help but laugh at the situation. Even a cow walked by our stuck taxi as we got out and pushed it." For Rachel, the side journey reflected who they had become. Surrounded by poverty and inequality, they were only able to lie on *la playa* for so long before their inner sense of duty called.

Hanley's occasional vacations included at least one trip to Haiti, the deeply impoverished Caribbean nation where poverty and child malnutrition surpassed Guatemala. Indeed, Haiti is considered the poorest country in the western hemisphere. In Port-au-Prince Hanley also visited the city landfill and later joked with Paul Sutherland that, "for fun, she liked to visit garbage dumps." Hanley also spoke occasionally of adopting children from Haiti. But through all this, another idea germinated in her mind. Launch an educational reinforcement project in Haiti, perhaps even following Safe Passage's model.

"When she talked about Haiti she swooned, like the way she talked about the *guajeros* in the dump during those first days of Safe Passage—like the girl who went to work in the dump with her baby in a box," said Lety, who imitated the playful, exuberant way Hanley pronounced the word "Haiti" in Spanish. Like "HIGH-T."

Hanley told Lety she wanted to launch a program there. That's where she felt she could make a profound impact. It broke her heart to see how the children lived. The environment in Haiti was totally different than Guatemala, but the need was the same. Those children needed love. She wanted to adopt two boys from there.

"She said she was preparing us, because when *Camino Seguro* was in good shape, and everyone knew their job, she would go to Haiti," said Lety. "But, we thought, we'll never be ready for her to leave us."

OVER TIME HANLEY SPENT MORE and more time in the States to raise money. In the beginning, she would come for a few weeks at a time, later she visited for a month, said Rachel, who felt she was growing closer to her as a friend. But 2006 was a tumultuous year for Hanley, and her relations with key staff suffered.

There had been too much rapid growth, development of interest from volunteers and groups who wanted to go to Guatemala, and spin-off Friends groups around the world. "Issues among families and kids were becoming more complex, and infrastructure and staff capacity were being outpaced by the growth," said Rachel. "Pressure was being put on Hanley to make really hard decisions, the board was requesting more accountability, and she had less privacy. This all took a toll and also strained our relationship and a lot of relationships."

When conflicts arose that involved supporters, or volunteers, or staff, Hanley often assigned someone else to deliver bad news. "It was too hard for her to play that role," said Rachel. "She hated being 'the bad guy.'" Instead, it was often Lety, Hanley's right-hand employee in Guatemala, who did the thankless work of firing people or bringing them into line with Hanley's orders.

As Safe Passage grew at a breakneck pace, Rachel and others recognized that certain structures needed to be put in place, staff needed to be trained and capacity built, systems and costs needed to be streamlined. This required difficult decisions and for Hanley to let go at certain levels. But according to Rachel, "Hanley saw herself as having to make those changes on her own. She was receiving a lot of consult from board members and other individuals, yet there was no internal management team that was pulled together to discuss ideas and strategies."

Some key relationships fizzled. Mary Jo Amani, whose husband Todd worked with USAID, had volunteered with Safe Passage since 2001. She introduced Montessori teaching materials to the project and became Hanley's main curriculum consultant, along with Amina Lacour. But time and time again, Mary Jo observed that Hanley couldn't take criticism, not from her, not from anyone. She refused to sway from her agenda on how things would proceed. Ed succeeded, on occasion, when he pushed back on Hanley for trying to initiate a project for which she had no money. "She didn't welcome other ideas, other than if someone suggested a pottery program or a welding program, and offered to pay for it," said Mary Jo, who decided to quit Safe Passage in December 2006. She said she had been fired one too many times. "Hanley had the tendency to fire someone immediately upon any dissent or questioning, then, realizing her mistake, would call within hours to apologize and implore the employee to return, offering more benefits even when not solicited," added Mary Jo.

Rachel had worked by Hanley's side for five years and had helped build up the Maine office and the U.S. support base. She wanted to bring Safe Passage to the next level. "I was frustrated because I felt she wasn't including me in her plans forward any longer. I felt as though she was keeping something from me." Rachel raised her concern to Hanley during a phone call in October 2006 as she stood in the sunshine outside the Maine office on Route 1.

Flustered, Hanley raised her voice on the other end of the line in Guatemala. "There are things you just don't know, that you wouldn't want to know!" she yelled at Rachel. "I have to be the lightning bolt."

The conversation struck Rachel, and she still remembered it years later. Hanley felt exposed at the top and didn't see she had partners, concluded Rachel. She and many others were begging to help her make the necessary changes to share the weight of the organization. "I felt greater empathy for the struggle she was feeling as the founder, leader, and future of the organization," said Rachel. "She was tired, yet knew she was carrying a tremendous responsibility. I told her, 'I'm here for you Han, I don't want you to feel you have to be the lightning all on your own.'"

DESPITE THE STRESS she carried on her shoulders and though her mind was never far from the project, Hanley pursued extracurricular activities in the anonymity of Guatemala City. Marina believed that she was taking classes in Buddhism. Hanley also made friends in the capital and sometimes even shared holidays together with them. She and Amina spent Thanksgiving 2006 with the family of Sandra González, where they ate a traditional turkey meal with all the fixings. "We offered a 'Cheers' for the work she was doing and told her we admired her efforts," said Sandra. Headstrong and stubborn though she was, Hanley blushed with humility at the attention, even from a table of no more than six people.

Hanley flew home to spend Christmas 2006 with her family in Yarmouth, Maine, while Guatemalan schools were closed for the holidays. She stayed at the place Marina rented on Cousins Island and relaxed just enough to grow philosophical about life. "Mom, what do you think the purpose of life is?" she asked one morning while she slowly brushed her long mane of blonde hair. Marina pondered the question as she scrambled eggs in the kitchen. It struck her as a strange question, given how much Hanley had already accomplished. "The purpose of life is a life of purpose," her mother replied.

Marina joined Hanley on the return trip to Guatemala so they could celebrate New Year's Eve together. The early months of 2007 would be an exciting time at Safe Passage with great possibilities on the horizon. The new school year was to begin on Monday, January 15, and culminate with the project's first graduations in the fall. The new *guarderia* daycare center was scheduled to open in early February. But first, Hanley, Marina, and Ed would enjoy a weekend trip to Lake Atitlán the weekend of January 5–7. After the several-hour car ride from Antigua, they caught a *lancha* motorboat from Panajachel and spent two nights at a hotel with a pool in the traditional Mayan town of Santiago. Ed remembered the mood as being very casual, almost like a real vacation, which was rare for Hanley.

HANLEY WAS SERIOUS about expanding Safe Passage into another developing country in Latin America. In fact, she was actively courting partners who could run an offshoot of her educational reinforcement program in another place of great need. Though her key staff and close family didn't know exactly why, Haiti was front and center. She wanted to adopt children from the impoverished, French- and Creole-speaking Caribbean nation, which she had last visited in 2004. On the afternoon of Sunday, January 14, 2007, she emailed Erdem Ergin, a former Safe Passage volunteer who was involved with the United Nations Development Programme (UNDP) in Haiti:

> Happy New Year (belated). I really appreciate the time and effort you put into helping to answer my questions. It was very informative. I have been thinking about what I could do in Haiti ever since my visit there 3 years ago. At the same time, I've been conscious of wanting to get Safe Passage in Guatemala in a manner that is sustainable and strong. Right now the project has completed 7 years.
>
> One big question I have for you is whether you might consider running something for Safe Passage in Haiti if I am ever able to secure the funding. I would need to go between the Guatemala and Haiti sites and would be thrilled with someone of your experience overseeing the day to day administration of the program. I know that is a big question and I have no idea what your future plans have in store. But I thought I would put it out there as something to consider. I would ask that you made at least a 3-year commitment to really get things up and running well. If you aren't able, would you be willing to help refer some potential candidates? I'm seeking a foreigner in the first 3 years to help oversee things...with the goal of identifying a trustworthy, competent local administrator as we go on.
>
> Anyway, I hope that we can perhaps meet and talk this year as I hope to get to Haiti to begin some planning.
>
> I am thinking of trying to devote the next 2 years to fundraising and then launch the program. I started Safe Passage without any funding to speak of and really struggled.

I am thinking of the following and would appreciate your ideas...

Starting a small residential program for children in preschool to high school who are identified as having the following:

Coming from an at risk and impoverished background which makes it difficult for them to afford school
Good conduct-behavior
Strong desire to attend school
Parental support to send them to the residential home

We then partner with American schools in Haiti ... I've read that there are a lot of Catholic or Christian schools or other non-profits running solid educational programs and send the children to private schools.

The residential home provides:

» Nutrition

» Medical care

» Educational reinforcement and tutoring

» Recreation

» Security, love and caring

» Leadership training

» Vocational training

» Life Skills

» Arts and music

» Values

Ideally we would have it somewhere where we could also house small groups of volunteers and a few long-term volunteers safely.

The goal would be to:

» create and empower leaders

» foster and encourage high aspirations

»   provide technical and vocational training

»   provide formal education as far as the student was able

»   promote self sufficiency

»   provide security and safety

»   comprehensive program

Based on my reading, most of the private schools are in Port-au-Prince so I guess it would be based there. The first year we would start really small....

The housing and meals for the volunteers would result in income generation to help cover expenses....

At the same time, we would have a product for kids to make we could sell for additional funding

What are your thoughts?

BACK IN ANTIGUA, Fredy Maldonado seemed to know everyone. His connections were crucial when Safe Passage needed to add new staff and needed them to start immediately, which was often the case. A donor had paid for a Jeep which Hanley could drive on the hour-long journey between Antigua and Guatemala City that followed a winding, mountainous road. But she was afraid of driving in Guatemala. Plus, during her time in a vehicle was when the *gringa* preferred to think to herself, take notes and write instructions for herself or others on her team. The car was sold. She needed a personal driver instead.

The first one Fredy found refused to work the unpredictable hours when she needed rides. "The *gringa* wants to go into the city at five in the morning," he protested. The second driver was shot and killed eight days after Fredy hired him—in an incident unrelated to *Camino Seguro*. The third person had experience both as a driver and as a security guard. He carried a gun with him in the car and projected an air of fearlessness. But one day he told Fredy that he had an omen and couldn't continue as Hanley's driver. "I feel like something bad is going to happen," he said. Days before school would resume in January 2007, Fredy met an acquaintance in the Parque Central in Antigua who sought work for his son, a driver. And so it was that Bayron Aroldo Chiquito de Leon, 26 years old, began working as Hanley's driver.

As invaluable as Fredy's connections in Antigua and his knowledge of other nonprofits including God's Child Project were to Hanley, she sometimes vented her frustrations on him. On Tuesday, the day after schools resumed, she learned that a wealthy professional basketball player from the United States had visited Guatemala and sought out Safe Passage to donate money. But with her staff stretched thin, no one had reciprocated the communication. The opportunity had been lost. Hanley called and yelled at Fredy. He remembered her saying something that bordered on insulting like, "This is why Guatemala doesn't progress, doesn't make the correct choices. You need someone to make decisions." Later that day Hanley called him back to apologize. "Can I buy you a chocolate or something?" she asked. "If I buy you a chocolate, will you promise me you'll stay with the program?"

THE FRIENDSHIP AND WORKING RELATIONSHIP between Hanley and Rachel had improved again since their "lightning bolt" argument the previous October. During that third week of January 2007, Hanley called her throughout the day with updates about the *guarderia*, which was to open in February. She wanted Rachel to be there to help with the grand opening.

"I've got to get my ticket. When should I come?" Rachel asked Hanley.

She'd call back at all hours of the day to say, "I know, I know, I still have to figure out if you should come earlier or stay longer."

At about 9 p.m. on Wednesday, January 17, Hanley called Rachel, who was at her boyfriend's house in Maine watching television. "Can't you let it go?" he implored Rachel. "Doesn't she know these aren't working hours?"

Rachel chuckled and answered the phone. She thought Hanley would finally tell her the dates for her upcoming trip to Guatemala. Instead, Hanley shared that one of the girls had run away from the Casa Hogar dormitory—again. "She asked me to call her sponsor the next day and explain the situation (he was extremely invested)," Rachel remembered. Hanley promised she would go into Guatemala City on Thursday to locate the girl. Her staff had been looking all night in Antigua and expected she had returned to the capital.

Hanley promised she'd call Rachel the next day with travel dates.

"I told her I was looking forward to getting back to Guatemala," Rachel told her friend.

PHOTOGRAPHS

Children in uniforms walking to school presents a striking contrast against the endless sea of trash, discarded tires, and vultures. (JOE DELCONZO)

In the early days of Safe Passage, Hanley was so skinny that some of her clothes didn't fit her. "I hate buying clothes," she told the Danish volunteer Joan Andersen. "I'm losing weight because I forget to eat. There's just too much work to do."

No matter how busy she was at the project, Hanley always made time for each child who sought her attention.

A boy delights in the innocent act of blowing bubbles in the garbage dump.
(JOHN SANTERRE)

Paul Sutherland realized that the strength of what Hanley had built couldn't be quantified in one number. No, these were individuals—every one of those 500 kids was an individual.

The January 2005 fire in the garbage dump impressed upon Hanley the need for a guarderia nursery school for toddlers. It opened weeks after her death. (JOHN SANTERRE)

PART III

Crudely built shacks along a ravine where Hanley walked to visit guajero families blurred the lines of where the *barrios* ended and the garbage dump began. (JOE DELCONZO)

The Unthinkable

THURSDAY, JANUARY 18, 2007. Hanley's morning began, as always, with a flurry of phone calls. Some she made from her house while she played with C-Well and Lucha. Some she made from the office in Antigua. Vilma Garcia, the Antigua native who had worked at the Casa Hogar before leaving Safe Passage the previous year to get married, called Hanley and said she wanted to return to the program. She had looked for other work, but nothing else spoke to her. "You're a very important part of Safe Passage for me," Hanley told Vilma, whom she arranged to meet in Guatemala City the following day. Hanley also called and left a voicemail message with Rachel in Maine about buying her plane ticket to attend the opening of the *guarderia* in early February.

As always, there were a thousand things on Hanley's list to accomplish that day. Ed and his personal assistant, Amilcar de Leon, who had been with the project since 2005, visited the *guarderia* site with a team of maintenance workers who were finishing the daycare center. About once a week, Amilcar would travel into Guatemala City to make sure all of Safe Passage's buildings were clean and in decent shape. On that day, Ed and Amilcar planned to visit a store in the city to buy light fixtures for the daycare center. At about midday, Hanley arrived at the *guarderia* and stepped out of the passenger side door of a late

231

1990s teal-colored Chevy Blazer. Amilcar watched her walk from the daycare center toward the yellow *edificio* reinforcement center and stop to greet children who ran up to ask her for a hug. From a distance he watched her smile and giggle as she whispered something to them.

Hanley then spoke with Lety and asked her righthand Guatemalan employee to stay at the *edificio* and interview a Safe Passage employee who spoke excellent English about whether they wanted to work directly with the *padrinos*, the sponsor parents. Lety was reluctant at first to do the interview because she had a meeting back in Antigua, but Hanley bribed her with sweets. "When you arrive, I'll give you chocolate," she promised Lety.

"But Hanley, I won't get back to Antigua until 5:30 or 6 pm."

"No problem, Lety. I'll wait for you. With chocolate."

Early that afternoon, Hanley met Claudio Ramos, the program's first social worker, Beth Kloser, the long-term volunteer from Indiana who had house-sat for Hanley and taken care of her dogs, and an English long-term volunteer named Rob Tinsley. They walked through the *barrio* next to the dump and talked about adjusting the service-learning trip tours through the community so they would be less intrusive for the families served by Safe Passage. They wanted to continue to show visitors the level of poverty and the need for the project, but not in a way that was voyeuristic.

While on their walk, Hanley got a call from Fredy Maldonado who told her that Joe Delconzo, the photographer from New Jersey whose published images of Hanley in the early days of Safe Passage had won the project important recognition, was in town to photograph the *guarderia* and he wanted to meet with her. She couldn't, she said. Not until this evening in Antigua. Joe and his girlfriend Sharon caught up with Hanley and her entourage just as she was preparing to depart for Antigua. They observed that she held up two cell phones, one to each ear. Always busy. "See you for dinner," Sharon said as Hanley nodded and smiled at them.

Shortly before 3 p.m., Hanley hopped into the front passenger seat of the Chevy Blazer for the return trip. She invited Beth and Rob to catch a ride in the backseat. They wholeheartedly accepted. This was better than having to stand up on a chicken bus during the rush-hour trip out of Guatemala City, thought Beth. At the wheel was Hanley's new driver, Bayron de Leon. As usual, Hanley hadn't yet taken the time to eat lunch. Beth, who sat behind the driver's seat, watched her unwrap a square of tinfoil and eat whatever traditional Guatemalan food she had picked up from a nearby *comedor*. A taco or a tamale, perhaps. Hanley took a quick call from Lorena, the receptionist at Safe Passage, who wanted to make sure that Hanley had found her personal cell phone, which had gone missing earlier in the day. Yes, she had it with her now. Hanley also asked Lorena to walk over to the *guarderia* and make sure a couple small tasks there were complete. "Of course, right away," said Lorena. Then Beth lay her head back and fell asleep for the familiar, hour-long ride from Guatemala City to Antigua. The grimy air and cacophony of horns and motors would soon give way to the fresh mountain air as Bayron, Hanley, Beth, and Rob ascended out of the capital and into the hills.

No more than 15 minutes after she had last talked with Hanley, Lorena returned from her errand to the *guarderia* and answered the office phone.

"Buenas tardes. Camino Seguro. ¿En qué le puedo servir?"
Good afternoon. How can I help you?

A man at the other end of the line, whose voice Lorena didn't recognize, asked if she knew of a certain volunteer named Rob.

"Yes, is there a problem with him?" Lorena responded. But the call dropped.

A moment later the stranger called back.

"Señorita, lo siento, pero el volunteer was in a traffic accident. Hay fallecidos. *I'm sorry. The driver is dead.* He was driving a car with a Señora Hanley Denning in it ..." The caller didn't know any more details. He had seen two blonde girls in the car, one in the front passenger seat, and one in the backseat behind the driver.

Lorena froze in fright. She worried about Hanley and the volunteers. Lorena worried, too about the baby she was carrying in her own stomach, halfway to term, and if this shock would hurt her child. She quickly dispatched her colleague Julio to find Lety on the third floor of the *edificio* where she was conducting the interview and tell her there was a traffic fatality involving Safe Passage staff. Lorena also called Ed, who was at the *guardería* with Amilcar and the contractors. They learned that the car accident had happened in the Mixco neighborhood on the western edge of the city where the Pan-American Highway (known in Guatemala as CA1) heads up into the hills. Ed and Amilcar jumped in a car and immediately drove in that direction, but soon found themselves stuck in a gridlock. Traffic leaving the capital was always bad that time of day. The accident had closed down lanes of the highway and created a bottleneck. While their car inched forward, Ed fielded a call from Michael Denning in Maine. He had heard that there was a car accident, and Hanley was in the vehicle. What could Ed tell him? But Ed knew nothing. He promised he would call Hanley's father as soon as he had information.

It took them almost three hours to arrive at the scene of the accident. Once they did, Ed told the police they knew the people in the car, and they were able to get past the taped-off perimeter. The Blazer itself was a mangled wreck, its entire front crumpled where it was hit head-on by a chicken bus, full of passengers and coming from the Quiché region of western Guatemala, which lost its brakes and crossed the median into oncoming traffic. The driver of the chicken bus had fled the scene on foot. Bayron's body was still pinned between the driver's seat and the steering wheel. Amilcar, just 20 years old, had never seen a dead person before. When the bus hit their car and stopped its forward momentum, they were rear-ended by a pick-up truck. The driver of that truck, uninjured, spoke with Rob in the backseat, who asked him to call the Safe Passage office. For whatever reason, the police arrested the pick-up truck driver, and he was held for 24 hours. But Hanley, Beth, and Rob were no longer in the wrecked car. They had been taken away by ambulance.

"Where did they go? Where did you take them?" Ed asked the emergency workers and the police. But in the chaos of the moment, they weren't sure. Amilcar and Ed quickly concluded that, unless the victims were conscious enough to tell the emergency staff they had health insurance and preferred a private hospital, they would have been taken to the large public hospital, the Roosevelt in the Trebol district of Guatemala City, just a few kilometers from Safe Passage and the garbage dump. Ed and Amilcar turned around and headed back into the city, but traffic was horrendously slow once again. Michael called again and Ed described the accident, but he knew nothing more about Hanley's condition.

Meanwhile, back at the office, Lorena called the Safe Passage Maine office at 5 p.m. No one picked up. She dialed again and again. Rachel was there, trying to wrap up projects while the office was quiet before she left at 6 p.m. to have dinner in Yarmouth with a family whose daughter had just returned from a trip to Guatemala. The phone rang again and again. "Okay, someone is trying to get through," thought Rachel, who finally answered the line. Lorena told her that Hanley had been in a bad car accident. A bus had hit the car in which she was a passenger. Volunteers were in the car, too. But little more was known at the time. Rachel hung up and called Ed, who was once again stuck in traffic in route to the hospital. She understood that Claudio would meet Hanley at the hospital. Rachel told Ed she was going to dinner and that he should call her immediately with any updates. Before they ended the call, Ed encouraged Rachel to reach out to Hanley's family—in particular, Marina and her brother Jordan. Michael also called Rachel in a panic, but she said she knew no more than Ed. Rachel left the office and went to dinner with the Safe Passage supporters. Her phone didn't ring and she hoped this meant that Hanley was OK.

Lety fielded calls from staff on her way to the hospital. Everyone was trying to figure out where Hanley had been sitting in the car, and who the other blonde girl was. A backpack may have been thrown around the car during the moment of impact. Perhaps Hanley was sitting in the backseat next to Rob, and the volunteer was in the passenger seat. Were there more fatalities than Bayron the driver? Rumors swirled.

Key staff and important people across Guatemala City who knew Hanley and the project were called. Amina LaCour and Juan Mini, Jr., who were now divorced, received separate, near simultaneous calls from people at Safe Passage—perhaps from either Lety or Fredy. At that moment Amina was at Juan's mother's house picking up their son, John Marco. They left the boy with his *abuela* and together headed for the hospital. But afternoon traffic was at its peak, and to Amina it felt like 10 hours lapsed before they arrived at the Roosevelt, all the while holding onto hope that they would arrive and Hanley would be OK.

It DIDN'T TAKE LONG before the *guajeros* in the garbage dump and the surrounding *colonias* heard about the accident and the rumor that *Seño* Hanley was badly hurt. Las noticias salían rápido. *The news traveled fast by word of mouth.* Perhaps it was a child at *Camino Seguro* who heard about the accident and ran home to tell family and friends. Perhaps it was employees at the project. Either way, several dozen *guajero* families began knocking on the doors of each other's shacks and gathered together to make a spontaneous plan. Some pooled their money together to pay a pick-up truck driver to drive them to the Roosevelt. Others simply dropped what they were doing and began walking the two and a half kilometers south toward the public hospital. Hanley was their angel and they would do whatever they could to help her. They had to be near her. Irina Rodríguez, the mother of four who had sought out Hanley at the tiny church and confided in her even as other *guajeros* worried she would steal their children, was one of those who walked to the Roosevelt that day—through the late afternoon orange hues of Guatemala City as the sun began to set. When she arrived, she found many other *guajeros* waiting there in the paved parking lot. They weren't permitted to enter the hospital itself.

Ed and Amilcar eventually arrived at the hospital and had to push their way through a sea of nervous and emotional *guajeros* seeking answers. "¿Qué pasó? Dónde está Señora Hanley?" they asked. *What happened? Where is Hanley?* Marco Cobar, a well-connected building contractor who was supervising work on the *guarderia* warned Ed that he wouldn't be able to cut through the chaos and get into the hospital. "You watch, they won't bother me, I'm not Guatemalan. I'm going to play the *gringo* card," Ed told Marco and Amilcar. He entered the emergency department's waiting room and found a scene as chaotic inside as it was outside. People were everywhere, laying on gurneys waiting to be helped. These were passengers on the bus that had lost its brakes and collided with Hanley's car. Since the bus was arriving in the capital from the Quiche, some were likely Mayan Indians wearing traditional *huipil* outfits and dresses. Ed made a beeline for the staffed desk, which he perceived to be a nurse's station.

Suddenly, while walking along the gurneys, he heard someone say "Ed, Ed!" He turned and there was Rob.

"Are you alright?" he asked.

"Yeah, I think I just have a broken wrist or arm."

"What's going on with Hanley and Beth? Where are they?" Ed asked Rob.

"I don't know. I haven't seen them since the ambulances took them away."

Ed approached the nurse's station and inquired about the whereabouts of Hanley or Beth.

"Lo siento mucho." *I'm sorry*, but the *gringa* died," the nurse curtly replied in Spanish.

Ed stood in silence. This was something he never could have imagined happening. Like others close to Hanley, he had heard her express fear many times about traveling by car in Guatemala. But that paranoia felt abstract. Everyone worried about the safety of driving here. This situation unfolding now was all too real. He left the waiting room and returned to the parking lot to break the news to a far bigger crowd that had gathered there. Still more *guajeros* came, on foot and in pickup trucks. But once outside, Ed was approached by Brenda, a Safe Passage employee who said to him, "I don't think it's Hanley who died. I think it's Beth. They both have blonde hair." It was true. No one had any idea where Beth was at the time.

Lety joined Ed now as they went back into the emergency room and told the nurse, "There might be a confusion. Can we see the body of the person who died?" Ed remembers he was alone; Lety remembers she was next to Ed and witnessed what happened next.

The nurse led the way to a room with a wide closet which contained a gurney with a black body bag. She unzipped the bag just far enough to reveal a woman's face and neck. The victim wore a blonde ponytail and a pink blouse. Her eyes were closed, and her face suggested that she was merely sleeping. No injuries were visible. The damage had been done to her chest, not her head. "She looks so peaceful," thought Ed, who struggled to grasp the tragedy that had happened today, what was now confirmed before his eyes. He had no idea how he would tell the growing, anxious crowd gathered outside in the hospital parking lot. A meticulous planner though he was, he cringed at the thought of the 100 gut-wrenching tasks he knew he would now have to set in motion in the hours and days to come. Above all, he would have to tell Michael Denning.

Ed left the emergency room and once again stood in the parking lot, under a telephone wire, as the sun descended into the west, in the direction of Lake Atitlán and the western highlands. Hundreds of eyes focused on him like lasers. The crowd was tense and anxious for news. Some *guajeros* sobbed. Others struggled to stand in place as their knees shook. Mothers held babies and tried to keep them quiet. Toddlers hugged the legs of their *abuelas* and asked for a snack. They all looked to Ed for a sign.

IMAGINE A BEAUTIFUL, RADIANT LIGHT that leads you for the first time out of the damp darkness of a corrugated tin-walled shack next to the garbage dump. Imagine leaving behind the noxious smells of trash during the rainy season, the methane gases bubbling from the surface of the *basurero*, the rutted dirt paths where boys lay as they sniff glue to quell their hunger. Imagine walking suddenly on soft green grass while warm sunlight kisses your skin and magically melts away the smell. Imagine birdsong where there was only silence before. Imagine a world of color, and joy, and playful laughter. Imagine a strong and encouraging hand that stretches out to guide you forward. Imagine your face inadvertently explodes into a smile. Imagine. And then without warning, the scene goes dark again. You find yourself back in the shack next to the dump—only this time, having experienced the light, your body recognizes how painful, how unwieldy these tin walls are that confine you once again.

Standing among the families of the garbage dump gathered outside the Roosevelt hospital that day, the *guajero* mother Irena Rodríguez Cotto watched Lety, Claudio, the *Camino Seguro* social workers, teachers, and staff huddle together and begin to sob and convulse. The truth was now obvious to any observer. The unthinkable had happened. At some point, she or one of the other *guajeros* heard a staff member confirm their fears. "Hanley está muerta." *Hanley was dead.*

A silence followed. Then the cacophony of emotion spread throughout the crowded parking lot. Irena sobbed in disbelief.

"Why do good people have to die? Why in this way?" she wailed to the *guajeros* gathered around her. Others pleaded for Hanley's body to be brought outside so they could see her, touch her, mourn for her. At that moment, Irena was convinced that the *Camino Seguro* project would close—that her childrens' opportunity to escape the garbage dump and go to school would end. And who could blame Irena for thinking that? In the past 18 months, Safe Passage had established a board of directors and secured leadership mechanisms to continue even without Hanley, but Irena and the *guajeros* knew little of that. They didn't know Paul Sutherland, or Charlie Gendron, or Marty and Frank Helman. They knew Hanley, they knew her smile, her embrace, her encouraging words that she shared with each child who enrolled in the project. And now she was gone.

"Qué va a pasar con nosotros?" asked a *guajero* mother named Felecita. *What will happen to us?* What will happen with our children? What will happen with the abused kids who live at the Casa Hogar?

Lety shook her head in denial at the tragic irony of what had just happened. "Hanley always wore her seatbelt, and she always made sure the driver drove slow," Lety whispered to herself. "She always said the bus drivers in Guatemala are crazy. She would never let her driver pass other vehicles or drive aggressively. She always told them, 'I'd prefer to arrive late, and alive. I don't want to die.'" It all seemed so unfair, so unreal. There was no blood on Hanley's face, no signs of trauma. She looked like she was asleep, peacefully asleep. But Hanley was gone.

ED LOOKED TO AMILCAR AND MARCO and spoke only to them—deliberately in English. "It wasn't that I was trying to keep a secret, it was just easier to speak in English to people whose help I would need," Safe Passage's finance director reflected. "Marco said to me, 'This is what's going to happen. They're going to do an autopsy in the hospital, then they're going to move her to the morgue.'"

Marco told Ed the process could typically take days. Ed shook his head, found an ATM machine, withdrew wads of cash, and gave several thousand quetzales (equivalent to hundreds of U.S. dollars) to Amilcar. "Move this process along, pay whoever you need to pay. I don't want her here for two to three days," he said.

There was so much to do, and Ed knew it. His own mourning and processing of grief would have to wait. Meticulous by nature, Ed swung into gear. He called the U.S. Embassy and reached consular services and told them that an American citizen who ran an important nonprofit in Guatemala City had died. What steps must be taken, and how could they help repatriate her body to the United States? Within minutes of getting off that call, Michael Denning called Ed. "I have to tell him," Ed told himself. He did.

Several moments of silence, and then Mike began to wail into the phone, clearly distraught. "She's my only daughter! She's my only daughter!"

Ed listened, but had no words for the moment. "I'm sorry Mike, I'm sorry. I've got a lot I have to do right now. Can we talk later?"

Michael needed to talk about it. He had to tell people. But he was so shaken that he couldn't speak, he couldn't say the words. He called Hanley's brother Jordan, who was still at work at a law firm on Fifth Avenue in Midtown Manhattan. Jordan answered, and Michael blurted out something about a car accident and Han being in bad shape. But he couldn't say it, his voice kept breaking up. He hung up and called back moments later. "She's gone, Jordan. She's gone."

Jordan left his desk, and without a word to his colleagues he grabbed his jacket and left the building. He walked north, past the Pulitzer Fountain and Grand Army Plaza, and walked the perimeter around Central Park. He bawled, he felt like he was losing his mind. He walked for hours. At some point his girl-friend Mira joined him after canceling the dinner reservation they had with friends.

Michael and Marina were divorced and lived apart, he in Yarmouth and she on nearby Cousins Island. He needed to tell her, too, but he couldn't get ahold of her that evening. At four a.m. on Friday, Michael drove to her house and pounded on the door, screaming "Your daughter is dead, your daughter is dead!" Around the same time, a minister and family friend named Bill Gregory who had heard the news, was arriving in Marina's driveway.

Marina sat up in bed and thought about what Hanley had asked her the month before while she was home for Christmas. "What's the purpose of life, mom?" She thought of Hanley's vocalized prediction that something was going to happen to her in Guatemala. Marina looked down at her comforter and saw sparks lighting up all over the bed. It was a sign from Hanley, she thought. She walked downstairs and opened the front door to Michael. "Your daughter is dead!" he sobbed.

"I know," Marina said. "I know."

When she went back upstairs, the sparks still covered the bed. "Hang on, Han, don't die on me," her mother pleaded. But she knew Hanley was gone.

SHORTLY AFTER THEY HAD LEFT the Safe Passage office, Beth Kloser buckled her seat belt where she sat behind Bayron the driver. In Guatemala she didn't always do so, because they were sometimes broken or unavailable. On this day she did. When Rob Tinsley, who was seated next to her and behind the passenger's seat, saw her buckle up, he did the same. They were outside the city where the road starts to curve as it winds into the mountains. Road construction had narrowed traffic to two lanes.

An eerie silence followed the collision with the bus, and the pick-up truck hitting them from behind. The next thing Beth remembered, a man—probably the pick-up truck driver—was trying to communicate with them through Rob's window, the side of the car that hadn't been hit. He asked if they were able to get out of the vehicle, and if there was someone who he could call. Beth recited to him the number she had memorized and told him to call the office and speak to either Ed or Lety. She remembered snapshots from the scene. The bus that hit them was resting along a hillside as Mayan indigenous women stood nearby watching the rescue effort.

Beth was separated from Rob and put into an ambulance, which took her to a hospital near Antigua called Los Angeles de San Felipe. Strangely enough, a couple of Mayan women and a young boy joined them in the ambulance—she thinks they were hitching a ride to nearby Chimaltenango. The ride to the hospital was long and bumpy. The ambulance didn't slow down once it hit the cobblestone streets of Antigua, jostling everyone. At one point the EMTs—probably volunteers—got lost and argued with each other about which direction to turn. Despite her traumatized state, Beth nearly told the driver to pull over and let her out. Once she arrived at the hospital, she lay on a gurney in the hallway, waiting. She had no cell phone with her.

As far as she knew, no one from the project had any idea where she was.

Eventually, Safe Passage staff learned that Beth was at San Felipe. Ed gave one of his maintenance workers a wad of cash and told him to get to Antigua, hire an ambulance, and have her moved to a private hospital in Guatemala City, which was better staffed and had better supplies and would be better equipped to handle Beth's injuries. She remembers that her friend Gary and a few other volunteers visited her at San Felipe. "You do not want to stay here," they told her. The ambulance ride into the city was much smoother. But Beth's injuries were severe enough that she spent nearly three weeks in the private hospital and underwent several surgeries before she was flown back to Indiana to be treated there and undergo another operation. She wasn't told until a day or two after the accident that Hanley had died.

IT WAS AROUND 6 P.M. when photographer Joe Delconzo and his girlfriend Sharon heard a knock on the door of their hotel near La Iglesia de la Merced in Antigua. Before them stood Fredy Maldonado, who was to join them for dinner with Hanley at a local pizzeria.

"Where is Hanley? Isn't she going to come?" asked Joe.

"No, she's not," replied Fredy in a tone of voice as deadpan as if he was asking the cook to hold the olives on his pizza. "She's not coming because she died."

Sharon began to cry. Joe was dumbfounded. But Fredy showed little emotion. It wasn't his way. The soccer star had lived through the Civil War, he had seen fellow social workers and acquaintances disappeared. It wasn't that Fredy was numb to tragedy, he just processed it differently than others. Perhaps this was his way of protecting himself because he knew the truth about loss and the injustice of this death. Fredy explained what had happened, and Sharon and Joe asked if they could return to the city to help. No, answered Fredy. There's a long process that must be followed now. What do we do then, they asked?

"We go and eat pizza," said Fredy. "If she was here now, she'd be eating together with us. We might as well eat."

IN MAINE, RACHEL RETURNED to the office from her work dinner and saw she had no messages from Ed or Lety in the Safe Passage Guatemalan office. Radio silence. So she called Ed. "What's going on?" she pleaded to him.

What Ed said next scarred Rachel like a hot iron. Years later she could remember hearing each syllable he spoke over the phone. "So this is the plan," he said. "Her body's going to be brought to the morgue and then ..."

"Ed, wait, Ed, did Hanley ... die?" Rachel exhaled.

"Oh Rachel, I thought Mike or Jordan had called you. Yes, we lost Hanley."

Rachel's next moments faded into a blur. She remembered nothing else that Ed said. But before hanging up she promised she would make calls to the board members. The first was to Sharon Workman in Michigan. Sharon's husband Wayne answered the call. "It's Rachel. I need to talk with Sharon." Wayne could tell from the tone of her voice, and the late call that something bad had happened. Sharon emerged from her yoga room and took the phone. "Why are you still working at this hour?" she asked Rachel. Then she heard the news. There had been an accident, and Hanley was gone.

Rachel called office staff to tell them. She called her boyfriend, and he came to pick her up. She was in no shape to drive that night, and she left her red Jeep in the parking lot. A heavy snow had begun to fall on Yarmouth, and Rachel looked out the passenger side window at the flakes as she cried. Already, she was running lists through her mind of all the people she would need to call in the morning who deserved to be personally notified. She knew that word of Hanley's death would spread fast throughout Maine and through Safe Passage support communities around the world. A thousand hearts would shatter as the news was passed along.

The following morning, she was dropped off early at the Safe Passage office. Barb Davis and supporter Stacy Varney were already there, as were the Fralichs, the family with whom Rachel had eaten dinner the night before. They gave her a tight hug. She hadn't slept a wink, but felt like she was in stealth mode. On a blank sheet of white paper, covered front and back, Rachel had written a long list of names of volunteers, donors and friends of Hanley who deserved a personal call to break the news. Jim Highland, who had leant Safe Passage its initial office space in Portland, arrived and knelt beside Rachel sitting at her desk, and asked her, "What can I do? I'm here to help." Rachel handed him the list, which he delegated to others who had arrived unprompted in the office to help. Relieved of that task, Rachel retreated to a private space at the back of the office and called her mom on the West Coast to tell her that Hanley was dead. As soon as the words left her mouth, she let out a wail. The reality was sinking in. Jane Gallagher and Barb found her in the back of the office and told her that a donor had offered to pay for Rachel to fly back to Guatemala that night. "Yes," she said without hesitation.

Amilcar, who returned to the driver Bayron's body at the scene of the accident, tried to comfort his parents and two sisters when they arrived several hours after the crash. Bayron's father transported his body in a black bag in the back of a police pickup to the morgue in Zone 3, next to the cemetery on a cliff that overlooks the garbage dump—just a few blocks from Safe Passage and the *colonias*. At the morgue Amilcar observed how bribes could speed up the autopsy and release of the body. Late that evening Ed came to the morgue to wait out the process with him.

Local *guajeros*, too, were gathering on the street outside. By now they undoubtedly knew that Hanley was gone, but they wanted to be close to her. They longed to hold her body if they could. Ed and Amilcar were permitted to enter the morgue compound, but weren't given any information on when Hanley's body would arrive. They were asked to wait there through the night. Sometime later, perhaps around 11 p.m., they were standing by the ambulance entrance when Ed noticed a body-bag tag on the ground near his left foot. He bent down to pick it up. The tag read "Hanley Denning".

"At least we know where she is now," Ed told Amilcar.

Bayron's last trip was direct. Ed and Amilcar eventually secured a long, black funeral car to deliver his body to his family in Antigua, where they arrived at 1:30 in the morning. Bayron's mother threw herself on his casket and wept.

But Hanley's body would take a different journey. A wake, a funeral, and a long journey back to the United States awaited her.

"We Have Work to Do"

THOUGH ED AND AMILCAR DID WHAT THEY COULD to speed up the process, it took until five in the morning on Friday before Hanley's body was released from the city morgue. A hearse transported her to a funeral home in Guatemala City's wealthy Zone 9, where a *velorio*, a wake, would commence that afternoon. Ed returned to Antigua to get whatever restless sleep he could. He had asked Lety and Amina LaCour to make funeral arrangements, which included choosing Hanley's casket. In his sleep deprived state, Ed would later pull Lety aside and sardonically criticize her for the casket she chose. Ed knew that Hanley's body would be cremated once she returned to Maine. "I can't believe you bought the most expensive casket, it's just going to burn," he deadpanned, but apologized later. Even now, Ed tried to apply the brakes on Safe Passage's spending.

At the *velorio*, Hanley lay in a casket that was mostly closed but her face was visible. She wore makeup, her hair was pulled back in a ponytail, she looked peaceful, and the hundreds who came to see her that afternoon and late into the night could be forgiven for denying that she was actually gone. Marc Wuthrich, the Swiss accountant who worked for Ed, observed the wide range of mourners who came to pay their respects. In the parking lot of the funeral home he saw worn pick-up trucks, their mufflers hovering inches off the ground, parked between a

Mercedes-Benz and a BMW. Hanley touched the rich and the poor alike.

Officials from the Marriott Hotel, from American Airlines, from the Guatemalan business and NGO communities came dressed in dark suits. Juan Mini, Jr., accompanied Amina, his ex-wife, to pay his respects. Juan skipped the funeral the following day, as he had already experienced too much death and mourning within his family. His father, Juan Mini, Sr., and his brother had died in a helicopter crash three months prior.

But it was those without the means, the hundreds of *guajeros* who trekked to the decadent funeral home in pick-ups, in buses, and on foot who didn't fit the ambience of the place, though their hearts beat as loudly as the wealthy *guatemaltecos*, Marc observed. They wore old and tattered clothing that smelled of wood smoke, sweat, and the garbage dump. They huddled around Hanley's casket and sobbed openly, they sang to her, they thanked her, they told her stories of the first time they had met her, they promised they would continue going to school, they called her their angel, "el angel del basurero." *The angel of the garbage dump*. They touched the casket and wanted to open it. They wanted to touch her, too, but were told they couldn't. Throughout the day and night, the tone of their suffering changed, undulating between noisy sobs and periods of quiet. When Shannon Moyle, a long-term volunteer from Canada, visited the funeral home, she was struck by what she heard from the *guajeros* huddled around Hanley's casket. Gatherings in this culture—weddings and funerals, alike—were typically raucous and full of noise, loud music, singing, and dancing. But what she heard was absolute silence.

Doubt and fear hung over them. "¿Quién va a cuidar a nuestros niños?" the parents asked. *Who will watch our children now?* "¿Qué va a pasar con nosotros?" *What will happen to us*, the children of the Casa Hogar asked. Would their home in Antigua close? Would their educational reinforcement project cease to exist, now that Hanley was gone? Would they be forced to return to the garbage dump to scavenge for food? Would Nancy Gudiel be left on the street again to sell chiclets and fight off people who wanted to harm her? Would Daniél Osorio have to join the gangs who murdered his stepfather in front of him?

The people stayed late into the night with her body, until the funeral home staff told them they had to go. They didn't want to say goodbye to their angel.

Vilma Garcia, who was going to meet Hanley on this day and discuss returning to Safe Passage, reassured the *guajero* parents, "*You* will look after your children. *You* will help them continue to go to school and satisfy their dreams." What else could she say?

But at that moment, the doubt about the future of Safe Passage was very real. "A lot of families didn't know what the future held for them, what was going to happen," Ed admitted. "We didn't either. There had been no plan for this. It was heart wrenching."

EACH PHONE CALL, each pained announcement of the news sent shockwaves through families, through schools, through churches, through communities. The tremors shook southern Maine, New York, North Carolina, Michigan, Oregon, Germany, Denmark, England—everywhere Hanley had inspired people.

Michael Denning called Charlie Gendron, the real estate developer and philanthropist, on Thursday evening. His choked language was difficult to understand, Charlie remembered. His wife Teresa phoned other friends, including Jane Gallagher, who had set up so many fundraising opportunities for Hanley in the Portland area and had become a dear friend and confidant. Jane took the call in her kitchen, and before the shock set in, before the pain arrived, she thought about all the times Hanley had expressed fear to her about getting in a car accident in Guatemala and how she resisted pressure to drive herself between Antigua and Guatemala City. Then Jane pivoted to worrying about how her son Jake, a high school sophomore who had just turned 16, would take the news when she told him the next morning. She had first learned about Safe Passage at Jake's and Lucas Denning's soccer game. It was Jake who encouraged her that they needed to travel to Guatemala to see the project with their own eyes. It was Jake who organized a fundraiser and brought Hanley to speak to his middle school. "My first concern was my children and helping them to reconcile that this beautiful angel who gave her whole life for others was now gone," she reflected. After Jane told her son on Friday morning, he sat on the couch and sobbed for an hour.

Susanna Place in Boston got the call from Rachel at about 3 a.m. on Friday morning. The sound of the telephone woke her from a deep sleep. But the minute she heard Rachel say that something awful had happened she knew immediately that Hanley was dead. Rachel burst into tears and struggled to talk. Susanna's mind raced to her own experiences as a passenger in vehicles in Guatemala. The roads are terrible, people skip the line, cars are never inspected, and buses drive too fast. It wasn't a great stretch of the imagination for someone involved in Safe Passage to be killed in a car accident there. But Hanley! Susanna was stunned. "This is so hideous, so sad," she thought. "This is the worst possible thing that could have happened."

Arnie Katz in North Carolina got a call from fellow board

member Sharon Workman. He absorbed the news, hung up the phone, and walked into the living room and looked at his wife, Svea. When she saw Arnie's facial expression, panic surged through her body. She thought that something had happened to one of their two children. "That's the way I thought about Hanley, like she was another daughter," said Arnie. "I was a basket case." In tears, Arnie called his network of Safe Passage supporters in the Chapel Hill area who knew Hanley.

In Boothbay Harbor, Maine, Chip Griffin called and told Marty and Frank Helman, who were funding the daycare center, which was scheduled to be inaugurated in two weeks. It was Friday morning, and Marty was working on the computer in her home office. She was busy organizing the production of quilts for the babies who would spend time in the *guarderia*. Enthusiastic about her contribution, Marty had overestimated and ended up with 200 quilts. Now each child would get two quilts—"una para la clase, y una para la casa." *One for the nursery and one for home.* The *Portland Press Herald* had planned on Saturday to interview and feature Marty and a half dozen others involved with the quilt project. The newspaper photographer would capture their quilts laying in the fieldhouse of the local YMCA—which Marty described as "our version of the AIDS quilt which filled the National Mall" in the late 1980s.

"After I got over the shock [of Hanley's death], I thought to myself, 'What do I do with this event? Do I cancel it? Do I run it?'" thought Marty. "We ran it. It was an *up* experience in the middle of a *down* event."

Longtime Safe Passage supporters in Yarmouth who knew Hanley personally felt as if they had lost a close family member. "There was a sense that this was a total injustice," said Phil Kircher, who had met Hanley in 2003 when she visited his church and witnessed the *guajero* children roll in the strip of green grass in the educational reinforcement center. "This woman was doing so much good in the world, and yet she was taken away so suddenly."

Christine Slader had lost her mom, she'd lost friends to unexpected long-term illnesses, but no death affected her the way the news of Hanley's death shook her. During her service-learning trip to Safe Passage in 2005, Christine had seen a person sleeping in a pile of garbage in the street and had asked Hanley incredulously, "How do you do this every day?" Christine was at her book group on Thursday night when her husband Christian called and asked, "Have you heard the news?" A pause followed. "Hanley Denning just died." Christine collapsed in anguish. She was incapable of driving and friends had to bring her home that night.

Her son Wilson, who had joined her on that 2005 trip—his first experience abroad—got a call on Friday morning from Hanley's younger brother Lucas, who cried on the phone as he told him that his older sister was dead. "We were good friends, but I wasn't his best friend," recalled Wilson. "But because I had been down there to Safe Passage, he felt like he could talk to me about it.... I thought, 'Damn, what do I say?'"

JORDAN DENNING HAD WALKED for hours around Central Park on Thursday evening after hearing about Hanley. Eventually, he and his girlfriend Mira returned to their Midtown Manhattan apartment, where he sat on his couch in silence. He lay in bed through the night but didn't sleep. On Friday morning he rose, hoping that the news was only a bad dream. Instead, he faced the cold reality of facing life without his beloved older sister. Jordan and Mira left New York for Yarmouth, where he would meet and mourn with some of his best buddies from childhood who returned to Maine in haste to support him. Seth, now a lieutenant commander in the U.S. Coast Guard, also returned from the West Coast.

The remaining Denning family gathered at Michael's house on Friday and found many people there hugging and consoling him, including family friend Christine Slader. The community brought food, they brought flowers. When he arrived from New York, Jordan embraced his younger brother Lucas, a junior at Yarmouth high school, and observed that "he was in a mess, he was in shock." Nevertheless, Marina remembered that Lucas was extremely supportive of her and never left her side. "I was both shocked and crying," she said. "I kept saying to myself, 'You need to hold your head up high; that's what Hanley would want you to do. You need to honor her.' That's what I did."

Later that day, the *Portland Press Herald* reported that Michael was consoled by relatives and friends at Lindquist Funeral Home in Yarmouth. "Hanley's only desire," he said, fighting back tears, "was to keep it going. You try to raise your kids the best you can, and you don't know where they will go." The elder Denning told the *Herald* that he supported his daughter's project in Guatemala, even though he feared at times for her safety. "She is just a wonderful, brave, courageous human being," he said.

That Friday night in the Yarmouth High School gymnasium, Lucas, the basketball team's co-captain and point guard, suited up for the hoops game against rival Greeley, even though he had learned of Hanley's death just 24 hours earlier. Lucas had skipped school that day as he processed the grim news. But after talking with his coach, Adam Smith, and with Michael, Lucas concluded that Hanley would want him to play that night, to carry on. "It would have done me no good to just sit in my room while my team was playing," Lucas reflected later.

Lucas was not Yarmouth's best player, said Coach Smith, but he was by far the team's most important player. He had transferred that school year to Yarmouth from a private school where his father and his older brother Jordan had played, and he would play every minute of every game at point guard for the Clipper Ships, who were coming off a 1-16 season the previous year. With Lucas handling the ball in 2007, Yarmouth would win its first tournament games in 37 years, setting the tone for the next 15 years of Coach Smith's career there. "He had a smile, charisma, and desire to make other people better," said the coach. "The younger kids at school loved him. They followed him around."

The night of January 19, the Yarmouth gym was packed, and not just with basketball fans, but with those who knew the Denning family, who knew Hanley, and who knew of her work in Guatemala. The town was in shock. The town was in mourning. The visiting Greeley players stood up out of respect for her during a moment of silence before the game. Flowers were presented to Lucas before the game. Seated in the stands near midcourt, his friend Wilson described Lucas as a "floor general" who wasn't looking to score, but to facilitate the game, pass to open teammates, and make his team play as well as they could play. "You could see him playing and realize that, although this had just happened, he was able to put it aside and do what he had to do." Wilson's mother Christine described Lucas' grit and ability to play basketball that night despite the circumstances as a testament to the Denning family's resilience.

Greeley was a bigger, faster, and better team than Yarmouth, and Coach Smith didn't think his squad had a chance. "All the guys wanted to win that game for Lucas, but I wanted to tell them, 'We're not letting anyone down. We're not gonna beat Greeley, and Lucas shouldn't even be playing tonight.'" The mood in the locker room before tipoff was quiet and somber, with heavy hearts in every man. As Smith suspected, Yarmouth was down by 12 points at halftime, and he expected no improbable, fairytale victory.

But in the second half Lucas carried the team, executing a full-court press and shutting down Greeley's star point guard. "He was the only one not feeling the pressure," said Coach Smith. "He carried us even though that was the night we were supposed to carry him." Lucas remembered very little about the game. He felt like he blacked out, even though he played all 32 minutes as point guard. "It was one of the shittiest games I ever played," Lucas recalled. His memory was wrong. In fact, he posted a double-double that Friday night, scoring 10 points and posting 10 assists. Yarmouth cut the lead to single digits, and in the final minutes the lead went back and forth. During the timeouts Coach Smith didn't say a word. His players in the huddle clapped their hands together and shouted, "We're gonna do this for Lucas!"

Yarmouth lost, 56–52, in a game that everyone expected Greeley to win in a blowout. Lucas' teammates embraced him and cried after the final whistle. The game nevertheless lifted the team and propelled them into the tournament later that winter, and winning seasons in the years to come. Several days later, Lucas went into Portland and got his sister's initials, "H-G-D" for Hanley Graham Denning, tattooed on his right arm.

RACHEL CAUGHT A RED-EYE flight and arrived in Guatemala

City at 7 a.m. on Saturday morning. Valerie Lefebvre, who managed *Camino Seguro's* hotel Posada Lazos Fuertes in Antigua, picked her up in a Saab. "Val, do you think you could take me to the funeral home for a quiet moment with Han before it gets crazy?" Rachel asked Val.

Valerie shot her a look of surprise and responded, "Rachel, there have been hundreds of *guajeros* there since yesterday. There are no private moments here."

Hanley's friend tried to prepare herself, physically and mentally, as they arrived at the upscale funeral home in Zone 9. She wore a pink tank top, a green sweater, and jeans. Rachel had left Maine in such a flurry that she didn't pack anything nicer. At the *velorio* her eyes immediately met those of Amina and Juan Mini, Jr. Ed hung back against the wall nursing a cup of coffee. She hugged each person and then moved toward the casket, which was surrounded by *guajero* children and families she knew. By now the box was closed but Rachel felt a powerful energy swirling all around the room. Lety Roque and her son Angel, one of Hanley's beloved founding students who had been accepted at a private school, hugged her and whispered the heavy question, "¿Qué va a pasar?" *What will happen now?* Rachel stared into their tear-streaked faces and responded, "Miles de personas en todo el mundo van a ayudar." *There are thousands of people around the world who are sending their love right now, and will do anything to keep Camino Seguro going.*

Later that morning, footage filmed by Mike Glad that would be used in a memorial video for Hanley showed a somber parade of mourners leaving the funeral home. Some carried floral bouquets of pink and white flowers woven in wicker wreaths. A funeral home employee lifted an ornate floral arrangement of white flowers that spelled the words "GRACIAS POR TU APOYO HANLEY" (*"Thank you for your help, Hanley"*) with red flowers in the background and hues of green and yellow around the border of the arrangement. They placed the flowers in the bed of a white pick-up truck.

An impromptu team of Safe Passage staff, volunteers and supporters acted as pall bearers, carrying Hanley's light brown wooden casket out of the funeral home. On the front left side was Rachel. Exhausted from the bewildering past 36 hours, she sobbed and grimaced as she carefully walked down the steps into the bright sunlight of a day that no one could comprehend. Juan Mini, Jr., was a pall bearer in the back. So was Lety Mendez, her face caked in salty tears. When the casket neared the back of the hearse, Ed Mahoney, wearing a grey hooded sweatshirt and sunglasses, helped push it into the long car.

Guajero families and Safe Passage children, wearing sweat-shirts, skirts, and whatever clean clothing they could find for the ceremony, walked alongside the pallbearers, trying to stay close to Hanley but not get in the way. Behind the hearse, the children gathered, hugging each other in silence, tears dripping from their eyes. One boy held a long American flag in his arms, the red and white stripes tucked under his chin and the stars on a blue background dangling from his outstretched left hand.

"I want to accomplish my dreams, so she is proud of me from up above," a child told Mike Glad as she nodded in quiet affirmation. "She never talked poorly of us. She always liked us, she strived for us. She died striving for us kids from the dump."

The funeral procession left for Zone 3, a grey minivan lead-ing the way, followed by the long white hearse, followed by a white pickup carrying the flowers. As it arrived on Calle 30, the *Calle Sucia*, a yellow garbage truck pulled over to let it pass, a few onlookers waved as plastic bags blew in the breeze, and in Mike Glad's video, the air was heavy with grime and dirt. The cars turned on their flashing hazard lights.

"Hanley was a great person," a man on the sidewalk told the video camera. "She was the most valuable jewel, the most valuable jewel of the neighborhood and the whole capitol, because she was serving all the poor people. She is the golden jewel we have lost."

The procession arrived at Safe Passage's *edificio* educational reinforcement center, blocks from the dump. Her Guatemalan funeral would be here, near the squalid slums where she had changed so many lives. Lety had arranged a traditional funeral with a Catholic mass—perhaps not what the Denning family would have envisioned for Hanley, but nonetheless appropriate for the *guajeros* and Guatemalan staff in a deeply religious country. After all, funerals are meant for those who are left behind, not the deceased.

On a yellow exterior wall of the *edificio*, someone from the project had taped a white sheet of paper that read in printed black letters, "Hanley, tú vives en nuestros corazones, porqué tú sentir está reflejado en cada sonrisa" (*Hanley, you live in our hearts, because your feeling is reflected in each smile.*) Ed and Rachel waited there by the entrance. Ed carried a floral arrangement, Rachel squinted in the sunlight as she cast a steely look forward. No one had slept much since Thursday. Juan Mini and a long-term Safe Passage volunteer named Jeremy Scott carried the front of the casket now as they entered the Edificio's grassy courtyard, with Rachel and Lety in the middle, and Ed supporting the back. Behind them, the boy carrying the Stars and Stripes took care not to let it drag on the ground. Behind him, another boy carried Guatemala's blue and white flag. Both flags would lay over her coffin during the funeral ceremony.

"Hanley started this project seven years ago with a very little bit of money and a big dream. She started with 40 children, today we have 600," Ed told the camera after the casket arrived for the ceremony. "The children in this area would never have had the opportunity to the educational experiences they have today if it wasn't for her work. I feel extremely confident that her work will continue with just as much *corazón* as before."

FEW WHO ATTENDED the traditional Roman Catholic Mass that followed remember many details of the ceremony. Everyone had fallen numb. Claudio Ramos, the project's first social worker, remembered they sang one of Hanley's favorite songs, "Yo quiero tener un millón de amigos" (*I want to have a million friends*). But no one would forget the way the children reacted. Shannon Moyle, who lived at the Casa Hogar dormitory and would teach music and movement at the early childhood center, remembered that the *guajero* children were no longer silent. Now they approached Hanley's casket and asked her directly, "Why did you leave us? How could you do this?" as if they were speaking to their own mother. Their faces bore deep sadness and despair.

The casket was placed in the central dining area of the *edificio*. Hundreds crowded into the open-air courtyard for the service. Lety overheard *guajeros* walk up to Hanley and wail that they were "losing their angel del basurero"—*angel of the garbage dump*—losing the only hope that they had. "Hanley's gone now. Our help is gone. Who will listen to us?" Lety re-imagined the scene she had witnessed so many times before. Hanley would stop on the street, in the paths of the *colonia*, or in the dump itself, lean down and hug a child, and say the reassuring words "Todo va a estar bien." *Everything will be OK.*

Joe Delconzo, who had planned to meet Hanley for dinner in Antigua on Thursday, agreed to photograph the funeral for the *Portland Press Herald* in Maine, for whom Hanley's death was obviously big news. Joe felt emotionally distraught about the difficult assignment. Over the years, she had become more than a photography subject for him—she had become a friend. And yet, the *Press Herald* had called him while he was driving through Guatemala City the previous day and asked if he would take the job. "As a journalist, you're not supposed to get involved and be affected like that," he told himself, "but it's different once you develop a relationship with someone." Still, he said 'yes' to the assignment and maintained his composure throughout the entire mass, while he shot photos of the school, the ceremony, and the processional of her casket into the Edificio.

Toward the end of the service, Joe saw two small children sitting on steps leading into the courtyard. The girl in the foreground wore what looked like yellow and brown pajamas and sported a ponytail with a pink rubber band that did little to keep her thick brown hair out of her eyes. Tears welled in her eyes, and her mouth was locked in a worried grimace. Perhaps six feet away, a little boy wearing pants and a shirt that were too big for his small legs and arms buried his face in one hand. In terms of capturing the emotions of the moment and the sense of utter hopelessness that had befallen the garbage dump community, this was the perfect photo, and Joe knew it. He moved in close for the shot.

As soon as he hit the shutter button, Rachel came and picked up the girl, shot Joe a disapproving glance, and walked away with the girl, now crying, in her arms. "She may have thought, 'how dare you?', but she didn't say anything to me," Joe remembered. The photo ran on the top of the back page of the *Maine Sunday Telegram* the next day, alongside an Associated Press story about Hanley's death, and information about the Yarmouth funeral that would be held the following Tuesday. The story quoted

Yolando Campos, a 33-year-old mother of children enrolled at Safe Passage: "Before I met her, I never would have imagined that my children would get so far in school," she said.

After taking the photo, Joe found himself overwhelmed by the emotion of the day. He was finished. He sat down on the steps and began to sob. At one point he looked up and saw that the AP photographer was now taking pictures of him. "I knew that my time shooting down there (for Safe Passage) was over," he said. "Something died in me down there when Hanley died."

That night Rachel crashed in a guestroom at Ed's house in Antigua. Still wearing her clothes from the previous 24 hours and the impromptu early morning flight from Maine, she collapsed on a twin bed with C-well and Lucha. Hanley's dogs lay on top of her and licked her face as they whimpered. The three of them cried through the night.

ON SUNDAY MORNING, January 21st, Hanley's casket, still draped in the American and Guatemalan flags, left Safe Passage for La Aurora International Airport so her body could be repatriated to the United States. Once she was gone, the community of staff, volunteers, and supporters pivoted to Antigua to offer condolences and support for the family of the driver Bayron Chiquito.

Rachel and Lety joined Hanley's body on her trip back to Maine. A framed picture of Hanley that would be displayed at the next service was propped between them on the plane. They sat in first class, and it took nearly the entire flight before they realized it, as their state of mind was one of delirium and grief. Ed made the decision to stay behind in Guatemala.

"It was better for somebody well-known to be in place here,

so it didn't look like everybody just left the project," he said. "It was more important for people to see my face here. I didn't know what was going to happen (to Safe Passage). I just felt that it wasn't a good idea to leave. So I stayed here."

Ed became the leader in those first weeks and months after Hanley's death. Indeed, the Board of Directors soon named him the project's interim director. Ed was the obvious choice for his right-hand employee Amilcar, who had proved so crucial in navigating Guatemala City bureaucracy in those first hours after Hanley died.

"They adopted the figure of Ed as the leader," said Amilcar. "He had a very serious approach, and he was calm at that moment. Someone had to do it." The central question that now lingered was, "¿Qué va a pasar?" *What will happen to Camino Seguro*? "There was a sense that the program had to continue, somehow. It was her dream," said Amilcar.

THE STORY OF SAFE PASSAGE and Hanley's work in the Guatemala City garbage dump was spreading fast. On Tuesday, January 23, the documentary *Recycled Life*, which California director Leslie Iwerks filmed together with Mike Glad, was nominated for an Academy Award (the Oscars would take place in Hollywood on February 25). The filmmakers had interviewed Hanley at length over a period of four years. Iwerks told the *Portland Press Herald* the documentary was a "labor of love." Hanley's passion for her work as depicted in the film helped viewers identify with the lives of the *guajeros* she was helping, Iwerks said. "Through her eyes you get a sense of the place."

"We're fortunate that we have something that can aid in the

trail of what Hanley left, that we can help in some way," Iwerks told the newspaper.

On the day the Oscar nomination was announced, family, friends, and supporters of Hanley were gathering in the Yarmouth High School gymnasium for her second funeral ceremony—this one a chance for Mainers and Safe Passage supporters and board members from across the United States to say goodbye, to honor her legacy, and to grieve with the Denning family, who had learned of Hanley's death five days before via a string of telephone calls and had now received her casket and repatriated body.

After arriving from Guatemala, Rachel and Lety visited and spoke to several local television stations, which covered Hanley's death and reported on the need to keep her project alive for the hundreds of *guajero* families who depended on Safe Passage. Snow and ice covered the streets and sidewalks of Yarmouth and Portland, and Rachel locked arms with Lety as they walked across slippery parking lots to building entrances—both to hold each other from falling on the ice but also the grief that overwhelmed them.

Distraught and in no shape to plan his daughter's funeral, Michael Denning had called Paul Sutherland on Friday, the day after the accident, and asked him to deliver the eulogy and lead the service. Michael knew that, as board chairman, Paul had fought to make Safe Passage sustainable in a way that Hanley accepted, if not approved. He also knew that Paul had become a close confidant and friend of his daughter. Paul, who had sent Hanley chocolate and popular magazines. Paul, who had pinky swore that they would be confidants who would keep their conversations secret. Paul, who all but insisted that Hanley move into a real house, take a salary, and take a day off once in a while.

Paul, who promised that no child would be sent back to the dump. Michael realized that Paul was one of the people who Hanley most trusted.

But since the news of Hanley's death arrived on Thursday night, Paul had been busy. He spent the weekend on countless calls with fellow board members to decide what steps to take next and to reinforce the message that Safe Passage would not close. "We have 100 employees who all have jobs, and school's gonna open on Monday," Paul reiterated. "Yes, she died, and that's sad, but she would want the program to stay open, the kids to go to school, and the parents to be supported."

"In leadership you say the same thing over and over again," Paul reflected later. "The mothers and children had to hear that, the staff and volunteers had to hear that, the media had to hear that." Paul wrote a long press release within 24 hours of learning of Hanley's death. His goal was to convince his fellow board members to speak with one uniform voice. "Nothing's gonna happen," he told them. "We love Hanley. We have to go through with the funeral, but the world does not stop. The law of physics says you don't want things to stop."

On the airplane flights from Traverse City, Michigan, to Portland, Maine, Paul drafted his eulogy extemporaneously while his fiancé Amy transcribed, then wrote and rewrote his speech. He knew he wanted to share personal memories of Hanley—ones she felt comfortable with him sharing—and that related to her work with Safe Passage. He wanted to show a personal evolution within Hanley, and he wanted to show how she impacted so many people today. He wanted to describe a scene that would bring the families of the garbage dump directly to the high school gym in Yarmouth. He also wanted to honor Hanley's family, who would attend the service and who were traumatized by their loss. He wanted to show how Hanley's leadership and determination was unique. And he wanted to inspire the crowd of mourners to hold hands and speak in a unified voice.

Paul viewed this eulogy, leading this funeral, and directing the board to keep Safe Passage open, as a duty to Hanley. "There was no time for grief," he reflected. "I didn't have time to grieve when my dad died, or when my best friend died when I was 19. Then Hanley died. I had no time to grieve for Hanley before the funeral."

THE APPROXIMATELY 1,000 PEOPLE who crowded into the Yarmouth High School gymnasium on January 23 for a "Celebration of Life for Hanley Graham Denning" included many local teenagers who had volunteered for Safe Passage. They came from high schools throughout southern Maine, including Brunswick, Greely in Cumberland, and Waynflete in Portland, the *Press Herald* reported in the following day's paper. Some of those teens wore suits and ties. Others wore dark green t-shirts that sported the Safe Passage logo of a rounded doorway opening to a staircase. All bore solemn or tear-streaked faces.

"I've never loved more than when I was combing lice out of children's hair," Brunswick High School senior Aly Spaltro told a newspaper reporter before the service. Spaltro planned to return to Guatemala as a long-term volunteer before starting college.

All who attended Hanley's "celebration of life" received a printed program that featured Michigan photographer Beth Price's photo of a smiling Hanley wearing a pink blouse in the foreground, with Guatemalan children huddled in the background. The front page of the program also featured Safe Passage's black-and-white logo.

The ceremony began with music by Jim Highland's wife, Mary, and Dean DeBoer, the North Carolinian who knew Hanley from his time volunteering at God's Child Project as well as Safe Passage during its early days. Dean played songs he composed himself on his Native American flute, including a tune he called "In Celebration of a Life Well Lived."

The Reverend Bill Gregory, a retired United Church of Christ minister who officiated the service, said that visiting Safe Passage and seeing what Hanley accomplished greatly affected people's lives. "She changed the world and she changed us," he said. "We have been to Safe Passage and seen what love can do."

The mourners heard from Rachel, who felt almost like a sister to her, but who also witnessed Hanley's frustration and stress as the project grew beyond something she, alone, could control.

"She touched so many hearts. She was like an angel and a saint," said Rachel, who also shared funny personal stories with the mourners. She described Hanley as a delightfully down-to-earth person who would laugh when she woke up in a cloud of feathers because her dogs had chewed on her pillow. She described Hanley sitting on the beach, shielded by a big hat and reading *People* magazine, as she giggled with Rachel over which celebrity was dating whom.

"You snuck one last hug with a child and you whispered to him that he was your *amigo*," Rachel described Hanley's final hours before her death. And she made a pledge that was becoming a crescendo at this service. "My dear Hanley. We will keep your dream alive."

Next was Lety, the lone Guatemalan who traveled to Maine

for the memorial, and whose life Hanley changed when she pushed the relatively sheltered Antigua native beyond her receptionist duties in the *Camino Seguro* office and out of her comfort level to conduct tours into the garbage dump.

"Thanks for giving the Guatemalan children an opportunity to have an angel at the garbage dump," Lety sobbed as she addressed the Denning family. "I don't know how to stop crying and understand that God needed an angel. I don't know how to do that."

The cover photo in the *Press Herald* the next day showed Jordan Denning standing and leaning down to comfort his father Michael, who was seated in a folding chair and clearly bereaved. Marina sat beside Michael. Behind Jordan lay Hanley's casket, which was adorned with American and Guatemalan flags and a colorful bouquet of flowers.

Jordan said that although his sister died young, she had lived a much fuller life than most who live long lives. He said the legacy she leaves is to inspire everyone to get up each morning and "give every ounce of ourselves to what we truly believe in."

A moment of silence for prayers and reflection followed before Mary and Dean sang an adapted version of John Lennon's *Imagine*:

Imagine there's no heaven, it's easy if you try
No hell below us, above us only sky
Imagine all the people living for today.
Imagine there's no countries, it isn't hard to do
Nothin' to kill or die for and no divisions too
Imagine all the people living life in peace.
You may say I'm a dreamer, but I'm not the only one
I've been to Safe Passage and seen the good that
     can be done.

Paul Sutherland opened the speech that he and Amy had written on the flight to Maine by invoking a light-hearted story to bring a little laughter to the crestfallen mood in the gymnasium.

When I first visited Hanley at Safe Passage, I asked her what I could bring down with me for the project. She had a whole list in her head that she rattled off to me: lice shampoo, tooth brushes, handi-wipes, Spanish books, tools ... I listened to her list, and then asked, 'Hanley, what do you need ... for you?' It took her the rest of the conversation to admit that she needed anything. And when she did, her response was 'Licorice, chocolate, and American magazines—Us, People, Cosmo, Vogue. I'm embarrassed to say it, but I haven't been back to the U.S. in six months.

Then Paul named children in the garbage dump community who Hanley had helped, and he described what set Hanley apart—what made her capable of walking into the *basurero* and launching this program.

What would Hanley talk about?

She might start by mentioning Wilmer, Angel, and Tomas, who sat for the Kinal School entrance exam. She, with simple elegance, would tell us how they got into that tough private high school. She would talk about how they did it, how they worked, how they studied, and not even mention Safe Passage.

She would know in her heart that had she not CHOSEN to help Wilmer, Angel, and Tomas—these kids, today, might have been sitting on the street smelling of glue. Because Hanley was able to see what no one else could in these three boys, they are destined to be leaders—good, smart, educated citizens, for Guatemala and the world's benefit.

Hanley was a dreamer. She had giant, big dreams. But I think, really, Hanley saw everything different than you and I. I think her dream was that we could see what she saw.

Hanley saw each Wilmer, each Sandra, each Angelica, as if they were the only child in the universe. In every child, and adult for that matter, Hanley saw brilliance, creativity, love, compassion, joy, curiosity, and knew each child had within them a natural tendency toward good, and that through discipline and the right environment—mainly people who care— they would become hopeful.

Paul encouraged the crowd gathered in the gymnasium to show their gratitude for Hanley's parents.

Mike and Marina, somehow you nurtured something in Hanley that is rare, a sincerity that sees the goodness in everyone.... I would like everyone to repeat after me:

With sincerity and love, Mike and Marina, Thank you! Thank you for doing your best! Thank you for supporting your daughter Hanley. Thank you for being supportive parents when Hanley went off to do this wild thing in Guatemala. We love you. We love your daughter Hanley. We are committed to helping Hanley's kids.

Paul described Hanley's adoration for each child in the program, and how she pushed back against any attempt to quantify or limit Safe Passage's impact.

For Hanley, it was about the children. It was never about numbers! It was always about each child as a unique, special person.

Once someone mentioned the idea of reducing the number

of children we serve. Hanley, red-faced, called me into a side office, through tears, and she spat out, 'Paul, what are we going to do? Throw 'em back in the dump? Which one do we throw back? Who?'

She then gave me a Hanley look—chin out, eyes that equally melt and create ice, and I said 'Hanley, every child will stay in school. Don't worry.'

Hanley's love for each of her children matched that of every single child's parent. She just happened to have a heart big enough for you, and me, and 545 or 1,000 children. She would feel no comfort if 544 kids were okay, and one was suffering or threatened.

Paul concluded his eulogy by describing what he believed was Hanley's dream.

Today, Hanley's dream is ... about us in this auditorium. Her dream, I think, was for us to see what she sees. If we saw like Hanley, it would allow us to feel connected to the world's poor, to the kids everywhere that need loving, committed help. We are here because we got a glimpse of the world through Hanley's eyes.

"So, Hanley, you need to know that we'll be there for your kids. We'll be there for Eduardo, who has come back off the streets, back to school, and wants to finish his education. And for Angelica, you know, the 14-year-old girl in the first grade. We are carrying on your work.

Paul invited everyone in the gymnasium to hold hands and repeat the words he quoted from the last email he had received from Hanley—*"We have work to do."*

As Hanley's casket was carried out of the gym at the con-
clusion of the service, Dean DeBoer played a haunting flute
melody he wrote called *"Un Lamento de los Latinos."*

Later that night, Paul and other board members and key
supporters joined the Denning family at the upscale Royal
River Grill, which sits next to the Yankee Marina and Boat
Yard on the river that empties into Casco Bay and the Atlantic
Ocean. In a private dining room upstairs, the board chairman
encouraged those seated around the table with him, including
Rachel, Lety, Charlie Gendron, Sharon Workman, and other
board members, to each share a few words and reaffirm their
support for Safe Passage.

Paul raised his glass and made a toast and a pledge that they
would keep the project alive in Hanley's name. They would continue the safe passage for her beloved *guajero* families.

A Ribbon Cutting,
a Presidential Visit, and
a Graduation

THREE WEEKS AFTER HANLEY'S DEATH, on Thursday, February 8, the early childhood center officially opened. Another one of her dreams had come true. Marty and Frank Helman, whose Otto and Fran Doonan Walter Foundation had helped fund the construction of the *guarderia*, traveled to Guatemala City to speak at the building's dedication. It should have been a moment of triumph, of wonder and of hope. Instead, a palpable sense of fear hung over the festivities.

"Everybody there was basically in shock," remembered Marty. "The moms didn't know if the program would continue. They thought of Safe Passage as Hanley, and now Hanley was gone. They didn't know ... We didn't know."

Frank remembered the trip as a blur. He saw more blank looks on faces than he saw crying or outward signs of emotion. Frank gave a dedication speech, both in English and in Spanish after he worked with a teacher from a local language school to help him translate the words, which he committed almost to memory.

We are gathered today to dedicate this project—a dream of Hanley Denning that has now become reality—in two senses," said Frank. *"First, we dedicate it to the benefit of the children of this neighborhood—those here now and the generations of those to come. And second, we dedicate it to the memory of Fran Doonan Walter ... Fran Doonan was born into a desperately poor family in the United States. (Yes, we too have poor people.) When she grew up she married Otto Walter, who had a long and very successful career as a lawyer in New York City. So Fran became a wealthy woman. But she never forgot the poverty of her childhood.*

The building is completed, but not the mission of Safe Passage," Frank's speech continued. *"That mission will never be completed as long as one child is denied an education because of poverty. With Hanley Denning no longer here to lead, it is up to us—all of us—to build on her legacy and move the mission forward.*

Despite the shock and the blanks looks on faces, Marty also felt and perceived an emotion of pride at the *guarderia* dedication. Though she wasn't with them for the actual ribbon cutting, Hanley had lived to see babies being cared for in that building. She lived to see six of her Safe Passage boys pass the entrance exam to attend Kinal and walk into the prestigious technical school located blocks from the garbage dump when the schoolyear resumed in the first days of January 2007. "Hanley lived to know that so much was happening, that her program accomplished so much," thought Marty. "But what an absolute, incredible loss."

Rachel also returned to Guatemala for the opening of the *guarderia*—just as Hanley promised she would. She stood with Marty and Frank, with board members, staff and volunteers in the beautiful new gardens which radiated a rainbow of bright colors. Rachel chatted with Marty, who suddenly said "one minute" and disappeared to talk with Chip Griffin. When she returned, Marty asked if she and Ed could attend Boothbay's Rotary meeting in March. Though she felt exhausted, Rachel had been trained by Hanley to take advantage of all opportunities. When they presented about Safe Passage the following month in front of the Boothbay Club, Ed and Rachel were honored with the Paul Harris Award for Service—Rotary's highest award. "It was unexpected and completely validated all the work together over the years," said Rachel.

The Helmans continued to support *Camino Seguro* and sponsored Juan Carlos, one of the six boys who attended Kinal, but he needed to repeat a grade and chose to do so at a less rigorous school. Marty quickly learned that, thanks to Safe Passage, they had the academic skills to succeed at the technical school, but they lacked a supportive home environment and background to survive the experience.

On a subsequent visit to Guatemala, Marty and Frank ordered fried chicken from the popular Pollo Campero chain for Juan Carlos, his two siblings, and his godmother, Angela, who raised them. All the kids in the family had sponsor parents except Juan Carlos' older brother José, whom the Helmans decided to sponsor as well. José persevered and, at age 28, eventually graduated from high school—becoming one of approximately 17 percent of Guatemalans from this part of the capital—and 36 percent nationwide—who have a high school diploma.

The Helmans later reacquainted with Angela, who was 63 at the time and enrolled in Camino Seguro's adult literacy program, where she sat at a computer learning to read for the first time. They offered to treat the family to a meal in Guatemala

City, and settled on a restaurant which offered menus with pictures of food in addition to words. Marty and Frank learned that Angela had worked as a domestic maid since she was five years old. Her father had married another woman, so she was sent to the capital to work for a different family. They asked Angela why it was important to her to learn to read and write, to add and subtract numbers. She replied, "If you don't know how to do that, people are mean to you." Marty understood that meant people would cheat her in the markets.

Despite the adversity she had faced in her life, Angela lived long enough to see Juan Carlos and José graduate from high school. "As long as they live under my roof, they can't have girlfriends," Angela once boasted to the Helmans. Because then they would father children and wouldn't be able to continue in school.

ALSO IN EARLY FEBRUARY, the Board of Directors traveled south to visit Safe Passage and reaffirm their commitment to keep the project open. Sharon Workman and Deb Walters—a fellow Rotarian whom Chip Griffin had introduced to *Camino Seguro*—came to Guatemala about a week after Hanley's funeral in Maine on a fact-finding trip to interview staff and parents, learn how the organization worked on a daily basis, and what it needed next. Deb was surprised to learn that, "many of the families didn't realize there was an organization. They thought when Hanley died, that was it," she said.

"We structured the interviews so we got information from everyone about what they experienced, what they needed, what they would see in a new leader coming in," said Sharon, who quickly realized that everyone at Safe Passage had reported directly to Hanley. There was no management hierarchy in place. Creating that structure from scratch would be one of the first tasks for the incoming leadership.

The challenges facing the board of directors in those early weeks after Hanley's death were daunting. Sharon's husband Wayne, who later joined the board, said that many board members and Safe Passage supporters just sucked it up and stepped forward to help. They had no other choice. Meanwhile, other board members were forced to reexamine their long-term relationship with the organization now that the individual who personified it was gone. Some, like Jim Highland, who had leant Hanley his office space in Portland, Maine, in the early days of Safe Passage, confessed that he was burning out. Sharon remembered Highland saying in one of their conference calls that his son had broken his arm and he was overwhelmed.

"I've been hanging on by my fingertips," Jim told his fellow board members. "This is it, I can't keep doing this."

Paul Sutherland left the board about six months after Hanley's death, and Sharon became board chair. Deb, who took over as chair after Sharon several years later, also learned that Guatemalans with whom they spoke were uniformly opposed to Safe Passage hiring a local executive director. "No, it had to be an American or European, and preferably a female," Deb heard. "The issue was corruption in Guatemala. If we had a Guatemalan executive director, people might lose faith in the organization."

Hanley's vision continued to move people and bring them into her orbit, both in life and in death. As so often happened during the seven years she carried Safe Passage, people would rise and then fade from her story, then others would show up and take their place. Sandra González, who had hosted Hanley and Amina Lacour for Thanksgiving dinner at her home in

Guatemala City two months before, invited the board members for lunch during their February 2007 visit to Safe Passage. They ate homemade Pepian de Pollo, a Guatemalan specialty, in her garden as the board talked about how to move forward.

"These people from the U.S. cared so much. We Guatemalans need to step up," Sandra thought to herself. Not long after that, Deb visited Sandra at her home and invited her to join the board. At first Sandra was reluctant. She was raising five kids and wasn't sure she could devote the time. But Deb insisted, and by the end of 2007 she joined the board along with Juan Mini.

Before their trip ended, the board convened once again at an upscale restaurant to affirm their commitment to keep Safe Passage afloat. This time it was at Fonda de la Calle Real on Antigua's 5th Avenida, just steps from the famous yellow arch, where U.S. President Bill Clinton famously ordered "de todo un poco"—*a bit of everything*—when he dined here in the late 1990s. Rachel Meyn, who attended the dinner, remembered that board members mingled with volunteers and staff. Paul Sutherland and others stood and made toasts to Hanley, to the project, and committed to lead it forward.

IN MID-FEBRUARY, about a month after Hanley's death, Michael Denning visited Guatemala for the very first time together with Marina. They had divorced eight years ago but remained amicable. Now they had a mission to complete together. Hanley's body had been cremated, and her parents drove through a snowstorm from Portland to Boston's Logan Airport, then flew to Guatemala City to deliver some of her ashes to the country and community to which she had devoted her life. On the plane with them they carried Hanley's remains in a plastic bag inside a thick cardboard box the crematorium had given them. Marina wrote "Han's Ashes" on the top of the box and cried when she explained to customs officials what was inside the box.

Ed Mahoney picked them up in an old, grey Mitsubishi, and the trio drove around Zone 3 so Marina and Mike could sprinkle Hanley's ashes in significant locations—next to the little church where she had started the drop-in center, at the *edificio*, at the *guarderia,* and as close as Marina could get to the garbage dump, itself. Hanley had changed the lives of these *guajeros*, and they had changed Hanley too. Now a small physical part of her would remain among them forever. They also sprinkled Hanley's ashes near Paramos, a community between Antigua and the town of Chimaltenango, where a Safe Passage donor and real estate developer had fronted the money late in 2006 for Hanley to buy a piece of land to one day build a home for herself. The final purchase papers hadn't even been signed when Hanley died, but Ed pulled a few legal strings so that the Denning family would inherit the plot of land.

But on the drive back to Antigua, Marina accidentally spilled the remaining ashes in the backseat of Ed's car. They pulled over and frantically tried to scoop them back into the box. Several days later, Safe Passage employees Lorena and Carlos were riding in the backseat and Carlos asked Ed in the driver's seat, "Did you go spread Hanley's ashes with her parents?"

Ed nodded, and employed a little black humor. "As a matter of fact, you guys are sitting on Hanley right now." The passengers screamed.

ON FEBRUARY 25 the Academy Awards were held at the

Kodak Theatre in Hollywood, California. *Recycled Life*, the Oscar-nominated short documentary by Leslie Iwerks and Mike Glad about the *guajeros* and the Guatemala City garbage dump and which also featured Hanley, came up short and didn't win a trophy that night. The film nevertheless focused needed international attention on the vexing issues surrounding the *basurero*.

On March 9—the date that would have been Hanley's 37th birthday—Iwerks and Glad traveled to Maine, and *Recycled Life* played in front of a packed house of nearly 2,000 people at the Merrill Auditorium in downtown Portland. The event at the Merrill was the brainchild of Jane Gallagher and an informal advisory group in Yarmouth that had supported Hanley and Safe Passage before the board of directors was formed in 2005. Jane described the local advisory group, which was initially a "friends" group, as "handpicked by Hanley to just noodle on questions and help her solve sticky problems." Several of those friends, including Jane, simultaneously encouraged Hanley to also form an official board.

The idea to hold the Maine premier of *Recycled Life* on Hanley's birthday took hold soon after her funeral in the Yarmouth High School gym. At the service Jane ran into onetime advisory group member John Coleman, CEO of an advertising and marketing company in Portland called the VIA Agency, and he said to let him know if she needed anything. VIA designed logos for Safe Passage and donated 20,000 pieces of stationary and envelopes to help the organization raise funds through mailings. Once the idea surfaced to show the film in front of a huge crowd and generate awareness and money for Safe Passage, the friends' group couldn't let it go. "Hanley's only in the movie for like 45 seconds, but it's about her people and her community," thought Jane. "We cannot pass up this opportunity to raise awareness and raise money and tell the story. Plus, it was nominated for an Oscar."

In the seven weeks between her death and the showing at Merrill, Jane grieved openly with her boys, Jake and Bart—she described living in a "river of tears." But Jane also channeled the pain into activities and planning for Friday, March 9. Organizing an event that large, and doing so in a matter of weeks, consumed her. A professional event planner might have needed six months to pull everything together. As she worked, the hours passed like minutes in her second-floor office. She remembers that Jake would send her emails early in the evening from his laptop in the downstairs kitchen and ask, "Mom, are you going to make dinner? Because I know you're up there in your black hole again ..." Five minutes later Jake would follow that with another email: "Should I make us dinner? Because I don't think you're ever going to make us dinner ..."

The big event at Merrill Auditorium gained support and momentum as March 9 neared. The *Portland Press Herald* offered to sponsor the event, the Safe Passage board of directors threw its weight behind the initiative, and Iwerks and Glad announced they would travel to Maine for the screening of *Recycled Life*. Still, a crucial question remained unanswered: how much would tickets cost, and more broadly, would Safe Passage court many small donors, as Hanley had done, or focus their attention on attracting a few lucrative supporters. Questions like these struck to the heart of the debate over how the organization might change, or evolve, after Hanley.

As Jane remembers, the board initially wanted to charge $100 per ticket for the Merrill event. Some in the Yarmouth friends group countered that tickets should be free, with Safe Passage donations encouraged. Jane's goal was to sell out the

1,900-seat venue, not just a few rows in front of the stage. Some thought her aspiration was naïve and unrealistic.

"I had done enough work with Hanley at the grassroots level that I knew our constituents," said Jane. "I knew we were talking about people who maybe could pay $15 or $20 per month to sponsor a child—not people with deep pockets."

"That wasn't Hanley. It wasn't her inclusive way of doing things. I knew that Hanley would want the whole group to be included. That was why some people in our friends group thought the premier should be free."

In the end, the board and the local advisory group reached a compromise. Tickets went for $25. On March 9, the auditorium was packed.

Rachel walked into the Merrill dressed in a black ballgown to fulfill Hanley's dream. In January, before the accident, she and Hanley had received a call that *Recycled Life* was nominated for an Oscar. The young women squealed and dreamt of going to Hollywood for the Academy Awards. "What if we could go? We could wear gowns," suggested Hanley. "Oh my God, this is crazy!" Even though the film didn't win a trophy, Rachel felt compelled to wear the dress on Hanley's birthday.

Prior to the event, Rachel had fielded calls from all kinds of Safe Passage supporters who wanted to showcase their singing, dancing and creative talents for a magical night at the Merrill. Singer-songwriter and Maine native Kate Schrock played and sang several emotional songs on the piano. Rachel's heart pounded in her chest with joy as she walked across the stage to the podium and looked across the sea of 2,000 faces. "We did this, Han!" she thought. In the crowd were supporters from across Maine and New England, as well as North Carolina, Michigan, and California. Safe Passage was present.

Three days later, on Monday, March 12, *Camino Seguro* received its most high-profile guest when United States First Lady Laura Bush visited the project together with Guatemalan First Lady Wendy Berger.

Berger's husband Oscar had been mayor of Guatemala City through the 1990s, so he and Wendy were aware of the situation in the garbage dump and they knew of Hanley and her work with the *guajeros*. The U.S. First Lady joined President George W. Bush on a seven-day, five-nation Latin American trip that stopped in Guatemala, where the President and Oscar Berger discussed immigration, trade, and agricultural aid, and appeared at carefully staged appearances at a medical training center for military doctors, a town west of Guatemala City destroyed by an earthquake but rebuilt with U.S. aid, and a packing station for farmers whose irrigation system was funded by USAID (the United States Agency for International Development). The Bushs and Bergers also visited a sacred archaelogical Mayan site at Iximche, a one-time capital of the Kaqchikel before the Spanish arrived in 1524. (Mayan priests would later "purify" the site, saying they feared the effects of Bush's bad spirits, reported *The New York Times*.)

Days before Laura Bush visited Safe Passage, the Secret Service arrived to scope out the surroundings. Ed Mahoney remembered standing on the sidewalk outside the *edificio* shortly before noon, warning the agents that a couple hundred factory workers would suddenly appear from around a corner half a block away and walk up the street to a neighboring building where they ate lunch.

Ed described the intense security for the First Lady's visit. "They put up this huge tent in the street next to the building— big enough so that a limousine could drive into it so that no one would see her get out." The Secret Service positioned snipers on the rooftops and, according to Ed, forced every single business within three blocks to close before and during the visit. Pre-screened and vetted adults had to be in the building before Laura and Wendy arrived. The Safe Passage kids would enter through a side door, with a metal detector swiping each child.

Once the dignitaries arrived, Ed led them on a brief tour of the project and explained Safe Passage's story and the organization's role. He remembered that Laura Bush and Wendy Berger offered their condolences for the loss of Hanley, adding that she sounded like a wonderful person. Following the tour, the First Ladies joined a carefully staged roundtable discussion, which included Ed, Lety, Fredy, and several *guajero* mothers and children in the project.

Lety remembered that the U.S. First Lady seemed impressed that an American woman had accomplished so much here in this rough environment. "I told her that a *guatemalteca* wouldn't have been able to do this," said Lety.

During the roundtable discussion, *guajero* mother Ingrid Mollinero leaned toward Laura Bush and bravely said, "que bonito su vestido." *Your dress is beautiful.* Ingrid's son, Christián Chiche, a student at Safe Passage, was rumored to have told the First Lady that he hoped to be president of Guatemala some day.

Ed was convinced the visit from Laura Bush, which lasted less than two hours, wouldn't have happened had Hanley not died. Nevertheless, he viewed the visit pragmatically as an opportunity to generate publicity, and ultimately raise money, for Safe Passage.

In fact, 2007 proved to be a fundraising bonanza for the organization that had just lost its founder. Barbara Davis, the accountant who had worked for Jim Highland when he offered to house the first Maine office, and then worked exclusively for

Safe Passage when Rachel Meyn opened a space in Yarmouth, said the organization went from raising approximately $500,000 or $600,000 per year to nearly $2 million in 2007—including $500,000 in donations made in remembrance of Hanley, on top of $1.5 million from regular donors.

Safe Passage's name recognition shot through the roof after greater Maine heard of Hanley's sudden death. Doug and Becky Pride's annual 5K road race in Cumberland, which Hanley attended in both 2005 and 2006, drew nearly 600 registrants for the event on April 28. By the end of 2007, some 5,000 different people and organizations had given money to Safe Passage, with about 40 percent of those funds coming from Maine, 45 percent from other U.S. states, and 15 percent coming from European countries including England, Germany, and the Netherlands.

What Laura Bush saw, or the stories she heard, when she visited Safe Passage on March 12, must have made an impact on her and her staff. On July 9, the First Lady spoke at a White House Conference on the Americas at the Hyatt Regency in Arlington, Virginia. Though she may have overexaggerated the role of the U.S. government in directly supporting the project, Bush's speech directly invoked Hanley and her legacy in Guatemala City.

I've seen the impact of these resources firsthand, at the Camino Seguro program in Guatemala. Founded by an American volunteer, and supported by USAID, Camino Seguro serves children whose parents earn a living picking through trash at the Guatemala City Dump.

Camino Seguro supports the children's education, and runs a medical clinic and nutrition program. Children receive healthy meals of vegetables, beans, rice, and meat. Little children also receive two daily cups of milk, and vitamins. For many of the children, Camino Seguro volunteers supply their only meal of the day.

Hanley had reached into the darkness and despair of the garbage dump and led children and families toward a hopeful future they never could have imagined. In life and in death, her dream and her vision had touched paupers and princes alike. From Mamá Roque and the first families who sent their children to the drop-in center at the little church next to the dump in exchange for bags of rice and beans, from Nancy Gudiel the orphan who sold chiclets on the street, from Daniél Osorio who went into hiding after drug-running gangs murdered his stepfather—to successful businessmen and philanthropists including Arthur Berg and Juan Mini, Charlie Gendron, Paul Sutherland and Marty and Frank Helman, to hundreds of volunteers of every age from all over the world who committed their skills, knowledge and money. Hanley's story reached from the hovels of the dump, to churches and schools, to elite corporate boardrooms, all the way to The White House.

EACH COMMUNITY that Hanley had touched mourned her death in their own way, at their own time, and contributed acts of service to keep her legacy alive. Safe Passage supporters in London threw a benefit ball on April 19; a "virtual visit to Guatemala" drew more than 350 people in Traverse City, Michigan, as guests walked through a replica dump and staged street scenes; University of Washington students came to Guatemala

City and completed a community garden at the *guarderia* that fall, and Columbian songwriter Marta Gomez performed at a Safe Passage benefit in Boston on December 1, 2007.

In Chapel Hill, North Carolina, Safe Passage supporters who knew Hanley held their own memorial service several months after the funeral in Maine. Arnie Katz remembered their gathering at the Church of Reconciliation taking the form of a Quaker meeting, with people sitting in a circle and anyone could speak if they felt moved to do so. Josh Lozoff, an actor and magician who had volunteered for Safe Passage in its early days, read a passage from the Irish playwright George Bernard Shaw. Arnie remembered one woman standing up and, through sobs, telling the group that she felt as though she had lost a best friend. "But this morning, thinking about it, probably over the last five–six years of knowing Hanley, we probably haven't had more than 15 minutes of actual conversation together," she said. Many in the group nodded.

"That was her magic, her connection," said Arnie, who admitted that, for years after her death, he couldn't talk about Hanley without crying.

Each friend of Hanley who traveled to Guatemala and visited Safe Passage in those first weeks, months, and years after her death faced the pain and bewilderment of suddenly being in the project without her. Jane Gallagher and her son Jake had planned to visit Ireland with his soccer team in 2007 instead of Guatemala, but after Hanley died, and after organizing the film screening at Merrill Auditorium, she decided they *had* to return to Safe Passage. "We have to go see our sponsor kids," she told herself. "We have to go back and see people we know like Fredy, because we want them to know we're still with you. We're not abandoning the program."

They traveled that summer as part of a group of six Mainers.

But this time when their van from Antigua pulled up in front of the yellow *edificio*, Jane got out of the vehicle and froze. She began to sob. She'd been to this place before, but never without Hanley. Jane slipped and fell, and suddenly felt the arms of Ingrid Mollinedo supporting her. Ingrid the *guajero* mother, whose son Christián was sponsored by Jane and her family to attend Safe Passage. Ingrid, who had summoned all her courage and spoke to the First Lady of the United States to compliment her dress. Ingrid who, like so many from the garbage dump community, had found the strength and dignity to send their children to school, to imagine a future for their family that didn't involve the *basurero*. She caught Jane and righted her.

Ingrid put her arms around Jane and asked her what was wrong. Using her broken Spanish, the emotional visitor from Maine was able to gasp that Hanley was a dear friend and she couldn't imagine being in Guatemala without her.

"Everywhere I went that entire week, those moms stayed right next to me," Jane said. "It's hilarious that I went on that trip thinking I was helping. But they were the ones making sure I was OK. It was unbelievable."

They may have called Hanley the "angel of the garbage dump" but at moments like these the *colonia* was full of angels. Hanley had merely helped these mothers dig deep and find their best selves.

ARNIE KATZ'S DAUGHTER LEAH, who had volunteered many times at Safe Passage starting in 2002, traveled immediately to Guatemala after learning that Hanley had died. Her heart was in that place and she wanted to help in any way she could. Leah's first moments and days there after the accident were a blur. "I

remember the shock and the sadness, but I can't grasp any specific interactions or sequences of events," she reflected. "I have
blurry images of hugging children, of seeing people like Fredy
and Claudio from across the room."

Leah stayed on for several months after Hanley died and got
involved in the process of hosting candidates vying to become
Safe Passage's new executive director. Each long-term volunteer
was assigned to host and interpret for a particular candidate
as they toured the project and the garbage dump community,
meeting children, families, teachers, and staff. Leah and others
collected and processed feedback questionnaires from everyone
who met the candidates. "It was an honor to be able to help
with that work, but it was also really hard," Leah reflected. "The
candidates were all impressive and qualified, but none of them
were Hanley, of course."

"I remember once talking with members of the board about
all the different qualifications they were looking for in a candidate, and realized that Hanley, herself, probably wouldn't have
been hired based on those criteria.... I understood it, based on
what was needed at that moment in time, but it still felt like a
big loss."

On June 12, 2007, after a global search, the board of directors announced that Barbara Nijhuis, a Dutch lawyer who had
launched her own nonprofit in rural Guatemala for impoverished villagers, would succeed Hanley as Safe Passage's next
executive director. Like Hanley, Barbara was 36 years old and
had a charming smile. She was stylish and would playfully tease
and joke with people. She had a direct way of communicating
that could be refreshing, but some who were used to Hanley's
style found it off-putting.

A month later, Barbara's uncle, Wim ten Wolde, completed
a 160-kilometer trek in the Netherlands to raise funds for Safe

Passage. According to a story in the *Maine Sunday Telegram*, board members were attracted to her experience working for companies such as a European power exchange. Barbara quickly made it her goal to run Safe Passage more efficiently without compromising the quality of education that children receive.

THE CULMINATION OF SAFE PASSAGE'S painstaking, roller coaster year of 2007 came on October 25 with the program's first sixth-grade graduation ceremony. The first graduate was none other than Nancy Gudiel, the tough girl who, orphaned at age 9, had sold candy on the streets of Guatemala City. Taken in by Hanley, she had lived at the Casa Hogar dormitory near Antigua and had run away over and over again. No one at Safe Passage thought she would graduate the program, remembered Lety Mendez. No one. It turns out, of the 50 or so street-hardened kids who lived at the Casa Hogar, Nancy was the first one, and one of very few, to complete her studies.

At Hanley's wake the day after the accident, Lety observed Nancy standing beside the casket throughout the evening, thanking the woman who had guided her off the streets. It occurred to Lety that the sudden loss of Hanley had hurt Nancy perhaps as much as any other *Camino Seguro* student.

"She was very strong," reflected Lety. "She fought. She hit. It was hard for her to show love because no one had done so with her. Her life on the street had been hard."

The day Nancy graduated, Lety took her aside and told her, "Mira, mija. *Look, my child*, I'm very proud of you." The girl shot her an incredulous look in return. She couldn't say a word, and just walked away.

The next day, Nancy returned to the office to find Lety. "I have a letter for you," she said.

"Why?" asked Lety. "What is it?"

"The person who I wanted to be at my graduation couldn't be there," said Nancy. "I wish that Hanley could be at my graduation. This letter I wrote for Hanley. Pero ella no está. *She's not here.* I wish she could be the one saying she's proud of me. But she's gone. She's gone."

Nancy presented the one-sentence, stream-of-consciousness letter to Lety instead.

Thank you, *Seño* Lety, all the hard work was worth the struggle ... Perhaps the person who hoped most that this day would arrive isn't here with us, but I know she's celebrating this along with me ... I never thought I would be here today ... but I also realize that the person most excited about my graduation is you ... for that I'd like to thank you for all your help so that I could reach this far."

As Lety wept she thought about what Hanley had told her. She could hear Hanley's accented, empowering words hanging in the air. "Con sólo una." *If we change just one life.* If just one graduates, I'll be happy.

Will the Project Survive?

IN THE YEARS AFTER HANLEY DIED, Safe Passage underwent significant changes, which the board of directors and subsequent executive directors felt were necessary to streamline the program and re-focus attention on the best ways to educate the children and families of the garbage dump community.

Soon after Barbara Nijhuis was hired, the board officially announced that it would close the Casa Hogar dormitory near Antigua for troubled Safe Passage kids who were orphans or came from violent homes. Ed Mahoney recalls that meeting happening at a hotel in Antigua.

"The Casa Hogar was too out of control, too expensive, and we couldn't demonstrate we were actually accomplishing anything other than warehousing kids, which shouldn't have been the purpose," Ed reflected. "The original mission for the Casa Hogar had swung 180 degrees, and it was costing us a ton of money. The kids were getting older, and there were some violent episodes there. We decided to get more mission-oriented."

Indeed, Lety remembered that the dormitory—with its swimming pool, green lawn, and bed for each child—was nicer than her own house. And yet the kids kept scaling the wall and escaping at night, and Safe Passage staff kept getting calls to track them down.

For some who worked directly with those students, closing

the Casa Hogar represented a monumental loss. Dorien Claessen, a social worker from the Netherlands, developed a program called "La Luna" which she implemented together with the social work staff in Guatemala City. For them, the Casa Hogar was a safe space to work with the most traumatized kids, and losing it and shutting down their program was devastating.

The board ultimately concluded that, of the approximately 30 kids living there, most could be returned safely to their families. Only a few truly needed the Casa Hogar for protection, they said. Furthermore, Safe Passage determined it didn't have the psychologists on staff to help the kids who were most traumatized.

Sharon Workman described the move as a difficult choice, but absolutely essential—even though some said they were going against Hanley's vision. Closing the Casa Hogar represented a separation of the vision from its visionary—perhaps analogous to separating a growing child from its mother. The board had made the pivotal decision during the search process for Safe Passage's new executive director. Once Barbara took the job in mid-2007, it fell upon her to close the dormitory, which she did by December 15. Stepping into Hanley's shoes and attempting to win the admiration and respect of the *guajero* community was perhaps a thankless job — perhaps even an impossible one. In the eyes of some local Guatemalans, shutting down the Casa Hogar made the task even more difficult.

The board also scaled back the carpentry and baking workshops, and technical training labs. None of these *"talleres"* were licensed with the government, so there were no certificates that would have helped the students land jobs in these fields. Those interested in technical trades would have more success enrolling in the nearby Kinal school—a less expensive option for Safe Passage. Plus, Susanna Place pointed out, the bread oven wasn't approved by the health department, so what the students baked couldn't be sold commercially. "Even if the kids did well with them and learned new skills, the *talleres* stretched us as a board and as a staff. In the end, we felt that those unrelated things didn't support the educational mission."

Some on staff also pushed to retool the week-long volunteer service learning trips visiting from the United States and Europe. Whereas Hanley had welcomed a generally laissez fair approach ("Come down and help"), the volunteer coordinators, Gary Teale and Ann Austin from Seattle, concluded that inserting a group of non-Spanish-speaking volunteers, who knew little about the program's day-to-day operations, into classrooms as "teachers aids" disrupted the educational process. The teachers were frequently forced to stop and translate or explain what activities the kids were doing, they said.

"We changed that so the volunteers would have a specific project to do while they were there for a week. They wouldn't necessarily be in the classroom every single day," said Ed.

In a meeting with the board of directors several months after Hanley's death, the volunteer coordinators made the analogy of a family always hosting friends and visitors until their home was a constant thoroughfare. But Rachel bristled at the comparison, which she considered misinformed. "I'm sorry but you have it wrong," she said with tears running down her face. "Supporters do not want to be a burden. We have been encouraging them to see Guatemala, to connect, to show the kids and families that they matter. This is one of the incredible assets of Safe Passage—that we have thousands of supporters who care so deeply about our organization."

Rachel and others saw the service learning trips to Guatemala as a vital part of engaging individuals as supporters so they would truly understand the stakes and invest themselves.

She recalled that Ed's response was, "Well, maybe we need new supporters then." The situation left her dumbfounded, and she left the meeting enraged. She agreed that changes needed to be made to the organization, greater structure needed to be put into place, but she felt the push to scale back, or eliminate, the service learning trips, and that volunteers were being seen as a burden, didn't take into account the full scope of Safe Passage. Ultimately, the number of trips didn't change. A new structure allowed each group to participate in a project with one classroom, which kept the service learning volunteers involved but reduced the day-to-day effect on the teaching structure.

The struggle for Hanley's legacy was underway. It came as little surprise that the decisions to close the Casa Hogar and the training labs, and retool the service learning trips met mixed reactions among the Safe Passage community, both in Guatemala and in the United States.

"Some people felt that we were doing too much, too soon, and destroying Hanley's legacy," Ed reflected. "Other people felt we should have made those moves years ago."

Several years later, Barbara initiated a coffee date with Ed and told him that they had to decided to also close Posada Lazos Fuertes, Safe Passage's hotel located on the traffic-heavy Calzada Santa Lucia, blocks away from Antigua's tourist center. This was where the program housed short-term volunteer groups and donors when they visited Guatemala, and where Safe Passage aspired to train students in hospitality and hotel management.

From his time as comptroller, Ed knew that Lazos Fuertes could be a financial drain on the project. Lodging revenues nearly covered the hotel's operating expenses, but Safe Passage had to kick in about $1,000 each month to pay the westerner who ran the hotel. Nevertheless, he told Barbara that he disagreed with the decision because he thought Lazos Fuertes was a fabulous marketing tool.

"At the time, the *Lonely Planet* guidebook rated it one of the best places to stay in Antigua. It got really good reviews," said Ed. "The hotel was loaded with pictures of the project, pictures of the kids. There were Safe Passage marketing materials in the rooms. Some people went there because it was a socially responsible hotel. It was a fabulous place for volunteer groups that came down to stay there.

"You don't know how much money you're getting from the hotel," Ed told Barbara, adding that Lazos Fuertes was a valuable tool for reaching potential funders, "whether they're sponsoring kids, or donating money to the project, or spreading the word about Safe Passage."

Meanwhile, Marc Wuthrich, the Swiss accountant, remembers troubling accounts of guests' valuables going missing while they were out during the day. And Antigua's raucous nightlife environment sometimes pitted student volunteers and 20-something guests partying late into the night against older volunteers and guests traveling on business who preferred quiet evenings at Lazos Fuertes.

The hotel had started off with a bang when it opened in 2005, but competition soon mounted from other small, socially responsible Antigua businesses, said Susanna Place. "It had been intended to be a hotel training school for kids, but it was hard to get permission to bring the kids from Guatemala City here on the weekends. There wasn't enough supervision," she added. "It was a good idea, but it wasn't panning out."

Ed also pushed back on discussions of moving Safe Passage's offices out of Antigua and exclusively to Guatemala City. "From a marketing standpoint, this is where people are, where the tourists are, where the volunteers stay, where you want to have a foot in the door," he opined. He succeeded for a time. Safe Passage didn't close its Antigua office until 2017.

FOR KEY STAFF WHO, FOR YEARS, HAD WORKED 60-hour weeks and poured their hearts into Safe Passage—and who adored Hanley—the months following her death were extremely difficult. The sudden absence of her vertical management style left a void that was filled by fierce competition and jockeying for power among the employees. In the ensuing year, many employees quit or were fired. It was a tense and awkward time. One volunteer called it a "bloodbath."

Claudio Ramos, the cousin of Maribel Cholotio from San Juan la Laguna who had become Safe Passage's first social worker though he lacked a degree in social work, and who, in the project's early days, was responsible for administrative duties when Hanley traveled to the United States to raise money, left in May 2008.

Lety Mendez lasted one year at the project following Hanley's death. Lety had become Hanley's Guatemalan deputy of sorts after starting as a secretary in Antigua, and she was the project's de facto legal representative, a dubious position to have in a sometimes-lawless country where justice is imposed by the strong onto the weak. She often worked as many hours as Hanley herself—she came into the office just hours after giving birth to her first child. Lety had traveled back to Maine with Hanley's casket and stood in front of the mourning crowd in Yarmouth as the face of Guatemala.

But Lety's steadfast confidence, and her proximity to Safe Passage's leader, also meant that she sometimes played the "bad cop" to Hanley's angelic, smiling persona. More than one insider observed that Hanley never fired anyone. It fell on Lety to "do the dirty work," and that made her unpopular among some staff. When Sharon Workman and Deb Walters visited Guatemala to interview employees and families and determine what the project needed next, it may have created an opportunity for some to settle scores and enact revenge.

"It was a hard time," Lety reflected years later. "A time to adapt to a new structure, to accept that things would be done differently than they had been with Hanley. I had to accept that it just wasn't the same."

"The numbers weren't Hanley's goal. Hanley's goal was to change lives. She'd say, 'If you miss a year of school, 'Está bien, amigo, pero el otro año vamos a lograr.' (*It's OK, but promise me you'll succeed the next year.*) 'Sí,' the kid would say. And he wasn't thrown out because he missed a year."

Lety offered an allegory to describe Hanley's approach for how Safe Passage should welcome children of the garbage dump.

"The floor can be white, but if a kid arrives with dirty shoes, you're allowed to clean them. It's not the goal that the floor has to remain white forever. The objective is that the floor is white so when the kid arrives, they are happy and comfortable. It's OK to arrive with dirty shoes."

Lety conceded that the new management style didn't work for her. "I wanted to do things the way Hanley had showed me how to do. She was my direct teacher," Lety said. "It would have been difficult for me to change my ways that Hanley taught me. The new people who came in, they didn't know Hanley."

"I think it was healthy for both sides for me to retire from the program."

As for Ed, he made a commitment to students at the Department of Landscape Architecture at the University of

Washington that he wouldn't leave Safe Passage until their garden at the *guarderia* was complete. Under the leadership of program director Daniel Winterbottom, they had designed, landscaped, and built the entrance and a playground area outside the new daycare center. The University of Washington paid for airfare, housing and food while in Guatemala; Safe Passage just had to buy the building materials. Daniel and Ed were planning a third project, in the courtyard inside the *guarderia*, when Hanley died.

"I promised Daniel, I won't leave this organization until your project is complete," said Ed. The team of landscape architecture students finished the "Peace Garden" in March 2009, and that's when Ed said goodbye to the program he had helped shepherd through the meteoric growth spurts, through Hanley's impulsive embrace of all initiatives that came her way, through the beer-soaked evenings with potential donors, through late-night phone calls and at least one email from Hanley he didn't answer, through those tumultuous hours after her car accident, and through the high-profile visits with dignitaries and First Ladies.

Before leaving, Ed reflected to volunteer coordinator Gary Teale how his time with Safe Passage had changed him and his view on international development: "You come in here to this project, you're a bleeding-heart liberal, aren't you?" Ed said in his thick Boston accent. "When you leave this project, you're gonna be a middle-of-the-road conservative. You see how much money is spent on handouts."

"The problem is that sometimes in the process of trying to do really good things, your heart gets in the way of your intellect. You end up doing things or tolerating things that you shouldn't."

It's worth noting that Hanley may have disagreed about the importance that there were handouts. Lives were changed, and that was what mattered most.

Rachel Meyn also left the project in 2009 after working as the project's U.S. Director since early 2008. She had hardly taken a day off work since she moved to Maine in 2003 to run Safe Passage's U.S. office. She considered Hanley to be nearly as close as a sister—despite the hurdles they faced in their personal and professional relationship in the months leading up to Hanley's death. Rachel didn't completely leave the organization, though. She served on the board of directors until 2014.

Fredy Maldonado remained at Safe Passage until 2011. He had picked her up at the airport when she arrived in 1997 to work for God's Child Project, he coached her not to give away food to local families without incentives, he voluntarily connected her with resources when she launched Safe Passage and became one of the most well-known faces of the project to international volunteers once he was officially hired.

But with Hanley gone, the long hours spent with the *guajeros*, organizing volunteers and courting international donors began to feel more impersonal, more like work, said Fredy. Furthermore, he didn't feel as safe as he once had in Zone 3, but he couldn't explain why. He was never assaulted or robbed there, but his instincts were more cautious.

Perhaps the Guatemala City gang members and street warriors who had known and respected Hanley, and had granted her and her team "safe passage" on more than one occasion—perhaps even guarded and looked out for her—personified the project in her. With the angel of the garbage dump no longer living, would they respect those who carried on her legacy?

HANLEY'S STRENGTH, BOTH IN LIFE AND IN DEATH as Safe Passage persevered as an organization, was her charisma, her passion, and the light she created around her, said Mary Jo Amani, the Montessori-trained teacher who volunteered at the drop-in center during the first years of the program and established a library for *Camino Seguro*. "No one else could have gotten so many people involved and committed to it without her spirit. That's what brought these incredibly strong donors who stayed with Safe Passage even after her death."

But Mary Jo added that, financially and administratively, the project was in poor shape when Hanley died. There was no evaluation system, no hierarchy other than every employee answering to Hanley, who seemingly wanted to remain involved in every facet of Safe Passage. Board members Sharon and Deb were surprised to learn how ineffectively it was run and to learn of the conflict among staff. It took a solid year for them to begin to straighten out and create a new structure.

"You don't need those things when you're small, but when you get big, you need structure and attendance systems, you need accountability," Mary Jo said. By not having structures in place, she put some people's lives at risk, she added. "Anybody like Lety could have been put in jail in a second if something happened to a child on our premises. We had no insurance, we had nothing.... It was one thing for Hanley to take risks. It would have been a Guatemalan who'd go to jail, not her.

"For all her complexities, Hanley was a beautiful, beautiful person," said Mary Jo. "But she wasn't a listener. When she had a thing in her head she kept going and going." There was the Casa Hogar, the hotel in Antigua, the carpentry workshop, the bread baking workshop, the ironworks facility ... it just kept mounting. "She was trying to do too much, too fast."

In some ways, Mary Jo considered Hanley a "tragic hero" because the very qualities that compelled her to launch Safe Passage and change the lives of hundreds of families in the garbage dump—her grit, her persistence, her fearless optimism, her determination, her stubbornness—were the qualities that nearly led to the project's downfall.

Mary Jo and her husband Todd drew a parallel between a nonprofit and a developing nation.

"There's a claim that at a certain time in a country's progress, you need a benevolent dictator," said Mary Jo. "In some stages it's not ready" to be led by many. "Hanley's spirit was proper and good in the beginning when, through sheer will, she got people to donate and give up their time." But at some point, "the burden of carrying it no longer falls on one person. It needs to be decentralized. You have the executive director, you have the board, you have a development director ... It won't flounder because you have people on all sides working together."

"Many organizations do start with a charismatic leader, and then it becomes clear that the strength of that leader is no longer what an organization needs," added Todd. "They need structure and rules, and different kinds of people to lead. At some point the tools are different. That seems true of Hanley." The project was her baby, but it was a baby that needed to be nurtured differently once it was up and walking.

Safe Passage *did* survive, and evolve, and continued to encourage and reinforce the education of Guatemala City's most vulnerable children. It survived because, before she died, Hanley had formed a board of directors—full of people with vision, and commitment, and checkbooks that could sustain the nonprofit through times of drought. But it also survived because of the seeds that Hanley had planted years ago. Those seeds germinated and created trust within the *guajero* community and created a passion among Guatemalans and ex-pats alike to keep the project alive.

Chip Griffin, the board member and Rotarian from Boothbay Harbor, Maine, who applied the expression "the life you change may be your own" to those who visited Safe Passage, drew a contrast between Safe Passage and a different nonprofit, on whose board he also served, which closed just months after its inspirational founder succumbed to a rare form of cancer. "Usually, when the founder dies so early on and at a critical time, there's no way it can be saved," he said. "That didn't happen with Safe Passage. That's a tribute to Hanley."

Who Will Carry Her Torch?

THOUGH IT EVOLVED, SAFE PASSAGE would remain a beacon of hope for children and families of the garbage dump community, and for foreign volunteers who heard of Hanley's story and traveled to Guatemala to see Zone 3 for their own eyes and to help for a few days, weeks, or months. The stories they told, the life-changing scenes they described, commanded as much emotion as Hanley's first foray into the *basurero*.

Hugh Taft Morales, a minister and ethical humanist with a degree from Yale, volunteered at Safe Passage in October 2007 and felt inspired to pen an unpublished essay about his time at the project. In "Camino Seguro from the eyes of a volunteer," he used arresting imagery to narrate his group's arrival at the project after a tour of the nearby cemetery and looking down on the garbage dump from above:

> We pass over a half dozen men passed out on the side of the road due to sniffing glue or whatever substance could put them out of their misery for the day. Many others watch the van pass with blurred eyes, clasping small plastic bottles with red caps—for the equivalent of a few U. S. cents they buy six ounces of pure alcohol. The van swerves to miss a dead dog in the middle of the road. I look back and see other dogs come sniff this curiosity. We turn into the day care center as a large metal door swings open—this is the new jewel of the organization, opened only a few days after the death of Safe Passage founder Hanley Denning. An automobile

accident kept her from seeing the opening of this site, an oasis, as [our guide] Lisa calls it, in a desert of poverty.

This metaphor of an oasis is painfully appropriate as we take in the view from the roof of the center—we are in a desert. On three sides of the center is nothing but patchwork tin roofs. They offer minimal protection from the rains, and turn the small sleeping quarters for large families into ovens. Eight people may sleep in a ten by ten room—little ventilation, mud floors, no plumbing, rats. Lisa explains that this squatter village of thousands is literally on top of the old dump, as it moved east over time. Living on compacted old trash leads to many health problems, some caused by the methane that seeps up through the soil sprinkled over the final layer of garbage. The gases cause an odd side effect for some children who breathe the noxious fumes all their lives—the tips of their hair turns orange.

Once inside the classroom and working as a teacher's aid, Hugh described the intimacy of helping children with the most mundane of tasks, and the powerful effect that helping the kids brush their teeth or wiping their noses had on him.

In the classroom, I am initiated into one of the daily rituals as Jessica asks me to help the children brush their teeth. They line up on tiny chairs in a small windowless bathroom. I move down the line squeezing toothpaste on their brushes. Most treat the blue gel like candy, eagerly sucking on their brushes before their turn at the sink. Two at a time they brush, spit, and bend over the sink to catch water running from the faucet. This is followed with a cap full of mouthwash that I pour into each mouth. They jostle to be the next to get the sharp tasting antiseptic. I feel like a cross between a mother bird feeding her young and a doctor administering a vaccine.

I wonder whether this is the only time each day the children practice dental hygiene. Which of them have functional homes, running water, and electricity? Which have none? There is a diversity of dress—some wear soiled and torn clothing, but most are neat and proper. None of them seem to care or notice the difference. But I notice, and am ashamed I do. Edgar is particularly dirty, and his nose runs like a faucet. He ducks and weaves to avoid Jessica's tissue. I take it as a small victory when he allows me to wipe his nose moments later and then gives me a hug. I gently scold myself for anticipating the shower later today that I imagine will wash away his cold germs."

Hugh observed the crucial role that volunteers play at Safe Passage. They offered individual attention that the children needed, they contributed money to the project's operating budget, and in many cases they visited Guatemala to fulfill a specific need—whether it was the architecture students from the University of Washington building the playground and garden outside the nursery school, or volunteer doctors from Shared Beat, a medical nonprofit based in Texas, who offered pediatric checkups, dental services, and eye checkups. Together with Shared Beat, Safe Passage would expand its health clinic in 2009.

What is most striking about the medical team visit is that despite the confusion about who goes where and who's been seen by whom, a remarkable calm pervades. The medical staff seems pleased to be here, at every turn smiling and gently examining each patient: some lice, a case of impetigo, a lot of runny noses. They make no comments about the crowded conditions or limited medical supplies, and move down the line, seeing first the smallest children, then parents and grandparents, who seem less at ease than the children....

More than anything else, the volunteers make the difference. In 2006–2007, 600 volunteers came through the program. Not only would the work be impossible without them, the volunteers make the children feel loved. They are the ones that give the one-on-one attention, tie a shoelace, give a hug, or read a story. It is not the President of Guatemala that makes a difference to these children. It's the volunteers. They are the best advertisement for Camino Seguro. They become invaluable ambassadors for the good that is done here.

ONE SAFE PASSAGE PROGRAM that a volunteer launched with Hanley's approval, and which thrived beyond her death was the adult literacy program, which Susan Attermeier had spearheaded in 2003. The adult literacy program now enrolled more than 80 mothers, fathers, and grandparents of children in the program and tutored them in learning to read and write. The initial goal was to help them earn a sixth-grade diploma in an accredited national program, though Safe Passage also encouraged them to study *beyond* the sixth grade.

Jane Gallagher, who had organized the showing of *Recycled Life* in Portland, Maine, weeks after Hanley's death, continued to visit and support Safe Passage together with her teenage sons even though the project's founder was no longer a physical presence in the garbage dump community. She noted a striking difference in the *guajero* mothers she met as the years passed. During her summer 2007 trip, Jane attended the monthly meeting of Safe Passage families when mothers from the community met with social workers as teams of volunteers cleaned head lice from their children's hair, before the families were sent home with bags of food. As a staff member made announcements, "I looked at these moms and I saw mostly people who were checked out—people who were so traumatized and hopeless than that they focused just on surviving," said Jane.

Fast forward to a visit in 2011, when more Safe Passage mothers were learning to read and write and create their own jewelry from recycled materials through the Creamos women's social entrepreneurship program, which earned them money that dissuaded them from working in the garbage dump. Once again Jane was invited by a long-term volunteer to attend a families' meeting. A few minutes after they arrived "the door opened and 24 women blew in with a different spirit and energy. They would look me in the eye, they were talking a mile a minute, and I just felt this electric current going through me, like 'Hanley, if you could see this!'"

Irina Rodríguez Cotto, who overcame early trepidations about Hanley within the *guajero* community and found her at the little church to ask for help and enroll her five children in Safe Passage, worked for a time handwashing laundry for others in the garbage dump after her 14-year-old daughter Sindy became pregnant and had to drop her studies. Then Irina joined the adult literacy program just as three of her kids continued their studies, and graduated in 2008 with a sixth-grade diploma, roughly equivalent in Guatemala to a GED.

At Irina's graduation, a long-term volunteer observed one of her daughters approach her and say, "Mom I'm so inspired by you! I hope I never disappoint you in my studies. I want to be as strong and as successful as you."

The following year Irina went on to the seventh grade.

A film that Safe Passage produced called "*Manos de Madre*" (Mother's hands) featured Irina and her family's journey from the garbage dump to literacy and education. She reflected on the role of working-class women in Guatemala and how they often lack self-esteem.

"Women have been greatly devalued and many times we think that we can't," she told the camera. "How are we going to know that we can't if we don't try?"

"I tell my children, 'If I don't respect myself, I'm not going to respect anyone else in the street.' You have to start by respecting yourself, respect your siblings, and if you learn to respect every-one in the house, you'll learn to respect everyone outside it."

As a young girl, before an abusive home environment sent her to the *basurero* to work, Irina dreamed of being a doctor or a secretary. Now at *Camino Seguro*, her daughter Irina, Jr., dreamt of being a biochemist, her son Kevin wanted to be a chef, and her son Eduardo aspired to be an investigator.

"My goal is that God permits me to see those dreams (real-ized) in my lifetime," she shared in *Manos de Madre*. "To be together with them when they see their goals realized. I want to leave my children my biography, so they'll know I fought for them."

Camino Seguro staff held her aloft as an example of a mother who overcame pain and hardship to push open new doors and opportunities for herself. Her ability to read and her diploma did wonders for her self-esteem.

"You can see it in their faces and body language," said the volunteer. Learning to read gives them a "new sense of empowerment."

BACK IN YARMOUTH, MAINE, the pain of Hanley's tragic death lingered not just for her family, dear friends, and those who had grown close to her through Safe Passage. An entire community felt a sense of kinship with the project in the Gua-temala City garbage dump—even if they had only heard Han-ley's speak once or shaken her hand for a moment. As such, Jane couldn't go to Hannaford's Supermarket off Route 1 for months without a cashier or a fellow shopper weeping as they brought up Safe Passage and the loss of Hanley, no matter that they were a total stranger. This was the same neighborhood grocery store which Jane had visited a couple years before and, overhearing the number of people in the checkout line buzzing about the project, she had emailed Hanley to boast "we've made it!"

"It was symbolic that I couldn't even go there because I just couldn't handle the overwhelming conversations," said Jane. "People tend to be kind and helpful, but it was just too much."

The publicity that followed Hanley's death—the incredible story of this "angel of the garbage dump" who gave up so much to devote her life to help the poorest of the poor in Guatemala—generated a flood of financial support, donations, and new child sponsorships in 2007 and 2008, in Maine, in Michigan, in North Carolina, and across Europe where former volunteers shared their stories and passed the hat. Safe Passage's revenues would top $2 million in the year after her death. The U.S. economy was humming, optimism abounded, and people wanted to travel abroad and do good.

Then on Sept. 15, 2008, in New York City, Lehman Brothers collapsed, bursting the subprime mortgage bubble. The bankruptcy sent stock markets on a downward spiral, which resulted in the largest global economic recession since the Great Depression. Americans lost millions in 2008 and 2009, some lost their life savings, and many clung much tighter to their checkbooks. The expression "When the U.S. economy sneezes, Latin America catches a cold" rang true in Guatemala, and particularly at Safe Passage, which relied on donations from supporters in the United States and all over the developed world.

According to a story in *Vice Magazine*, "Direct investment in Guatemala dropped 20 percent between 2008 and 2009 (it recovered the following year), and the bottom fell out of the economy. At the same time, the price of basic commodities began to skyrocket—the cost of providing food for a family in Guatemala grew 50 percent from 2007 to 2011. The construction jobs that many poor people had relied on disappeared, and remittances sent to Guatemalans from friends and relatives abroad plunged 10 percent from 2008 to 2009. Guatemala's rate of GPD growth dropped from 6.3 percent in 2007 to a low of just 0.5 percent in 2009. By then, the entire world was suffering the effects of a recession, and poor Guatemalans were hit especially hard."

Rachel, who officially became the project's U.S. director in early 2008, remembers joining a conference call from Guatemala with Betsey Anderson (who was then the board's development chair) and board member John Gundersdorf to review the budget and revenue projections. Safe Passage faced a $200,000 gap at a time when the global economic recession was shaking every sector. "Rachel, what are your thoughts on how we can close that gap?" John asked. Rachel felt paralyzed by the situation. Perhaps it was the first time she truly worried about whether Hanley's project would survive. Her voice cracked and she asked, "Can we have this call later?" The reality facing Safe Passage felt overwhelming. Not just the economic crisis, but also having an executive director who was difficult for some people to connect to as she was deliberately different than Hanley, and change after change to the program that could make it hard to engage supporters in the same way as before. Rachel knew that Safe Passage faced a moment of reckoning.

For Barbara Nijhuis, who had accepted the excruciating task of stepping into Hanley's shoes when she took the helm in the summer of 2007—and had to make the unpopular moves of shutting down the Casa Hogar, the hotel, and the workshops, and reducing the gifts that *guajero* families received for sending their kids to school—the financial crisis and dwindling support made her job all the more difficult. Nevertheless, Barbara ran Safe Passage with far more structure and organizational capacity than it had before. Under her leadership, the project was more formally divided into specific departments, each with their own goals and priorities.

"There was obviously no one else with the charisma of Hanley," observed the Swiss accountant Marc Wuthrich. "Barbara was not the same fundraiser [as Hanley]. We had to shrink the program a bit by closing these items."

She stayed until August 2010. John Gundersdorf took over as interim executive director until the end of that year. Meanwhile, Sharon Workman vacated her seat as board chair—which she had held since Paul Sutherland stepped down six months after Hanley's death. Sharon's husband Wayne filled her seat on the board of directors, and Deb Walters, who had conducted the fact-finding mission with Sharon just after Hanley's death, became the new board chair.

Deb, an avid long-distance kayaker and adventurous spirit in her mid-50s who had recently retired from a career in academia, took a hands-on approach and interacted directly with members of the community. On one visit to the garbage dump she met a *guajero* woman who had retrieved a gold ring by diving into the river that runs beneath the trash at the bottom of the ravine. "I could understand the excitement about what might be found," she later told *The Rotarian* magazine. "But that river is toxic enough to dissolve a boat."

Safe Passage Becomes
its Own School

A FAMILIAR FACE BECAME SAFE PASSAGE'S THIRD executive director in January 2011. It was Richard Schmaltz, a Canadian who had come to Guatemala in 1999 together with his wife Susan, who had dreams of providing educational support for impoverished communities in Central America. They had met Hanley through God's Child Project, the nonprofit near Antigua where she had first worked, and she and Susan became fast friends. In 2001 the Schmaltzs had launched a preschool program and clean water project in the village of Sacala, near Chimaltenango. Two years later, their project became Planting Seeds, which promotes early childhood education for those in extreme poverty, using a Montessori-based philosophy of child-centered, activity-based education. That same year they formed a partnership with Safe Passage to operate a two-room preschool pilot program for *guajero* children. The relationship with Planting Seeds was a win-win for Safe Passage. The Schmaltzs built desks and all the furniture and materials needed for the classrooms and the daycare center. Planting Seeds would help Hanley build her early childhood education program, develop the nursery school curriculum, and train teachers to employ that method in the classroom.

"From the standpoint of managing the facility, the only thing we were directly responsible for was providing the salaries of people who worked there and providing lunch," said Ed Mahoney.

Once he took over Safe Passage in 2011, Richard quickly realized that one of the project's biggest hurdles was that it was built around outsourcing education to Guatemala City's public schools. The students spent only half a day at Safe Passage's educational reinforcement program, where they received tutoring, meals, emotional and social support, and engaged in extra-curricular activities like music, sports and arts. But the other half of the day they wallowed in large class sizes run by poorly trained and underpaid teachers in often mediocre schools that taught in a way that Safe Passage had little control over. The homework they brought to the half-day reinforcement program, either before school or after school, often involved rote memorization of numbers, words, or sentences. Furthermore, the various schools attended by Safe Passage students required different books, uniforms, shoes, and workbooks. The project provided all school supplies, and it devoted vast resources to its staff running around Guatemala City gathering those supplies so the kids could attend public school, and its social workers constantly checking in with teachers at those schools. All these factors resulted in high failure and drop-out rates, said Susanna Place.

The six students accepted in 2006 at the prestigious all-male Kinal technical school—including Wilmer, Angel and Tomas, whom Paul Sutherland mentioned in his eulogy for Hanley—also didn't fare well. Sharon Workman remembered they had a difficult time adjusting to the cultural differences and academic expectations at Kinal and ended up dropped out within a year or two.

Richard favored keeping the project's approximately 550 students on one campus for the entire day so they could receive a high-quality education that would be more enriching than simply memorizing images on a chalkboard. "The Board believed that having a private school would give more control over quality of education and increase likelihood of academic success," said Sharon. With the board's support, in 2012 Safe Passage implemented a five-year transition that started with opening the "Hanley Denning Primary School" in 2013 with grades 1–3. In the following years, the program would add one more grade each year. Initially, Safe Passage used Planting Seeds' Montessori-based child-centered approach and in 2015 incorporated an expeditionary learning model as its guiding pedagogy. Richard spent much of his time at the helm laying the groundwork for Safe Passage's transition away from educational reinforcement and toward an actual school.

However, a downside that some in the *guajero* community and some staff perceived was that—when it became a school—Safe Passage no longer focused as much on social work, outreach, handouts, and meeting the psychological and everyday needs of the garbage dump community. As a school, Safe Passage now focused on direct educational attention, and it needed to produce results. More than half a dozen students who had learning difficulties were not invited back to the new Safe Passage school. "Se cambió," Hanley's project had *changed*, said some frustrated members of the community.

Another significant hurdle Richard faced was that he didn't speak Spanish, or at least not well enough to engage with the community as Hanley had. Instead Richard relied on certain Guatemalan staff members to interpret for him and to act as his eyes and ears. That created what some long-term volunteers described as a culture of mistrust among Safe Passage staff. The board of directors interacted mostly with Richard as executive director, which meant that the organization's leadership often seemed disconnected to realities on the ground, or at least that's how some *guajero* families saw it. To some who had known Hanley, Safe Passage now felt more businesslike.

Mary Jo Amani reflected on the challenges that Richard's language barriers posed for the organization. "The hard part if you don't speak Spanish—it's not so much the families that need to hear from you, but you could do that with an interpreter," she said. "It's the staff, because you don't get the nuances and information from them. How can you run a meeting and have things translated for you constantly? You don't know what's happening half the time."

By the time Richard stepped down in December 2013, Safe Passage was on a path to phase out its educational reinforcement model and operate schools at the pre-kindergarten, elementary and middle school levels. The program already had the early childhood education program including the newly registered "Escuelita Hanley Denning" for preschool-aged students, the Hanley Denning Primary School, the educational reinforcement center where children received nutritious meals and access to homework help, medical care, social and psychological services, sports and art programing, English and computer skills, a library, and a safe place to socialize. Safe Passage also had the *Próximo Paso* "Next Step" program which was created to assist high school graduates transition to internships, jobs and continuing education opportunities. And it had the Creamos women's social entrepreneurship program, which taught mothers income-earning skills and small business management. In 2014, the women's jewelry business which employed more than 30 mothers, including Irina Rodríguez Cotto, became its own registered NGO.

Mary Jo's husband, the former USAID employee Todd Amani, took over Safe Passage in 2014 and served until October 2017. After that, Mary Jo, herself, served as interim director for nearly a year until Safe Passage's fifth executive director, Trae Holland, was hired in 2018.

While he was inspired by what Hanley had started, Todd was also moved by his predecessor Richard's vision of turning the organization from a reinforcement program to the full-day school. That transition faced more obstacles under Todd's watch. In 2015, in fact, several dozen *guajeros* and community members protested and managed to shut down Safe Passage for two days. They were upset that some students with learning difficulties weren't permitted to continue at the school, and they called for certain Guatemalan staff members to be fired.

"Parents didn't feel like they were involved in decisions," remembered Wayne Workman, who was board chair at the time. "There was a feeling of families and networks breaking down. And a few senior Guatemalan staff members were not acting as team players, and staff underneath them felt disempowered and dissatisfied. That feeling translated out to the kids and their parents, and that caused an insurrection."

Some of those disaffected families met and negotiated with Todd, changes in management were made, followed by efforts to heal wounds, and the project reopened. Wayne described that as the "beginning of a better era."

Many *guajeros* and community members spoke of Safe Passage as a different organization than the one they had known while Hanley was alive. *"Ya cambió,"* they said. But that change was inevitable, and perhaps necessary. The project may not have survived its frenetic pace and impulsive decisions. The Casa Hogar and the hotel, as well as the ancillary workshops, had to go. And the program's educational reinforcement support to what students learned at local public schools sometimes yielded a tenuous relationship. It's true that Safe Passage was no longer exactly what Hanley had created, but it continued to do her important work of pulling children out of the garbage dump and off the dangerous streets, and offering them a chair in school and a path out of extreme poverty.

"She had a vision. She accomplished a great deal in the time that she had," reflected Susanna Place, who served on the board until 2012 and left after Richard was hired. "But her vision was like a flower. It was just beginning to take shape and had not fully bloomed or matured."

Mary Jo predicted that, had Hanley survived, she would have evolved along with the project. She also would have pivoted toward Safe Passage becoming its own school rather than acting indefinitely as an educational reinforcement project.

"Hanley was also a progressive, an excellent educator," said Mary Jo. "The values this school has are values we were trying to [uphold] even before we became a school. The very curriculum we have now she would have 100 percent supported."

In 2014, in preparation for adding future grades, Safe Passage purchased a new "Blue Building" property near the primary school. Two years later, the project's multipurpose center was built to house all part-time program activities, including after-school tutoring, the Next Step program, Creamos, skills building workshops, and Saturday clubs.

TODAY, IMAGES OF HANLEY are visible everywhere you look at Safe Passage and throughout Zone 3. Some say they feel her presence here. In the reception area of the administrative building, Michigan photographer Beth Price's portrait of Hanley in her pink blouse, smiling and staring into the camera, with a blurry landscape of kids in the background, hangs on the wall. The words "We have work to do" are printed underneath in bold letters. Before their official Safe Passage tour begins, guests and volunteers sit in the waiting room and watch Leslie Iwerks' and Mike Glad's brief video testimonial to Hanley—featuring scenes from *Recycled Life* and from her funeral processional in Guatemala City.

In the nearby medical clinic building, a drawing of a determined Hanley, her gaze straight ahead, her hands reaching down to embrace a child nuzzling their face against her stomach, is taped to the window next to bulletin board. In the main school building, a two-foot tall painting of a young Hanley, smiling, her hair pulled back in a ponytail, and wearing earrings and a grey-collared shirt, peers out from a blue wall. On both sides of the picture are Safe Passage posters that feature children in school uniforms while standing on the edge of the garbage dump. The words "vision" and "mission" appear in both English and Spanish. T-shirts worn by the students carry her name just above Safe Passage's logo of the doorframe opening to a staircase. The words "esperanza, educación, and oportunidad" sport the back of the t-shirts. *Hope, education, opportunity.*

"I see her picture and it inspires me now," said Mary Jo.

Another small but symbolic change that Todd Amani made at Safe Passage was to intentionally remember and celebrate Hanley on her birthday, March 9, not the anniversary of her death, January 18.

"When I started, there was an altar with flowers and a big picture of her [on the date of her death]. She wouldn't have done that," said Todd. "We wanted to celebrate her life, not her death. Instead, on her birthday we celebrate her and what she brought. In the Creamos program they show the video of her and talk about her values and how she worked with the community. We try to pull out an example of something for the kids, but not worship her as a saint. I think it was a little overdone, the sainthood."

More than 15 years after her passing, there are no students at Safe Passage, and very few staff members, who personally knew Hanley. She and her dream are shared through stories, through photos and artwork. Many of the project's major donors knew her and still tell stories of how she convinced them that supporting the *guajero* community in the Guatemala City garbage dump was a noble undertaking and deserved their support.

"Even now, a good portion of the base still has roots in Hanley," said Todd. "But every year it's less so."

For staff and volunteers today, the draw to serve Safe Passage isn't the founder, but the children and the community.

"If I ask why people are here today, it's rarely because of Hanley anymore," said Mary Jo. "It's the children who inspire them, just like the children inspired Hanley.... Hanley gave the structure for this to happen—a wonderful structure that allows us to use our skills and talents to help these students today."

The World Shuts Down

At 3 p.m. on Friday, March 13, 2020, Trae Holland, Safe Passage's gregarious and energetic executive director since 2018, met with his staff in the *comedor* cafeteria to discuss basic information about the frightening COVID-19 pandemic, which was spreading across the globe and killing tens of thousands of people in its path. The bright sunshine above the open-air courtyard seemed to defy the looming darkness. For several weeks, Trae had been following the news from China, Europe, and the Middle East, and making contingency plans within the organization in case the coronavirus came to Guatemala.

"We gave a science presentation. We wanted to shore up people's understanding of what the disease was," said Trae, who remembered the staff exchanging hugs, kisses, well wishes and salutations of "see you on Monday."

Trae, a Georgia native who grew up in Florida, had become the project's fifth leader in July 2018 at age 51 after running a nonprofit international school in Quito, Ecuador, for grades preschool through 12. Prior to that, he was a high school and middle school teacher, and development director at Polk Museum of Art in Florida. Trae's ambitious task was to continue the program's expansion of its all-day school, and eventually a high school, too. In 2018 Safe Passage added sixth grade to complete its primary school and implemented a Science,

Technology, Engineering, Arts, and Mathematics pilot in all primary grades. The school library also expanded to include bilingual books and online resources. The following year, Safe Passage inaugurated its middle school with the first class of seventh graders, and eighth and ninth grade in 2020 and 2021. All 36 students moved from ninth grade into "Oportunidades," which is Safe Passage's high school-level half-day program, with students spending the other half day in external schools.

Amidst the project's growth support, Trae took it upon himself to continue to incorporate Hanley's vibrant presence, love, and care within Safe Passage. Upon taking the helm, he understood that Hanley's figure was still everywhere in the DNA of the organization. Trae was so curious to learn about her that he reached out to people who had known her.

2020 was to represent Safe Passage's 20th year since Hanley opened the doors of La Iglesia and the addition of a full-day eighth grade as part of the project's middle school expansion. But the arrival of the coronavirus dealt what Trae called "a triple pandemic"—which included the viral threat, itself; a precarious economic situation in Guatemala, and the already prevailing danger of living in Zone 3.

Monday, March 16, never came. On the same day Trae met with his Safe Passage staff in the cafeteria, the country confirmed its first case of COVID-19—a Guatemalan man who had returned to La Aurora airport from coronavirus-ravaged Italy along with two family members and five Salvadorans on an Aeromexico flight. A day earlier, Guatemala had banned entry to citizens of all European countries, as well as Iran, China, and South Korea. On Sunday, March 15, the country registered its first COVID-19 death, an 85-year-old man who had arrived from Madrid with his family nine days earlier.

That weekend, Guatemalan President Alejandro

Giammattei, a retired surgeon who had taken office in January, canceled all public events and gatherings of more than 100 people. Public and private schools and universities would shutter for at least three weeks, and Easter holy week celebrations in early April would also be canceled. On Monday, March 16, Guatemala began restricting travel to visitors from the United States and Canada. Five days later, a nationwide curfew took effect. Giammattei had reason to worry about COVID spreading through Guatemala. The country reportedly had less than one hospitable bed available per 1,000 inhabitants and only 60 respiratory ventilators in swiftly constructed temporary hospitals to serve a population of nearly 17 million.

Guatemala shut down. The entire world was shutting down. Safe Passage faced yet another existential threat, and this time no one knew exactly what it meant or how long it would take to overcome this new and global tragedy.

FOR A TIME, THE DAILY CURFEWS imposed on Guatemalans and suspension of public transportation almost certainly slowed the spread of the virus. But for the nearly 70 percent of the Guatemalan population who live from day to day working in the country's vast, unregulated informal economy, the shutdown also risked putting them on a path to starvation. Many had no monetary savings and no stash of food to get them through the lockdown. The roughly 12 percent of the country's gross national product that comes from remittances sent from Guatemalan migrants in the United States dried up, too. Guatemala's children—now deprived of school—were in particular danger. More than 60 percent of the population lives in poverty, and the country has one of the highest rates of childhood mal-nutrition in the world.

In early April the village of Patzún, a large agriculture-producing community near Lake Atitlán, detected the first community spread of the coronavirus and was subjected to a strict quarantine, with no one entering or exiting the town of 58,000. Soon after that, people holding white flags began to appear on the streets of Guatemala City and elsewhere in the country. Their *banderas blancas* signified not surrender but hunger. As a story in *The Guardian* newspaper reported, flags of various colors reflected an entire lexicon of need. White meant the household had no food; red meant they needed medicine; black, yellow, or blue meant that a woman, child, or elderly person was in danger of violence.

With the promise of COVID vaccines still many long months away, protests soon erupted as trust in President Giammattei's government sank to new lows. By June, the number of people facing hunger in Guatemala had doubled, prompting demonstrations in front of the Guatemalan Congress that called on the government to ease coronavirus lockdown restrictions. MEANWHILE, IN THE MIDST OF THE PANDEMIC, three-quarters of members of the Guatemalan Congress approved a 2021 budget—which was later scrapped—that sought to cut health, education, and human rights spending, while increasing meal stipends for members of Congress and prioritizing major infrastructure plans. In early November, two massive hurricanes, Eta and Iota, pummeled Guatemala and disproportionally affected rural areas with high levels of extreme poverty. Against this backdrop, thousands protested in mid-November 2020 against Giammattei's government and the proposed budget. Some demonstrators lit the Congress building on fire.

Rudimentary government services broke down during the pandemic. Guatemala City residents in Zones 3 and 7 could rarely count on daily access to water even before COVID— sometimes it flowed only once a week. They often had to buy it from water trucks which visited the *barrio* near the garbage dump and charged them 12 quetzales, or $1.50, for a barrel of water that wasn't necessarily potable. Water trucks sometimes ran out before they could serve residents on the next block. But with the economy shut down and travel restricted, the water trucks no longer serviced the garbage dump community. Zones 3 and 7, among the poorest areas of Guatemala City, received the lowest priority from city government. And yet the importance of water to drink, water to cook with, and water to wash hands, was amplified during the pandemic, particularly for the community served by Safe Passage.

The garbage dump itself closed down in March, depriving thousands of *guajeros* their only source of income. It opened a couple times during the early months of the pandemic, but then closed just as suddenly. Sometimes garbage trucks just came and left trash in the streets around the *basurero* to let the workers pick through it there. By some estimates, the *guajeros* lost 60 percent of their income during 2020—a burden exacerbated by the fact that they were forced to pay as much as 33 percent in extortion money to gangs. With an unstable economy, and a day-to-day power structure that was severely altered, the gangs who dominated the garbage dump *barrios*—grew more violent, and they acted in less predictable ways. "The gangs have lost their minds and engaged in ultraviolence," observed Trae Holland. When they couldn't extort money, the gangs sometimes demanded that a family hand over their daughter instead. Girls around Guatemala City disappeared.

INTO THIS VOID left by a lack of social services, education, and nutrition, Safe Passage stepped up. The project had overcome one deeply personal tragedy and survived an economic recession. In some ways, *Camino Seguro* applied the resilience it learned from those experiences to this new and more widespread threat. After the country shut down on March 13, Trae's teachers and staff worked around the clock to find innovative solutions to communicate with their students, even as they could no longer meet in person. The *guajero* families didn't have computers in their homes, but most of them did have mobile telephones—70–80 percent of them, estimated Trae. Those that didn't have phones could borrow them from neighbors in the *barrio* who did. So, when Safe Passage sent the first food disbursements and care packages, along with cleaning supplies, to families in late March, two weeks into the lockdown, they included educational curriculum packets to help the students learn.

During a two-day stretch in early April, Safe Passage staff distributed 400 bags of food from the temporarily-opened Colegio facility. During Easter week, when the project closed, families received vouchers to shop at local bodega markets. Later in the spring, *guajero* families stood socially distanced and took temperature checks before they picked up food supplies to bring back to their home. The innovative outreach helped lift people like Wendy Navas, the mother of a student at Camino Seguro whose husband works in the *basurero* but was unemployed for five months when it shut down. Those students whose families couldn't help them with their homework also received "second-chance" study guides. The social worker team also set up a phone/text message "tree" with families in the *colonia*. During the shutdown, social workers contacted each family at least once a week to monitor their health and stress levels. A teacher ambassador checked student performance and the level of parental support in the homes.

In June, Safe Passage published a video filmed in the home of a second-grader named Santiago who thanked the project for a table full of essential foods delivered to his family's home in the *barrio*, including flour, beans, salt, sugar rice, "atole" corn-meal, masks, toothbrushes, toothpaste, oil, toilet paper soap, shampoo, sanitary wipes, a towel and detergent. "And thanks to my teachers that sent me my homework. I'm learning a lot at home," Santiago added. "I miss you so much. I want to be with you."

In an effort to maintain the connection with their students, teachers also wrote personalized notes of encouragement to each of their pupils. Many students responded with their own letters. "I work hard studying and doing my homework," said Santiago. "And thank you for my letters. They were beautiful."

Meanwhile, Safe Passage teachers created digital videos and Zoom-style Google classrooms that were accessible from mobile phones through WhatsApp, so they could continue to interact with their students, whether or not they had access to a computer, or even electricity at home. Safe Passage established a telemedicine model, too, and the program's pediatrician worked with two local pharmacies each time a critical medical situation arose in the community. New packets of educational materials, study guides, food and hygienic supplies were sent to families every two weeks, and by June the mobile curriculum included hands-on learning projects and even home science experiments. In keeping with the flexible expeditionary learning model, sixth graders were able to complete at-home projects which included creating their own model butterfly gardens or 3D cityscapes out of newspaper, cardboard, glue and other available materials.

"I will forever be inspired by the images of our students crafting their homework expeditions in the dim light of their homes," Susanna Place was quoted in Safe Passage's Fall 2020 newsletter.

At the end of the 2020–21 school year, according to Trae, 552 Safe Passage students (92 percent of the total student body) passed the Ministry of Education's strict requirements for passing into the next grade. Almost that same number were expected to pass during the 2021-22 school year. Each year since Safe Passage became a formal school, approximately 40 students continue to graduate to elementary and middle school, as well as adult education programs, and COVID didn't stop that.

The project helped the community in other ways, too. On several occasions, when the municipality faced a worker shortage at the water plant and shut off water access to Zones 3 and 7 for days, Safe Passage collaborated with the local municipality and REDES, a group of Guatemalan nonprofits, to pool their resources and bring in water tanks. During 2021, the partnership delivered roughly 117,000 gallons of water to the community. Trae's staff also provided N95 masks and personal protective equipment to Ministry of Health workers active in Zone 3 when the government ran out of them. And when an officer at a local police station tested positive for COVID-19 and the city all but abandoned him at his post, it was Safe Passage that brought him food.

"When the virus started, the dump closed and fear began to mount, our community members looked for solidity somewhere," said Trae. "The government wasn't supplying enough news, but Safe Passage was able to be a lynchpin of the community. We've leveraged 20 years of trust building here. That investment paid off during the COVID crisis. The *guajeros* believed in us."

The pandemic posed as Safe Passage's second great existential crisis, said Trae. The first was Hanley's death 13 years prior. Here, once again, the relationships and trust that she helped build among the *guajero* community when she walked into the garbage dump as a skinny, naïve, and hopeful gringa with her backpack and telltale blonde ponytail—this trust allowed her organization to act as a hub for the community during these frightening and bewildering months.

Trae credited Hanley's enduring legacy with helping to guide the project through its response to the pandemic, even as many other nonprofits and non-governmental organizations ran into walls, fired staff, and sometimes closed entirely during COVID; an Associated Press story in March 2021 reported that more than one-third of U.S. nonprofits were in jeopardy of closing within two years because of the financial harm inflicted by the pandemic. Meanwhile, Safe Passage thrived. During 2020, the project netted its highest fundraising year ever, reaching approximately $2.5 million. He lauded the bedrock relationship with stakeholders, donors, and organizations that supported Safe Passage even after face-to-face learning was shut down.

"We're not a distant, theoretical concept," said Trae. "They give support because of the hands-on relationship we have with them. We don't just want your money, we want something deeper."

Safe Passage teachers and staff continued to work with students and families as well as they could through online learning throughout 2020 and much of 2021. Nevertheless, the lack of face-to-face contact and the inability of students to leave their *barrios* and come to the project to learn in a safe environment hurt students in a variety of ways. Families involved with Safe Passage lost more people to suicide and alcohol poisoning than to COVID itself, said Trae, who added that the project saw a 50-percent increase in child abuse and spousal abuse in the homes. Gang warfare affected neighborhoods across Guatemala City, Zones 3 and 7 in particular, as a former Safe Passage student was murdered and a current student was arrested for carrying a gun in her backpack to a funeral. Isolated from the physical school setting, more and more students were falling prey to gang recruitment.

"Every day that passed, we were losing our relevance," said Trae. "The key to Safe Passage is creating hope and a sense of one's self. This crisis has isolated students so we couldn't mentor them, we couldn't intervene in their lives. We had students running away from home. We had spousal abuse. We had three suicides among fathers."

The pandemic lockdown also threatened to derail Safe Passage's hard work to implement sexual and personal health trainings. When Trae arrived in 2018, many female students in the project were still getting pregnant and dropping out of school, but the first months of 2020—before the pandemic shut down the school—yielded not a single unplanned pregnancy. Then the daily contact with the community was severed. "We went months and months without seeing the kids," lamented Trae.

The lockdown and frequent closing of the garbage dump wrought havoc on the local *guajero* economy. Trae counted more than 10 Safe Passage middle school students who took jobs to help their families make ends meet. One worked at a bakery, another in a mechanic shop. In addition, the shutdown adversely affected their scavenger microeconomy. The money they got for selling plastics had declined; earnings from tortillas sold in the *barrios* had also plummeted. Meanwhile, the cost of fresh fruit has risen.

Despite these COVID setbacks, Safe Passage continued to adapt and find innovative, new ways to serve its communities. On September 28, 2021, the project hosted its first vaccination clinic, which the Guatemalan army held in its multipurpose center. Between 8 a.m. and 8 p.m. on that day, military doctors administered 600 Pfizer vaccines while local staff facilitated the flow of people. By Trae's estimates, that number who received jabs represented around 30 percent of the total *Camino Seguro* community and roughly 1.5 percent of the total garbage dump community. On November 30, Safe Passage held another *jornada*, or medical clinic, and this time administered 450 vaccinations. And in early February 2022, the national *Centro de Salud* health center vaccinated 211 students, ages 12–17.

"This was a huge step for us," reflected Trae. "We've always seen ourselves as life-saving in our education, in our health and outreach. But to be actively involved in making sure shots were put in arms was a game changer for us and the community."

A whopping 97 percent of staff at Safe Passage got vaccinated, in large part because they and the community trusted the organization. For them, that trust overcame rampant misinformation they may have heard in the community, such as falsehoods about vaccines inserting a microchip into one's arm or even changing one's sexual orientation. Lies like those affected the vaccination campaign elsewhere in Guatemala. In early October 2021, in Alta Verapaz province north of Guatemala City, anti-vaccine villagers attacked and temporarily took hostage nurses who were administering COVID vaccines. The mob eventually released the nurses, but destroyed 50 vaccines doses they carried. By July 2022, 45 percent of Guatemalans had received at least one vaccine dose.

The vaccines that reached Safe Passage didn't come a moment too soon. A staff member was hospitalized in critical condition in January 2021, but survived. To date, the project has not lost any students or employees to the pandemic.

I spoke to Trae via Zoom on November 3, 2021, as he rocked back and forth in his chair out of joy while sitting in his office two blocks from the entrance to the dump. Students had just returned for face-to-face learning the day before, a couple weeks after Safe Passage received a special waiver from the Ministry of Education to resume in-person learning, albeit with students practicing social distancing and wearing masks. They would attend classes for a week before taking a six-week break for the holiday season—as per academic tradition in Guatemala—and resume school on campus in January 2022.

After 20 months of isolation, they were finally out of their *barrios* and back in the school building. The children sat, masked and socially distanced, at every third or fourth small brown desk—with the unoccupied tables between them marked with X's—raising their hands and interacting with teachers standing at the front of the classroom, just as they had done before the pandemic.

Trae had joked to me during an earlier conversation that Safe Passage might need to stock up on extra belts once in-person classes finally resumed because malnourished and hungry kids might not fit into their uniforms. In fact, when they did return on Nov. 2, teachers didn't immediately recognize some of their students. The pandemic had affected everyone in profound ways. Their voices had changed, they were older.

Much of the staff workload that first week focused on doing academic assessments and diagnostics, and checking the students' health, their weight, the condition of their teeth, and looking for any visible signs of abuse.

"They had to relearn what it was like to be in a classroom. It seemed alien to them at first," said Trae, who noticed how quiet the campus felt during those first few hours. "But as the day progressed, the volume in the classrooms increased. They started to laugh more."

Trae wasn't sure yet when volunteers and service-learning groups from North America and Europe would be permitted to return to Safe Passage. Their role had been a central part of Hanley's dream for the project, whether they came with classroom skills or not. She wanted them to come and see for themselves, and help while they were in Guatemala, but also become ambassadors and spread the word back home.

But now they had been gone. Nearly two years without volunteers had given Safe Passage the opportunity to rethink the program and take it back to the drawing board.

"I believe it's time to professionalize our volunteer program," said Trae. "We've got to get away from 'voluntourism.'"

"It's hard to take an 18-year-old with no Spanish and no pedagogical training and put them in the classroom. I think it's time to actively recruit certain profiles of volunteers." That could include college students who create their own social-service learning components who fulfill a distinct need at Safe Passage, and get academic credit for it, he suggested. "There's nothing you can't study here. We've got sanitation issues; we've got gender equity; we've got gang violence. There's so much community need, and we're a prime place to be a source."

Trae emphasized that he also recognized the importance of support teams who visit for a week and engage in a particular Safe Passage project, albeit not always in the classroom, as well as gap-year students who volunteer for longer stretches. "They come down and see the students. That's how we build a future wave of support," he said.

Safe Passage had not set a date, but hopes to welcome back volunteers sometime in late 2022 or 2023—potentially in concert with the opening of the project's new Basico building for high school students, which was slated to be completed in June 2023. Trae spent much of the pandemic lockdown working with his staff to reinvent the high school program, assess each student, and craft programs that fit the interests of those students. They also used the time to grow Safe Passage's *Próximo Paso* "next step" program which matched students with corporate partners where they could intern or work. The project's aim was to land 15 students with internships in 2022. Other lofty goals, as Safe Passage hoped to emerge from the pandemic, could include a daycare center, a community center, and a teacher training institute.

Trae didn't sit long in his office during those joyous early days of November 2021 when students returned to school. His habit is to travel frequently to Safe Passage's other campuses, including the *Jardín*—the community garden built by University of Washington students outside the *guarderia*—and the multipurpose center on the edge of the *basurero*. Wherever he walks he hears the garbage trucks, all day and into the evening, permeating the air with their noxious fumes, their rumbling a constant reminder of the dump's presence, and that down below, in the belly of the landfill, the *guajero* families await their arrival.

"But the most ubiquitous image and symbol of the dump

remains the vultures, flying back and forth in swarms and reminding us of the filth a mere stone's throw away from the paradise we are trying to maintain right in the midst of it all," Trae wrote to me. The vultures, these predatory scavengers, embody everything about the dump. They arrive with the wind that sears down the valley of the dump, filled with dust and particles, creating a veritable miasma. "I will never forget being told that when Hanley first saw the dump, she saw mothers placing their infants in covered cardboard boxes while they worked to keep the vultures from attacking their babies."

"If Hanley could see what we've become, how we weathered this storm, how all the members of the community stepped up and leaned in, she would be so proud," said Trae. "The organization is not just making it but thriving in this difficult time."

"I want to take the kids on a day trip to the beach," Hanley once told Lety Mendez, seemingly out of the blue. The children of the garbage dump had probably never visited Guatemala's black sand Pacific coast, with its hatching turtles and mangroves. Transporting dozens of kids out of the capital on a daylong trip on buses the project didn't own seemed like a logistical nightmare. But on numerous occasions Hanley pulled it off. "Her imagination was enormous," said Lety.

Michigan photographer Beth Price's portrait of Hanley in her pink blouse smiling in the foreground, juxtaposed against a blurry background of guajero kids huddled in the back of a room, is prominently displayed at Safe Passage today. (BETH PRICE)

Ripples in a Pond

HANLEY DENNING HAS BEEN GONE for more than 15 years now. *Camino Seguro*, the educational reinforcement program she birthed in the abyss of the Guatemala City garbage dump has lived longer *without* her than it did with her. Her closest students, employees, volunteers and many of her supporters have moved on. But inspired by her and by their own experiences at the project, many have continued down the path of humanitarian assistance and nonprofit development work. The time they spent with Hanley—intense, jarring, scary, empowering, joyful, overwhelming, committed, tragic—forever changed them. This blonde-haired *gringa* from Maine tossed the stone. Her students and families, employees, volunteers and supporters are the waves that continue to ripple today.

AFTER HANLEY'S DEATH in January 2007, her mother Marina volunteered at the Safe Passage office in Yarmouth for a time. She offered an emotional and spiritual bridge between the project and its founder. (Hanley's brother Jordan also served on the board of directors) Marina ran errands and made phone calls, and she offered a warm shoulder to cry on whenever a supporter needed to mourn about Hanley. In particular, she consoled Jane

Gallagher, the grassroots organizer who rallied many Mainers behind Safe Passage and who organized the showing of *Recycled Life* to a sellout crowd at Merrill Auditorium just weeks after the accident.

But the omnipresence of Hanley, and her death, in southern Maine became too much for Marina. Like Jane, she began to avoid Hannaford's grocery store. "Everybody knows me. I don't want to talk to people anymore about it," Marina reflected later. The tension within Safe Passage about how close to stay to Hanley's original mission, or let the project evolve, also took their toll. She began to feel as if she didn't belong in Yarmouth any longer.

In 2016 Marina moved to Guatemala. She first settled in Antigua, but the late-night partying and frenzied tourist pace of the town didn't suit her. She soon settled in Panajachel, the village on Lake Atitlán, also dubbed "Gringotenango," where expats shop for Mayan artisan clothing and where they embark on *lancha* motorboats to more remote villages around the *lago*. Like so many visitors before her, Hanley had also fallen in love with this deep, freshwater lake surrounded by active volcanoes. In his 1934 travel book, *Beyond the Mexique Bay*, writer and philosopher Aldous Huxley wrote about Atitlán, "it really is too much of a good thing." For centuries legend held of a sunken city in the middle of the lake containing valuable treasures.

It was as though Marina was embarking on her own odyssey into the land where her lost daughter had discovered her "life of purpose"—to borrow her response after Hanley asked Marina during her last Christmas at home in Maine, "What is the purpose of life?"

Marina stayed in a hotel in Panajachel for the first month and discovered that the store in the lobby sold goods made by women in *Camino Seguro's* Creamos program. Over time she began to meet expats and Guatemalans, alike, who had known Hanley. One Christmas she found an abandoned puppy outside the gate to the house she rented and adopted it. "Charlotte" joined Marina on jogs along the rutted roads between Panajachel and Santa Catarina Palopo to the east. She loved the warm weather, and she found the locals to be warm and friendly. One invited her to a traditional Guatemalan wedding, another owned a motorcycle, and she would sit on the backseat for exciting rides.

"Wow, that was fun. I'd never do this in the United States," she said. "There was no reason for me to go back to Maine. I felt like I belonged here."

Marina returned to the United States for a couple years after she was assaulted and robbed in Panajachel, and Jordan, Seth and Lucas insisted that she was too far away and needed to come home to Yarmouth. For a time, she took care of their father Michael after he suffered a stroke and slipped into dementia, even though they had been divorced for 20 years. Michael has since moved into an assisted care facility and only vaguely remembers that he had a daughter who passed away, and does not remember her name. Marina returned to Lake Atitlán in the spring of 2021.

SISTER REGINA PALACIOS, the nun who joined Hanley on her first visit to the garbage dump in late 1999, returned to the United States after spending seven years in the western Guatemalan highlands and six years in Peru. She currently works as a therapist for unaccompanied minors of Central American immigrants in a shelter run by the Catholic Charities of the Archdiocese of San Antonio, Texas. Regina and her team provide the minors with basic needs and work to reunify them with identified sponsors.

"Being a therapist, I have the privilege of hearing their stories of lack of educational opportunities, poverty, violence, gang and cartel oppression, and the resulting trauma," Regina wrote in an email. "They are only with us a short time but for me it is an opportunity to begin their process of healing and integrating into the North American culture. Our clinical team and program staff assist them in fulfilling their 'journey toward a future of dignity, respect and fulfilled dreams.'

"I know that my first experience with the marginalized families in Antigua, as well as my years in San Marcos, Guatemala, serving in a project for survivors of civil violence, and years near Lima, Peru, counseling and giving workshops on mental health issues, motivated me to choose this current ministry.... Hanley's untimely death was a tremendous loss and a tragic shock to many of us. However, I am sure that Hanley is smiling down on us as we pass on the gift she gave to so many, and acknowledge 'If you dream it, it can happen.'"

THE WHEREABOUTS OF PADRE LUÍS Gonzalo Pérez Bámaca, the priest who lent his small yellow, rat-infested church to Hanley and her project on non-Catholic worship days, are unknown. A secretary I met in 2018 at the nearby parroquia office heard that he may have moved to the United States. I was unable to find and interview him. A website maintained by the Guatemalan Archbishop for a time included the priest's name on a page cryptically titled "Sacerdotes Suspendidos por Otras Razones" (*Priests suspended for other reasons*).

Joan "Juanita" Andersen, the Danish woman who became Hanley's first volunteer and helped welcome *guajero* families into the yellow church next to the garbage dump for the first monthly food giveaway, returned to Denmark in 2003 and, inspired by Hanley, studied international, intercultural social work. She returned to *Camino Seguro* nearly once a year until 2011 when her first child was born. Her visit in 2008, which marked the one-year anniversary of Hanley's death, was marked by tearful speeches and balloons released into the sky over Guatemala City. Joan graduated from Copenhagen College of Social Work in 2007. Today, she works for WeShelter, an organization that supports the homeless in Copenhagen get back on their feet and return to their communities.

MARIBEL CHOLOTIO, Hanley's first employee at *Camino Seguro*, returned in 2005 to her native village of San Juan La Laguna to be closer to her daughter "Hanley" and to escape the toxins of the garbage dump which affected her health. She worked for a different educational reinforcement project called *"Viviamos Mejor"* that helped children become better leaders in their communities. In 2011 she took a job with the Ministry of Education working with 8–9-year-olds at a local school in nearby Tzununa.

"I sometimes tell my kids about my first job in the capital," said Maribel. "Sometimes they don't want to work. But I tell them about working with children in the dump and helping give them what they didn't have. Sometimes the trucks arrived and threw out fruit and vegetables, and the kids ate that. I tell them about how the kids were able to leave the dump and go to school."

Maribel has four children between ages 20 and 8. Her eldest, Hanley, who was born in Guatemala City while she worked for *Camino Seguro*, now has her own daughter named "Haley" whose father, Pedro, drives a tuc-tuc taxi in the village.

"I'm proud to have her name because of the stories my mom has told us about her," Hanley Cholotio told me about Hanley Denning. "I'm proud to have the name of someone who was great with kids, who gave them education. I'm proud of her, even though I don't know her, proud of what she accomplished."

Maribel's cousin Claudio Ramos, the project's first social worker, left Safe Passage a year after Hanley's death and also returned to San Juan. When I met him in 2018, he was driving a tuc-tuc to make a living. Claudio nearly died of COVID-19 in late June 2021. He received supplemental oxygen at home for 10 days, was diagnosed with pulmonary fibrosis and spent more than four months in therapy. He still struggles to breath normally. Maribel estimates that the pandemic has claimed five lives in San Juan, where tourism has been slow to return after the 2020 shutdown.

FREDY MALDONADO, who picked up Hanley the first night she arrived in Guatemala in 1997 to work for God's Child Project and trained her to limit handouts to families—and who later joined *Camino Seguro*, first as a volunteer then as an employee—lives today in Antigua, where he works with, and assists, several nonprofits. Gregarious, well-connected, and fluent in English, Fredy is a bridge between many ex-pats and international donors and development organizations in Antigua. On some days he gathers hundreds of pounds of vegetables and distributes them to schools, hospitals, and orphanages in villages between Antigua and Guatemala City. Following deadly mudslides caused by torrential rains, in 2018 Fredy joined ConstruCasa, an organization that builds concrete block houses, schools, clinics and community centers, and supplies stoves and water filters, to affected rural areas outside Antigua. He also works with a Michigan-based organization called Buckets of Rain to supply food to local families in need.

AFTER HE LEFT *Camino Seguro* in 2010, Ed Mahoney stayed in Antigua and worked for Viaventure, an inbound travel company, until he retired in 2018. Though he cherished his relationship with Hanley, the experience also burned him out, and he never returned to the nonprofit realm. He also never returned to Zone 3 in Guatemala City to visit the project. Ed lives today with Carlos and Lorena Quisquina, whom he met while working for Hanley, in a house they built several years ago near Guatemala's Pacific Coast.

"We had our ups and downs, we had our differences," Ed reflected on Hanley. "But I always respected her. I knew what she was trying to do. Somehow we were always able to put things aside."

LIKE ED, LETY MENDEZ has not visited the project since she left a year after Hanley's death. Today she and her husband operate a print and copy shop in their town of Jocotenango, near Antigua. Over the years, they have on occasion printed fliers, trifolds and business cards for *Camino Seguro*, though the secretary who calls to facilitate the transaction doesn't know Lety or the important role she played beside Hanley. Once in a while Lety smiles when she recognizes a child featured in one of the photos she prints.

In December 2017, Lety sent her 15-year-old son, Pablo Manuel, along with their company's driver, to deliver a package to *Camino Seguro*. When he was just days old, Lety had relented to Hanley's urging and come into the office to work while tiny Pablo Manuel slept in a cardboard box. The boy no longer remembered the project, but when he entered *Camino Seguro*'s main office, he instantly recognized the enormous photo of Hanley Denning on the wall. When Pablo Manuel returned to Jocotenango, he told Lety, "Yo sé quién es Hanley." *I remember Hanley*. His mother smiled.

"We changed lives," Lety reflected. "She changed my life. She showed me compassion. She was also crazy, but her craziness changed the lives of so many kids."

Several years ago, Lety made a routine visit to a bank in Guatemala City to deposit money. Following the quick transaction, the well-dressed young woman behind the counter asked, "¿Algo mas, Seño Lety?" *Do you need anything else?*

"How do you know my name?" She didn't recognize the bank teller.

"*Seño,* you don't know me? My name is Anita. I graduated from *Camino Seguro* and left the garbage dump. You gave me the opportunity and I work here now, thanks to Hanley for believing in me."

Lety simultaneously broke into a wide smile and began to cry. Hanley would be so thrilled to know that another one had made it out.

OF COURSE, NOT EVERY CHILD MADE IT OUT. Some got pregnant or fathered children before they graduated, and had to drop their studies. Ángel Roque, the son of Mamá Roque and one of the very first to be enrolled in *Camino Seguro* that first day when the doors opened at La Iglesia, was reportedly one of Hanley's star pupils, and she held high hopes that he would continue all the way to university. Angel was one of the stand-outs who received a scholarship to study at Kinal. But soon after Hanley died, he impregnated his girlfriend when he was 16 and dropped out of school. If it weren't for the accident, "Hanley might have intervened and convinced him to stay," predicted Mary Jo Amani. Some returned to the dump to help their *guajero* parents in the scavenger economy. Some who left the Casa Hogar after it closed took to the streets and quelled their hunger by sniffing glue. Some joined gangs. Some were killed.

The success stories warm hearts and show the impact of Hanley's work. Stories like Anita, who holds down a stable job working at a bank.

Stories like Nancy Gudiel, the nine-year-old orphan who sold chiclets on the streets, the tough girl who ran away from the Casa Hogar, the program's first graduate, who now works as a clerk in an electronics store. She lives with her husband Daniél, whom she married in 2010, and their two daughters in a far safer neighborhood in Zone 13 of Guatemala City.

Stories like Daniél Osorio, who Hanley put in a safe house after his stepfather was executed by gangs in front of their house, and who fell in love with video while studying at *Camino Seguro*. After graduating, he shot and produced much of the project's marketing footage. Daniél recently received a scholarship to attend a film school in Michoacán, Mexico.

Stories like Iris Ramírez, who once sorted paper and nylon together with her mother in the garbage dump, who stuck with

Camino Seguro—thanks to the support of her "padrino" Phil Kirchner from Yarmouth—graduated from high school at age 18, and received a scholarship from Shared Beat, a Texas-based nonprofit that supports Guatemalans who want to work in healthcare. She is now in medical school in the capital doing clinical rotations at Roosevelt Hospital and attends to a rising number of COVID patients, though the hospital and medical personnel lack sufficient supplies and resources.

"I learn more every day, I love what I do," Iris wrote to me via email. "I love serving people in this way, I love studying medicine, and even after I graduate as a general practitioner and surgeon, I will continue studying." In 2018 she told me she dreamed of one day working in Guatemala's western highlands, where her grandparents lived and where *campesino* peasants with few resources could come and receive care. "When I can do it, I want to set up a hospital that cares for people with low resources ... or I'll go with a group like Doctors Without Borders to care for the neediest people.

"Because of Hanley I am here, and I will be a doctor," wrote Iris. "Hanley gave my life a path and a meaning. I wish I could stand before her and ask what she saw in me."

Stories like Irina Rodríguez Cotto, who worked in the dump after an abusive husband left her and five children to fend for themselves, who joined the adult literacy program, and advanced through the sixth grade just as three of her children had done, and who joined Creamos, *Camino Seguro*'s women's jewelry business.

Not every success story features a student with an advanced degree. Many children stayed in Zone 3 of the capital and their families remained in poverty, but Hanley's light and the years of schooling they received taught them to dream of a life beyond the garbage dump. Some used the skills and connections they acquired at the project to land solid jobs for them or their families. Wayne Workman remembers that one boy he sponsored gave up his spot to study at Safe Passage to his little brother when an opportunity arose for him to work as a mechanic.

HANLEY'S IMPACT RIPPLED beyond the project she started to others who felt inspired to serve the *guajero* community. Fifteen years after her death, Safe Passage is only one of several nonprofits that change lives in Zone 3.

Shannon Moyle, the Canadian who joined *Camino Seguro* as a long-term volunteer and moved into the Casa Hogar in Antigua just two months before Hanley died, worked as a music and movement teacher at the project's early childhood center for nine years. She took over the family nurturing program and used breakdancing and hip-hop music as a way to connect with the older children. In 2016, she and another long-term volunteer, Illinois native Mac Phillips, took over Planting Seeds, the nonprofit founded years earlier by Richard and Susan Schmaltz, which promotes early childhood education using a Montessori-based philosophy of child-centered, activity-based education.

As Safe Passage transitioned toward a formal school, Planting Seeds allowed Shannon to immerse herself directly in the *barrios*, enter families' homes, and become part of the community. Like Hanley, Shannon also arrived in Guatemala speaking hardly a word of Spanish. Where Hanley once walked with tennis shoes, khaki pants, her pink blouse, and a backpack hanging from one shoulder, here was Shannon, another seemingly fearless, tall, fair-skinned North American woman. Shannon wore tight leggings and a black t-shirt as she and a teenage girl breakdanced to hip-hop music pumping from a portable boom-box on the open concrete in front of a Pentecostal church in the *colonia* as curious toddlers looked on.

Hanley's style this was not, but you could almost feel her spirit and connection to the families reincarnated in Shannon.

"The kids really identify with the way I dress, the way I speak, the fact that I know what music they listen to," said Shannon. "It has helped me gain the respect of the kids. It's not like I walked in wearing a dress and carrying a briefcase. This has been my gateway into their community."

Through her early childhood work, the kids of the *barrio* went home and talked about Shannon, her music, her dance moves. Soon the parents began to ask about her. Through their children they began to trust her, in the way that Hanley gained the trust of *guajero* families years before. Soon Shannon was invited to birthday parties, and she would share meals with families.

"I'm not here for the paycheck," she said. "I'm here for them."

I had to hurry to keep up with Shannon on a walk through the *colonia* in March 2018, as excited children and families jumped out from houses on both sides of the narrow lane to greet her—just as volunteers had struggled to keep up with Hanley during her busy jaunts through the same neighborhoods 15 years earlier. Just a few months before my visit, a gang shootout had left bullet pockmarks in the concrete walls. An innocent family was hit, including an eight-year-old girl and her older sister, a Safe Passage graduate. Miraculously, no one was killed.

Nevertheless, Shannon told me, life in the *colonia* is far better now than it was when Hanley launched *Camino Seguro* in 2000. A different nonprofit had built block concrete houses to replace the sheet metal shacks that offered little protection from the sun, the rain, and the mud. The paths were now paved. The majority of the children were in school.

We came around a corner and met Lety (Mamá) Roque, the first one to enter the little yellow church the day Hanley and Juanita the Danish woman signed up children for the drop-in program, and the first one to protest when bags of rice and beans were given only to those families whose children had attended school. Holding Mamá Roque's hand was her grand-daughter, 11-year-old Hanley Emilia—yet another Guatemalan girl named after the program's founder. Hanley Emilia's father, Juan Luís, had lived at the Casa Hogar and studied at *Camino Seguro* until he became a father after Hanley Denning died.

WHEN I VISITED SAFE PASSAGE on March 9, 2018—the date that would have been Hanley's 48th birthday—students had created a poster featuring a woman with long blonde hair and large pink hearts on her green dress, standing atop a miniature globe. The words "Super Hanley" appeared at the top of the poster. A smaller poster in a classroom depicted Hanley as a flying superhero, her blonde hair falling down past her flying cape, paired with the words "Hanley es una heroina de la espe-ranza" (*Hanley is a hero of hope*). The words "Feliz Cumpleaños Hanley" appeared on a light blue brick wall, with paper cut-outs underneath that were meant to depict balloons, clouds, and a colorful rainbow. Strings attached to the balloons car-ried a cutout of a single red backpack (Hanley's backpack) with dozens of photos of Safe Passage's founder taped to the wall. A message written in the balloons said "Gracias Hanley."

To these hopeful and exuberant young students whose

doors to education and opportunity now lay open, the founder of their school was as abstract as Wonder Woman. And yet they celebrated her.

That afternoon I caught a ride with staff and volunteers on the Safe Passage bus from the campus in Zone 3 to Antigua, where most foreigners stayed. The project had long since forbade employees and volunteers from taking the public "chicken buses" between Guatemalan City and Antigua. It was the beginning of Semana Santa, *Easter week*, a spectacular festival of parades and crowds in Antigua, and Safe Passage was going on holiday. During the bus ride, some staff and long-term volunteers put on their headphones and stared out the windows as we left the capital and began ascending the hills. Their days were intense, and the poverty of Zone 3 could be exhausting, even for those seasoned veterans who had worked many months at Safe Passage.

Meanwhile, a small group near the front of the bus lead by Donnica Wingett, the volunteer program manager who had spent 4.5 years at Safe Passage, broke into clapping and song as they celebrated and thanked a group of volunteers whose stint had ended that day. The following conversation became a sort of debrief: How was your experience? What were your most powerful memories? How can we fine tune the experience for the next team?

Donnica, a social worker by training who worked at a social services agency in Washington, D.C., before coming to Guatemala to learn Spanish, described to me how she fell in love with this community, how this culture made her feel alive. (She had to dissuade her mother from thinking she was having a midlife crisis.) At first she worked as Safe Passage's math and literacy tutor in the reinforcement center before the volunteer program manager position opened.

The volunteer corps now included a handful of local Guatemalan college students who helped at the project on Saturdays and international volunteers who committed to serve a minimum of five weeks and worked as classroom assistants, as English tutors, or if they had special skills, in public relations or development. Long-term international volunteers who came for six months or more received a monthly housing stipend.

"We want folks to feel effective and engaged," said Donnica. "Our motive is to fit the needs of the project first."

Each of the volunteers, whether they stay for five weeks or six months, also became an ambassador of sorts for Safe Passage in their home communities.

"We focus on the relationship between the volunteer and the affiliates with whom they're working. It takes time for those relationships to develop," she explained. "We have a lot of international volunteers who extend their time and stay longer because they fell in love with the project. Some folks come for their five weeks and return the following year."

Safe Passage also welcomed support teams—usually high school or university groups from the United States—who came for one week at a time, typically in May, June, or July. Their itinerary might include spending a morning in the preschool, a morning in the elementary school, and doing activities with the Creamos artisans. Once their week was over, said Donnica, many of them returned for a longer period as volunteers or become child sponsors.

"We get a lot of volunteers who come, and serve, and care," she said. "They recognize that they, too, learn, and grow and change. They stay connected with the program, which is optimal, or they return to their home communities, having been changed and are more capable of being their best self. The life you change might be your own."

The day before, Donnica told me, she received two emails from previous Safe Passage volunteers. One was a 19-year-old, recent high school graduate from Maine who had come for several months the previous year and wrote, "I want to come back!" He wanted to see how "his kids" had grown in the classroom. The other was a Bowdoin College alum who had volunteered at Safe Passage back in 2005, when Hanley was alive, and wanted to return.

Donnica never knew Hanley, but she could recite by heart her legacy as part of the Safe Passage origin story. She shared with volunteers and prospective volunteers how Hanley saw the children toiling in the garbage dump and it touched the *gringa* from Maine and initiated in her a personal call to action.

"That's the story we share at the start of the project. How Hanley came and she saw, and her heart was immediately opened. It changed her and she understood her purpose. She came to this community and said, 'I'm going to work with people here to create positive change. Life can be different for folks here with an education.' I share that the spark happened within her. However instantaneous it was, it happened and then it spread to others."

"People hold her spark as an inspiration. How one person can change the world."

TWICE A YEAR—ON JAN. 18, the anniversary of Hanley's death, and March 9, her birthday—Jane Gallagher and Christine Slader visit the memorial bench next to Yarmouth High School, for which Jane's son Jake raised the money, and where Marina sprinkled a few of Hanley's ashes. They leave flowers and they reflect on Hanley and what she meant to them and their families.

Christine's son Wilson, a close friend of Hanley's brother Lucas, first traveled to Safe Passage in 2005, and the experience forever changed his life. He returned to the project eight times and lived and volunteered there for a year after high school. "Before that he only cared about sports," said Christine. "He came back and realized there's so much more to life than what he knew in Yarmouth, Maine." Wilson studied social work in college, and later backpacked through South America.

Jane thinks about Hanley nearly every single day during her morning meditation and her moment of gratitude for those who have influenced her life. She frequently feels Hanley's presence, and sometimes talks to her. Hanley has visited or spoken to Jane in multiple ways over the years, she claims. On the day of Hanley's memorial service at the high school, she and her son Bart were in their car at a stop sign, with no other traffic and no other people in site, when a deer trotted out of a side street and right up to their windshield to look at them. After a few seconds, the long-legged animal calmly turned and ran into the woods. "Oh my God, oh my God," she and her son reacted, convicted they had just seen Hanley.

On another occasion, when Jane felt burned out and unable to continue her work for the project, she called her husband and confessed, "I can't do this anymore." While she sat at a traffic light she said out loud to Hanley, "If I leave Safe Passage, please don't leave me. Don't leave me." The next day she came to the office in Yarmouth, where Marina worked as the receptionist. "I have something for you," Marina told Jane. "It's from Hanley. I'll leave it on the front seat of your car."

Jane rushed around to prepare a presentation about Safe Passage. When she returned to her car she found a coffee mug from Wheelock College with a note from Marina stating this was Hanley's favorite mug, and she wanted Jane to have it. "Thank you," Jane shouted to Hanley. "Not only did you hear me, but you responded really fast!"

While Jane remains in awe of Hanley's devotion and what she accomplished, she believes that her friend would struggle with being depicted as an angel or savior.

"She wouldn't want the focus to be on her," Jane told me during a walk in 2019 along one of Hanley's favorite running trails in Yarmouth. "She never felt comfortable being thought of as a savior. I watched Hanley squirm in her chair when people would put too much praise on her. She tried to deflect it. She did what she did because it came from a very deep place."

"But I think she would be happy to be known as a catalyst or a person who brought attention to a really hostile situation [like the garbage dump]. Her job was almost like a matchmaker—she found the beauty that people had to offer, and then matched it with the need and with Guatemala. She was an incredible conduit. She wanted to build something that would last."

AFTER SHE LEFT THE BOARD of directors, Deb Walters hatched a plan over a bottle of wine with friends in Antigua one evening to continue to promote Safe Passage by embarking on a kayak trip from Maine to Guatemala. "I wanted to combine my passion for long-distance kayaking with my passion for the kids in the garbage dump," said Deb, who had previously kayaked in the Arctic Circle. "The story here is the old lady kayaking," a public relations firm in Boston recommended as the hook. The challenge didn't faze Deb. "Navigation won't be a problem. Just keep the land on your right," she told herself. She left Yarmouth in July 2014, but a herniated disk in her neck a few months into the voyage forced her to suspend it. Following spinal surgery in South Carolina and rehab, she returned to the water and completed the 2,500-mile journey in January 2016. Though she had originally hoped to paddle all the way to Guatemala, the threat of drug cartels active off the Mexican coast convinced her to break up the journey and catch a ride in a yacht from the southern tip of Florida and across the Gulf of Mexico to Belize, Guatemala's neighbor to the northeast. *Camino Seguro* students followed her trip on a big map of North America in the dining hall. Along the way, Deb appeared at numerous speaking engagements, teamed with other Rotarians to raise money, and ultimately donated $425,000 to Safe Passage.

"Before the trip I met a woman in the literary program who told me the story of her life, of growing up with her uncle, and working in the garbage dump. She supported herself by making beads in the Creamos program," said Deb. "I asked her what message I should share on her behalf. She responded, 'If you believe you can do it, you can do it.' That was what she learned at Safe Passage." Deb chose to amplify that same message on her journey.

Hanley occupies a spiritual place for many who knew her and worked with her.

Sharon Workman, who helped establish Safe Passage's first board of directors, has small, beaded Guatemalan angels hanging in her yoga room that remind her of Hanley whenever she sees them. "Every time I think about Safe Passage I think about her. When I'm in Guatemala, there are so many sites that for me are connected with her."

PAUL SUTHERLAND, the first board chair, and one of Hanley's closest confidants who gave the eulogy at her funeral in Maine, has given hundreds of motivational speeches across the United States and in developing countries such as Uganda, where he and his family lived for a time while adopting a child.

"In my speeches I tell people, 'Anyone in this room could be Gandhi, or Mandela, or Hanley Denning.' Everyone. We all have those attributes," Paul told me. "The problem with the world is that we're indifferent. We know [environments like the Guatemala City garbage dump] are happening. We *choose* not to do anything about it."

"Hanley saw each child as an individual. She didn't get caught up in the past, and she never looked at anybody as a victim. She said to each one of them, 'You're a child of God.' ... Why couldn't one of these kids be the next president of Guatemala?"

BETH KLOSER, the long-term volunteer from Indiana who survived the car accident that killed Hanley and Bayron, sets aside time each January 18 to think about them. "The first few years that day was very much a time of grieving," she said. "Now it's more a time of remembering and honoring them." Beth didn't learn for several days after the accident that Hanley had died. She recalled that she didn't react well to the news. "But there was no way I was going to get to the memorial service. That was really hard." Beth's injuries from the accident were serious enough that she spent several weeks in a Guatemala City hospital before she was flown back to the United States and received another surgery months later in Indiana. She has fully recovered.

Beth visited Guatemala about five years after the accident

to see friends and stop by the project for a day, just to say hello. "Enough time had passed that I knew a few people but there had been lots of turnover," she said. "A lot of people I knew had moved on. It was good to come back, but also bittersweet." For 12 years she worked in Detroit with the Jesuit Volunteer Corps, a program for young adults and recent college grads who commit to a year or two of full-time volunteer work with nonprofits, social service agencies, under-resourced schools, or health clinics. "Volunteers commit to four core values: social justice, growing in their own values, living simply, and living in intentional community," said Beth. "A lot of the work I did was to help young adults look at the unjust structures in our country and do a social analysis." Beth stepped back in 2019 to be a fulltime parent.

RACHEL MEYN stepped down in 2009 from her position running the Safe Passage U.S. office in Maine after two very intense years following Hanley's death. But Sharon Workman and Deb Walters soon convinced her to join the board of directors, in order to help "provide stability to the organization in a time of changeover from older staff to new," said Rachel. That same year she took time to decompress, traveled to Haiti, and stopped in Antigua to celebrate *Camino Seguro's* 10-year anniversary. There she crossed paths with a former Guatemalan boyfriend, and the arrow stuck. Rachel and Rafa married in 2010 and over the next three years had a son and a daughter. They moved to Washington, D.C., where Rachel got a Master's in International Development Management from American University, then west to California to care for her chronically ill mother. Rachel served five years on the Safe Passage board.

Since 2014 she has worked in the nation's capitol as the Chief Development Officer for La Clinica del Pueblo, where she oversees a robust grants and contracts program, fundraising, volunteers, and communications. La Clinica provides health services primarily to Central American immigrants and their families as they work toward greater health access and health equity. "Due to my work with Safe Passage I understand what our patients have left behind—the sense of home, culture and belonging, and the plight of navigating that here in the U.S. I understand the bearing that has on health."

When she first walked into La Clinica, Rachel said she felt at home. "Hearing Spanish, the bright colored walls, the music and food ... it was all familiar from my time living and working at Safe Passage," she wrote. "I came to Safe Passage at a formative time in my career and was able to be part of a start up, to build and grow something. That has been important to my professional purpose. I must align deeply with the cause, feel I am part of building something, and the impact must be real and tangible. Hanley hooked me that way."

But Rachel's time with Safe Passage taught her something else—not to overwork herself. "One thing I have been absolutely mindful of since Hanley's death is the imporance of balance. I will never work 80 hours a week again. Work is important, but so is family, friends, self-care. I've learned to re-balance and still find I am able to make big differences in this world."

SOME DAY IN THE FUTURE, when he's a little older, Hanley's brother Jordan will bring his son, Campbell Hanley Denning, who was born in 2014, to Guatemala. They'll spend a day in the project so Campbell can interact with kids his age at *Camino*

Seguro. They'll walk through Hanley's garden, they'll join art projects, play sports, learn a little Spanish, and take in the old buildings and architecture of beautiful Antigua. "The chicken buses, alone, will be exciting for him," Jordan chuckled.

"I think about her every day, literally. What makes me think about her the most is when I'm going through something difficult. I say to myself, literally, 'Hanley would do it. Just think what she had to go through!' In those times when I think things are difficult, that's when it's time to put my head down and plow forward."

THIS STORY OF HANLEY DENNING shining a light into the darkness of the Guatemala City garbage dump and beaming hope into the hearts of the destitute *guajero* families wasn't my own story. I wasn't one of her hard-working staff members, financial donors, or wide-eyed volunteers on a service learning trip; I knew Hanley only briefly in Antigua after we met during one of her fundraising trips to Michigan. My role was merely to recreate and retell her remarkable story in this book.

And yet, maybe this is my story, too. Maybe this is the story of everyone who Hanley's dream touched or inspired—whether they walked through the *basurero* or rode the chicken bus with her, or learned of her journey many years after her tragic death.

When I launched this book project, my family began sponsoring a 4-year-old Safe Passage student named Kateryn Elizabeth Flores Virula, who lives on the periphery of the garbage dump with her mother, her aunt, her elder brother, and grandparents in a 13-by-13-foot cement block house with a roof of corrugated sheet metal. The Safe Passage sponsorship coordinator wrote to us at the time that "Kateryn is a sweet and chatty little girl. She is a girl who enjoys to color. Her favorite class is Literacy, her favorite color is mulberry, her favorite food is pizza and her favorite sport is soccer. When she grows up, Kateryn wants to be a teacher because she likes children. Her favorite activity at Safe Passage is Literacy. Her best friend is Kari from the project."

I showed the picture of Kateryn we received via email to my then-3-year-old daughter Nina. They both shared December birthdays, though my daughter was a year younger than our sponsor child. Nina immediately noticed that Kateryn was wearing a pink shirt featuring the Disney character, "Sofia the First." In subsequent emails from the Safe Passage office with updates on Kateryn, Nina noticed that her new friend always wore the same clothing. This is poverty, I wanted to tell my daughter, but couldn't find the words. This represents the lack of material wealth that we in the United States take for granted.

During bedtime stories I tell Nina, and later my son Leo, how we will someday visit Kateryn in Guatemala City—how they will sit side by side at a table with her and color a picture together, how we'll kick a soccer ball in the narrow paths of her *colonia*, how we'll visit her mother and grandparents and thank them for keeping her in school, and maybe we'll take her family out for pizza afterwards. The experience will open my children's eyes and challenge their assumptions. What they see at *Camino Seguro* and the garbage dump neighborhood might break their hearts a little, but it will also make their hearts grow larger. Perhaps it will compel them to a lifetime of action—just as the experience has changed the lives of thousands who have witnessed, and taken part in, Hanley Denning's dream.

Acknowledgments

THE POWER OF HANLEY'S STORY is that she possessed saint-like qualities—even though she was as human as you or me. As such, each of us could commit ourselves to acts of service in poor and disenfranchised communities in order to create a more equitable world. For pushing me to understand that universal truth and the power behind Hanley's journey, I want to thank Judy Barrett-Walters and Paul Sutherland, in particular, for urging me to write this book.

To my parents, Mimi and Norm, for raising me to see humanity as one community, even though I grew up deep in the woods of northern Michigan.

To my wife Sarah, for the time and patience.

To my daughter Nina, for listening to me read first drafts of these chapters before bedtime.

To Nina and Leo, please bear with us as we work to create a better world.

To Ann Hosler, Anne-Marie Oomen, and Rachel Meyn, thank you for reading the manuscript and for your helpful edits and critiques.

To Joe Delconzo, John Santerre, and Beth Price for letting me reprint your photographs of Hanley.

To Heather Shaw and Mission Point Press, thanks for giving this project a home. To my mentors and teachers in Guatemala, who helped me fall in love with this beautiful land so long ago, and for teaching me its haunted history: Jessica Ohana González, Carlos Sanchez, Eduardo Elias, Brenda Morales, and the staff at Proyecto Linguistico Quetzalteco in Xela. In my restless dreams I pine for your volcanoes, your lake, your highland villages.

To the characters of this story, Hanley's family, friends, coworkers, volunteers, the children and mothers of the Guatemala City garbage dump, and the staff at Safe Passage, I'm grateful for the time you spent with me, for your memories, meals and tears you shared, for answering my barrage of emails, Facebook and WhatsApp messages as I pieced together the past, and above all your patience as I wrote this book. Fredy Maldonado, you are a Robin Hood of Antigua. Your connections around town when I visited in 2018 were crucial for my research. Thank you for hosting me.

To Mary Jo and Todd Amani, Ed Mahoney, Lety Mendez, Vilma Garcia, Susanna Place, Maribel Cholotio, Claudio Ramos, Shannon Moyle, Amilcar de Leon, Juan Mini, Lety Roque, Irina Rodríguez Cotto, Daniél Osorio, Iris Ramírez, Nancy Gudiel, thank you for your time and reflection. While memories wane as the years pass, I benefited greatly from your ability to analyze what your time with Hanley meant. To Joan "Juanita" Anderson in Denmark, thank you for letting me quote from your moving memoir, *Drømmenes Losseplads*.

To Trae Holland, Safe Passage's current executive director, for our Zoom calls and for narrating how the project has survived and thrived through the pandemic.

To the supporters I met in Maine in 2019, thank you for your time and reflection: Jane Gallagher, Marty and Frank Helman, Phil Kirchner, Christine Slader, Doug Pride, and Barbara Davis.

You were the first supporters. Without you, Hanley's dream wouldn't have happened.

To Paul Sutherland, Sharon Workman, and Marilyn Fitzgerald, thank you.

To all those I interviewed via phone, Beth Kloser, in particular, thank you for your willingness to share those painful memories of the accident with me.

To Rachel Meyn, your guidance, your list of contacts, your input was indispensable to this project. Thank you, also, for reviewing an early draft of my manuscript.

Above all, to Hanley's family, Marina, Michael, Jordan, Seth and Lucas, for trusting me to write Hanley's story, and for the time you spent with me in Yarmouth and on subsequent phone calls. You were guarded and protective of her legacy at first, and I completely understand why. What a gift you gave the world. Thank you for sharing Hanley with us.

"In the early days we saw her leaning into the children, brushing their hair out of their eyes, giving them unabashed hugs, and listening to all they had to say," remembered Rachel Meyn. "The modeling of this quickly grew to how Safe Passage became Safe Passage: a nonjudgmental safe space to be seen and validated. This was the essence of the program."

Further Reading & Films

Books about Guatemala and international aid work that informed my research and writing of *Angel of the Garbage Dump* (listed in alphabetical order).

Between Light and Shadow: A Guatemalan Girl's Journey through Adoption, by Jacob Wheeler, 2011, University of Nebraska Press

Bitter Fruit: The Story of the American Coup in Guatemala, by Stephen Schlesinger and Stephen Kinzer, 1982, Harvard University Press

Drømmenes Losseplads: Blandt engle og skraldebørn I Guatemala Citys slum ("The Garbage Dump of Dreams: Among angels and garbage children in Guatemala City's slum"), by Joan Juanita Anderson, 2016, EgoLibris

Mountains Beyond Mountains: The Quest of Dr. Paul Farmer, A Man Who Would Cure the World, by Tracy Kidder, 2003, Random House

Open Veins of Latin America: Five Centuries of the Pillage of a Continent, by Eduardo Galleano, 1997, Monthly Review Press

Silence on the Mountain: Stories of Terror, Betrayal, and Forgetting in Guatemala, by Daniel Wilkinson, 2004, Duke University Press

Film list:

Recycled Life, documentary directed by Leslie Iwerks, 2006. Nominated for Academy Award

Manos de Madre, short documentary produced by Safe Passage, 2009

About the Author

AUTHOR AND JOURNALIST JACOB WHEELER lives in Traverse City, Michigan, with his wife Sarah and children, Nina and Leo. He publishes the Glen Arbor Sun newspaper and teaches at Northwestern Michigan College.

Wheeler fell in love with the Central American nation while studying Spanish in Quetzaltenango in the Guatemalan highlands. His first book, *Between Light and Shadow* (University of Nebraska Press, 2011) covered Guatemala's child adoption industry.

Wheeler's reporting has won awards from Project Censored and the Michigan Press Association. A native of Denmark, he has filed stories from five continents, and his work has appeared in such publications as *The Rotarian, Teaching Tolerance, Utne Reader, In These Times,* the *Christian Science Monitor, Detroit Free Press,* and *San Francisco Chronicle.* As a storyteller, he is attracted to narratives that feature ordinary people taking on herculean tasks and succeeding against great odds.

For more information about this book, visit:
AngeloftheGarbageDump.com and SafePassage.org.

CPSIA information can be obtained
at www.ICGtesting.com
Printed in the USA
LVHW022317211122
733714LV00002B/253